AUG 2 9 2017

At Home in the World

At Home in the World

WOMEN WRITERS AND PUBLIC LIFE,
FROM AUSTEN TO THE PRESENT

Maria DiBattista and *Deborah Epstein Nord*

PRINCETON UNIVERSITY PRESS

PRINCETON AND OXFORD

Published by Princeton University Press, 41 William Street, Princeton, New Jersey 08540
In the United Kingdom: Princeton University Press, 6 Oxford Street, Woodstock, Oxfordshire OX20 1TR

press.princeton.edu

Jacket art: *Nocturne*, 1948. Oil on canvas. Ernest Fiene (1894–1965) / Private Collection / Photo © Christie's Images / Bridgeman Images

Jacket design by Kathleen Lynch / Black Kat Design

ISBN 978-0-691-13811-4

Library of Congress Control Number: 2016945501

British Library Cataloging-in-Publication Data is available

This book has been composed in Sabon LT Std

Printed on acid-free paper. ∞

Printed in the United States of America

10 9 8 7 6 5 4 3 2 1

We dedicate this book to the memory of our mothers,
Jean (Giovanna) and Gayola,
and to our daughters-in-law,
Eva and Rachel, Erin and Minoosh

Contents

Preface

COLLEAGUES AND FRIENDS FOR MANY YEARS, we began to think about the possibility of writing this book when we first taught a course together in 2004 on women writers. With the awkward and likely outdated title of "The Female Literary Tradition," the course itself had a history. Our former colleagues Elaine Showalter and Sandra Gilbert, two pioneers of feminist literary criticism, invented it when they both taught at Princeton in the mid-1980s. When we devised a new iteration of the course in 2004, we extended its reach further into the twentieth century and, eventually, into the twenty-first. We also chose to focus on political themes and the pull of public discourse for women writers.

This was the era when a spate of film and literary adaptations of Jane Austen's novels began to appear, and we observed, along with many others, that they tended to reduce the author's appeal to matrimonial giddiness. The term "chick lit," coined in the late 1990s to refer to novels from *Pride and Prejudice* and *Jane Eyre* to *Bridget Jones's Diary*, evoked a niche group of readers with a clearly—and narrowly—defined set of interests and expectations. At the same time, some contemporary women novelists complained that their work never received the serious critical attention from reviewers that their male peers garnered. In the midst of a popular cultural slide into the idea that the great nineteenth-century women writers devoted themselves almost exclusively to dramas of the marriage market, we wanted to convey to our students that the "tradition" was both weightier and more varied than they might have imagined.

In 2005, energized by the prospect of locating women writers in the clamorous midst of public life rather than at the quiet margins, we organized a small Princeton conference, "Women, Art, and Politics in the 20th Century." We invited scholars from an array of disciplines to explore the diverse and complicated responses of women novelists, playwrights, poets, political theorists, sculptors, and photojournalists to the cataclysmic events of the two world wars; totalitarianism in Europe; the Depression, McCarthyism, and race in the United States; and the roles of women and gender in the representation of political life. Our keynote speaker was Joan Didion, one of our most trenchant commentators on American political life and its institutions. Although we could hardly anticipate it at the time, the title of Didion's last major work of political critique—*Where I Was From*, an autobiographical rumination about her shifting notions of and allegiances to the idea of a home (West or East Coast)—encapsulated the recurrent preoccupations of this book: how women writers reimagined the dynamic relation between home and world, private and public life. Didion's lecture was complemented by a reading given by Eavan Boland, an Irish poet of pronounced and proud feminist convictions. One of Boland's poems, "That the Science of Cartography Is Limited," a searing and yet resolutely lyrical indictment of the Irish famine, also came to resonate with the political and aesthetic issues that our readings of women writers insistently uncovered and often deliberately left unresolved. The poem seemed to invite and encourage a remapping of the literary landscape we had inhabited for so long, one in which women were seldom pictured in the wider world of public actors deliberating on the uses and abuses of power.

What most interested us as our work progressed, however, was not solely the impulse toward public life and political themes in women's writing, though we found this a fascinating and indeed inspiring avenue of inquiry, and one that surely animates this book. Rather, we kept encountering, both in our teaching and in our thinking about the writers and artists the conference included, a persistent preoccupation with the idea of home. Again and again we found a simultaneous rejection of domestic life and a search for some ideal place of settlement, what we have called in our conclusion a "promised land." Setting off for unknown realms, strange and risky adventures, and a life emancipated from oppression or old familial forms, heroines invented by writers from Austen to

Edwidge Danticat engaged in explorations—or perhaps utopian imaginings—of a heretofore unimaginable dwelling place. While male writers also, of course, dream of heroes' liberation from private and familial constraints and long for expansive new worlds, lighting out for the territories, leaving the provinces for Paris or London, seeking personal transformation through politics or war, women writers contend always—and still—with the myths and meanings of home, their bodily and psychic ties to family life, and their unauthorized desires for independence and equality.

These characteristics—ambivalent ties to home and persistent impulses toward an engaged life beyond it—help us delineate our sense of the traditions of women's writing. If, as we have said at the outset, the term "female" seems awkward and outdated, it is primarily because we eschew any essential and transhistorical meaning of femininity, though we also recognize that for some the biologically inflected term itself has become vexed. But neither do we accept the notion that the category of woman has been emptied of its meaning and usefulness, either because there are too many other aspects of identity that impinge on it or because the two "sexes" have splintered into an infinite number. There is indeed more uncertainty now than there was in the 1970s and 1980s about womanhood as a primary affiliation, and about whether the common experiences and aspirations of women are sufficiently powerful to override differences and constitute a literary tradition. Believing in the efficacy of the notion of women's experience and of a literary tradition that absorbs and accommodates distinctions, we have chosen our writers and texts in an eclectic and wide-ranging manner. Always hewing to the themes and idiosyncrasies of private and public aspiration, we have intentionally avoided the kinds of segregation by nationality, race, sexuality, religion, geography, and even historical period that might otherwise organize our writers. We hope that unlikely juxtapositions—Elizabeth Gaskell and Toni Morrison, Willa Cather and Mary Antin, May Sinclair and Martha Gellhorn, Grace Paley and Joan Didion, Nadine Gordimer and Jhumpa Lahiri—might offer new ways of seeing each of these individual writers and of imagining a lineage that accommodates all manner of difference.

This lineage, unsurprisingly, reflects a lineage of our own. We have dedicated this book to our mothers and daughters-in-law out of abiding love and affection. As daughters, we honor mothers who gave us our first and fundamental sense of home and also our impulse to face outward toward the wider world; as mothers of sons, we look to our daughters-in-law, who have their own home to make in the world. Our dedication is thus meant to reflect our critical but also deeply personal investment in a vital female tradition that we have inherited and hope to bequeath—enriched and expanded—to a new generation of women.

Acknowledgments

WE WISH, FIRST OF ALL, TO THANK our undergraduate and graduate students, who have inspired and taught us and who have kept the tradition of reading the work of women writers going in new and unexpected ways. More than anything else either of us has written, this book has been influenced by our teaching and by successive and varied cohorts of students. Christine Stansell, dear colleague and friend, read an early draft of our proposal for this project and helped us to sharpen it. Our predecessors, among them the late Ellen Moers, Elaine Showalter, Sandra Gilbert, and Susan Gubar, established a feminist critical tradition from which we have benefited and learned. We owe a great debt to Hannah Winarsky, our first editor at Princeton University Press, who encouraged us to write this book and responded to it with enthusiasm. Anne Savarese, our current editor, showed patience and gave us welcome advice throughout the final stages of writing. We are grateful for the intelligent and careful copyediting of Cathy Slovensky.

Maria never found the occasion to present any portions of this book to a professional gathering. But over the years she found encouragement, guidance, and inspiration in conversations with friends, especially Suzanne Nash, Brigitte Peucker, Cynthia Avila, Martin Karlow, and the late Barbara Rietveld. She is also supremely grateful to her sons, Daniel and Matthew, and to her coauthor for their unfailing love and forbearance during the writing of this book.

Deborah wishes to thank the planning committee of the British Women Writers Conference (spring 2007) for inviting her to give a keynote address that year. The result was a talk titled "Outward Bound," which turned into the germ of chapter 1 of this book. The following fall, she was fortunate to spend the semester at the National Humanities Center as an M. H. Abrams Fellow. The first sections of her contribution to *At Home in the World* were crafted there in the company of a wonderful group of fellows and under circumstances ideal for thought, conversation, and writing. Matt Steding helped her with sources and footnotes. Colleagues in the Princeton English Department's Faculty Seminar responded in helpful and lively ways to early versions of her writing on the "multinationals." Finally, she wishes to thank her beloved husband, Philip, and sons, Joseph and David, and her close friends—including her coauthor—for support, love, and encouragement during years of both loss and gain. This book came to completion because of them.

At Home in the World

The Peripatetics

IN HER MEMOIR OF THE FIRST WORLD WAR, the British pacifist
and feminist Vera Brittain remembers the period leading up to the
outbreak of war as a time of self-regard and absorption in her own
private life. Bright, ambitious, and twenty-one, falling in love for
the first time and newly admitted to Somerville College, Oxford,
she became aware nonetheless that "public affairs" were imping-
ing on private lives in a way that rendered the two inseparable.
She records in *Testament of Youth* that this difficult conjuncture of
public and private preoccupations called to mind a passage from
George Eliot's novel *Daniel Deronda*, published some four decades earlier: "There comes a terrible moment to many souls when
the great movements of the world, the larger destinies of mankind,
which have lain aloof in newspapers and other neglected reading,
enter like an earthquake into their own lives—when the slow urgency of growing generations turns into the tread of an invading
army or the dire clash of civil war."[1]

These lines come at the end of Eliot's novel, when the solipsis-
tic and blinkered Gwendolen Harleth comes face-to-face with the
alienation of a people—in this case European Jews—and their aspirations for a homeland. Eschewing Gwendolen's role and choosing Eliot's legacy instead, Brittain was soon to give herself to public service, working as a nurse throughout the war, and becoming
involved in political causes, both domestic and international, for
the rest of her life. From here she was to face outward, in full, en-
ergetic pursuit of a heroic life and in rebellion against the narrative
of domestic contentment and romantic love.

Our book argues that the dominant image of Anglo-American
women's writing in the late eighteenth through twentieth centuries

as a largely domestic literary tradition is itself a resilient fiction or myth, and that Brittain's narrative of going forth to meet "the great movements of the world, the larger destinies of mankind" comes closer to the truth. This domestic myth casts women's writing as inevitably—and conservatively—preoccupied with the mundane and circumscribed aspects of home, personal relationships, sexual mores, marriage, and the taming of refractory men, and it has been perpetuated by a variety of critics, popularizers, nostalgic audiences, and even devotees of those novelists who have inspired the staunchest followings.[2] Early twenty-first-century Austen audiences, to name one example, revel in her romantic plots, seeming to miss Austen's ironic stance toward the habits and rituals of courtship and matrimony and her dim view of family life in general. We offer a very different account of the history and trajectory of women's writing, one grounded in the notion that its impulses largely ran toward public engagement rather than domestic entanglement.

Readers and critics, especially those of eighteenth- and nineteenth-century novels, have often tended to focus primarily on female experience of the world as defined and limited by personal relations and the private sphere. Our rereadings and reassessments chart the ways women's fiction takes its heroines, however briefly or impermanently, outside the confines of the domestic into public domains, where they directly confront the social and political obstacles to the well-being of others and to their own personal emancipation. In our most powerful and influential women writers, a critique of domestic life was more common than its celebration, the embracing of public debate and the social questions of the day more frequent than their avoidance. From Austen, Charlotte Brontë, Elizabeth Gaskell, Harriet Beecher Stowe, and Harriet Jacobs to Virginia Woolf, Willa Cather, and Edith Wharton and then on to Tess Slesinger, Mary McCarthy, Joan Didion, and Nadine Gordimer, women's fictions (as well as poems and essays) faced outward, often chomping at the bit of domestic expectations and cultural constraints, and tackled the subjects of class formation, slavery, warfare, feminism, political economy, labor unrest, democracy, tyranny, globalism, and the clash of cultures. Until relatively recently excluded from classic or official forms of public life—suffrage, journalism, organized politics—women were nonetheless always active participants in debates about the crucial concerns of civil society.

For the new millennium, with its heightened sense of intersecting cultures across the globe and increasing awareness of the multiple struggles of women in far-flung and yet eerily familiar societies, we offer an account of the female literary tradition of the last two centuries that recognizes and evaluates its engagement with public life. The foundational texts of feminist criticism—Virginia Woolf's *A Room of One's Own*, Mary Ellmann's *Thinking about Women*, Ellen Moers's *Literary Women*, Sandra Gilbert and Susan Gubar's *The Madwoman in the Attic*, and Elaine Showalter's *A Literature of Their Own*—demonstrated the existence and defined the contours of a distinct and coherent body of female writing with characteristic themes, preoccupations, and tropes. They identified the founding "mothers" and canonical texts of this literary corpus, thus endowing it with the lineage, authority, and historical endurance that are the hallmarks of a vital tradition. Woolf focused on the material circumstances—money, time, and space—that women lacked and sorely needed if they were to produce great writing. Ellmann took aim at the sexual stereotypes that govern cultural attitudes toward the writing of both men and women. Moers offered a gallery of heroines—traveling, loving, performing, educating— and cast her net wide, bringing together multiple centuries and national literatures through dominant themes of women's writing. Showalter proposed stages in the development of women's fiction in Britain, from feminine to feminist to female. Gilbert and Gubar posited a nineteenth-century "feminist poetics" with anger and rebellion at its heart.

We undertake to build on the work of these feminist foremothers by insisting on and extending the idea of a distinctly female literary tradition and by zeroing in on strains of public consciousness and ambition and on narrative tensions and exchanges between home and abroad. It is our aim, first of all, to suggest continuities between the themes of what Virginia Woolf called the "golden age" of women's writing in the nineteenth century and the fictions of women who wrote in the wake of the political and social emancipations of the modern age. As Vera Brittain's invocation of Eliot's final novel suggests, women writers of the twentieth century maintained a powerful consciousness of this continuity, just as mid-nineteenth-century writers like Eliot, Elizabeth Barrett Browning, George Sand, Charlotte Brontë, and Harriet Beecher Stowe imagined themselves to be co-conspirators in a common literary project.[3] This project, like Brittain's and Eliot's insistence on the individual's widening sphere of curiosity and engagement, was fundamentally both political and activist.

For us, the tropes and themes that most saliently express women writers' impulses toward a role in public life involve travel, sailing forth, escape, adventure, going westward, exodus, dissent, and emigration. But they also include settlement and home, a radical remaking of the domestic, and the discovery of new places of belonging that often bear little resemblance to the home left behind. We find in these women's texts, then, a recurring dialectic of home and abroad, a complicated relationship that changes over these two centuries but nonetheless remains central in the literary expression of women's experience. Home must be rejected but also recreated, sometimes, as in the case of Linda Brent's hiding place in Harriet Jacobs's *Incidents in the Life of a Slave Girl*, in a startlingly counterintuitive form, and sometimes in a radically utopian vein that entails the total abandonment of family and nation, as in Charlotte Gilman's *Herland*, which envisions a matriarchal society, governed by "Over Mothers," in which child-rearing, considered the primary work of the nation, is a public and collective rather than a private and familial undertaking.

The one meaning of home that the "great writers" (as Ellen Moers called them) refused outright was a sheltered and isolated one—home as a retreat from the pressing and controversial matters of the day. For Elizabeth Barrett Browning, this posture of withdrawal and self-cloistering seemed tantamount to giving up the vocation of writing, because for her, the idea of speaking out and authorship were one and the same. When the art critic and memoirist Anna Jameson complained that in *Uncle Tom's Cabin* Harriet Beecher Stowe had taken on too incendiary a subject for a woman to tackle, Barrett Browning scolded her in heated prose: "Is it possible," she asked, "that you think a woman has no business with questions like the question of slavery? . . . Then she had better use a pen no more."[4] For Barrett Browning and many of her peers, writing was not only equal to activism but also to leaving the domestic realm, what the poet called the "women's apartment," contrasting her own Ulysses-like literary venturing forth to the stay-at-home Penelope. Not to write, not to speak out, was to be satisfied with the life of the woman left behind and, even worse, it was a form of slavery.

This book shows women writers at their "business," grappling with the most pressing questions of their day. The history of their imaginative enterprises in a public and geographically extended (and ever-expanding) field spans the surprisingly active, unsettled plots and mobile heroines of the early nineteenth-century novel to women's fiction written in the late twentieth and early twenty-first century. The compass of women's fiction becomes ever wider as women gain the confidence and material means to enter into previously inaccessible or forbidden domains of experience: politics, warfare, revolution, and nation making. In contemporary works we encounter plots that follow heroines as they explore wider geographical and cultural territories, that experiment with new ways of seeing and living, and that offer new definitions of what it means to have and create a home. In interpreting the female literary tradition through its impulse to face outward, we suggest the ways women's fiction not only tried to document the lives of women but also sought to displace conventional narratives of inner strife and yearning, and to create, instead, narratives of self-extension, political activism, and spiritual adventure. We regard and characterize writers in this tradition as instinctive and inveterate peripatetics, women seldom at home in the place they were born or that custom has allotted them—women moving, if only imaginatively, from place to place in search of greater freedom and a greater part in directing what Eliot called the "great movements of the world." The errant Eve of Eden, not stay-at-home Penelope, is the model and pattern for their curious character and creative ambition.

Ours is not an exhaustive study or survey of female peripatetics in their various historical and cultural avatars, but will, rather, engage representative moments, writers, and texts in the interest of suggesting the broad sweep and scope of women's writing and its resolutely public impulses and ambitions. We select and concentrate on issues—emancipation, war, democratic politics—that summoned the most passionate and eloquent responses of women determined to make their views known and their voices count. What we lose in comprehensiveness we hope to gain in altered outlook, especially in determinations of literary prominence. Women writers currently patronized as provincial and minor talents, like Sarah Orne Jewett and May Sinclair, or languishing in relative obscurity, like Tess Slesinger and Iris Origo, or whose literary reputation is often overshadowed by their fateful marriages to literary giants, like Mary McCarthy and Martha Gellhorn, emerge as bold figures in high relief when read against the panorama of women's literature devoted to public themes. Thus, for example, the Mary McCarthy who attracts our attention is not the young woman of shrewd but untethered literary intelligence who found her vocation as a novelist only after her husband, the redoubtable critic Edmund Wilson, locked her in a room until she produced her first work of fiction, but the fearless satirist of the beliefs and manners of America's intellectual and political class. Martha Gellhorn, once separated from the legend of Hemingway, stands on her own as a novelist whose fiction rivals male accounts of the mass dislocations, battles, and soul-sickening discovery of the death camps that made the Second World War so hard and so necessary to write about. It is our contention that these women writers should be ranked among the thinkers and speakers who imaginatively ventured into the public marketplace, where the ideas propelling the greater movements of the world are voiced, debated, modified, embraced, or discredited.

If we think back through intrepid and outspoken figures like McCarthy and Gellhorn, we can see how different even the canonical examples of late eighteenth- and nineteenth-century fiction appear. We would expect the polemical writings of someone like Wollstonecraft to face outward to engage with public concerns, but so, too, does her travel writing and so, too, do the novels—courtship plots and bildungsromans alike—by Austen, Brontë, Gaskell, and Eliot, which have for so long defined the female literary tradition. We focus on narratives of itinerancy, movement, and uprooting, elements that challenge the idea of a circumscribed domestic domain. For so many of these female adventurers, travel itself meant emancipation. Mary Wollstonecraft's *Letters Written during a Short Residence in Sweden, Norway, and Denmark* (1796), a travel memoir with commentary on prison reform, property rights, and capital punishment, revisits some of the preoccupations of her *Vindication of the Rights of Woman* (1792), though in a different key. Jane Austen's last novel, *Persuasion*, imagines emancipation along different lines. The novel literally gives us a ship, a vehicle of travel and exploration, as the future home of Anne Elliot. Before she speaks up and asserts her right to be heard and to be happy, Anne seemed fated to be one of the great stay-at-homes of the English novel. The arrival of navy officers on *Persuasion*'s domestic shores not only imports a prospective (and retrospective) suitor for its isolated and languishing heroine but introduces into the English novel itself the possibility of a more mobile existence for women and the chance to confront and address the critical issues of the day—war, class mobility, and the ascendancy of companionate or, as Lionel Trilling characterizes it, intelligent love.[5]

Female impatience to secure a future redolent of adventure and needful, healthy change is the motive force animating the more visibly restless heroines, who yearn for the world and experiences beyond the threshold of home. The adventurous young women of these fictions are easily recognized and well remembered, even loved by many readers. Their eagerness for enlarging experience is crystallized in Jane Eyre's reveries of travel from the top of Thornfield Hall and in her almost constantly peripatetic state, and in Lucy Snowe's abrupt departure from England, home, and all that she knows in the early chapters of Charlotte Brontë's *Villette*. A slightly different, although complementary, paradigm informs Elizabeth Gaskell's *North and South*, in which the heroine's inquisitiveness leads her to an open engagement with class conflict and the strife of industrial workers, just as Gaskell's first novel,

Mary Barton, emboldened her to enter debates about "political economy" and the exploitation of laborers. Gaskell's abolitionist colleagues across the Atlantic saw themselves engaged in a related fight—the cause of emancipation—and combined a like-minded Christian belief in the relatedness of all peoples with a militant assault on slavery. George Eliot created a string of heroines who chafe at convention but seem ultimately to succumb to it, who long for escape but are repeatedly brought back and reined in. We see in *Daniel Deronda*, Eliot's last novel, a form of delayed release.[6] In taking her narrative literally across the Mediterranean to Palestine, a place that is at once historic and messianic, Eliot, inspired by Stowe's *Uncle Tom's Cabin*, makes the imaginative leap into uncharted territories in the person of her male protagonist.

By the turn of the twentieth century, women's growing responsiveness to "the great movements of the world, the larger destinies of mankind," resulted in a burgeoning of fiction explicitly concerned with the social and moral fate of entire populations displaced by war or fleeing persecution, political upheaval, or centuries of economic penury. These migrations were stressful but also hope-filled ventures into new lands that tested and inevitably transformed traditional notions of nationality, home, and identity. Willa Cather, the moral historian of the American frontier and its settlement, represents the urge to find a new home in foreign and unsettled territories as an urge indigenous to modernity in general, but she also shows how that pioneering spirit can express itself beyond the confines of traditional notions of what women can do. Cather's early works, *O Pioneers!* and *My Ántonia*, represent the opening of the American frontier as a historic opportunity for women to participate in the geographical expansion and political consolidation of a new nation. But Cather was also aware that the national destiny the pioneer helped manifest was accomplished by the dispossession and sometimes wholesale liquidation of Native Americans, who thought of the land not as a wilderness but as a tribal home. This is the underlying theme and lament of Cather's *The Professor's House*, a novel that, despite its staid, academic title, advances the radical notion that home is a spiritual idea that modern life may frustrate more than fulfill. Written at a time when

America, the uncontested victor in a war it entered late but decisively, had secured its place and its future as a leader among nations, *The Professor's House* is a historical fiction that elegizes the vanished Indian cultures of the Southwest and ponders the moral future of an American homeland forged out of conquered and often despoiled native lands.

Tom Outland, Cather's hero in *The Professor's House*, dies in the First World War, a plot development that further complicates Cather's vision of America's manifest destiny as a world presence and power. She, like so many other women writers who imaginatively and often literally ventured into battlegrounds at home and abroad, became more aware and more articulate about the conduct, as well as the political purposes, of war. The literature of women written in and about wartime has been recognized, even honored, but not appreciated for the way it expanded on preoccupations, techniques, and moral stances inherited from the female tradition of writing on public themes. Vera Brittain, May Sinclair, and Rose Macaulay, among others, entered the fray, both as volunteers for service in a war that saw unprecedented participation by women and as witnesses to the painful moral ambiguity of the Great War.

Yet even those who were skeptical that the Great War would, as promised, make the world safe for democracy were sometimes moved beyond their own disillusionment to envision—or simply hope for—a postwar future that would eventually mean more than "so many beautiful old things smashed."[7] Thus, even as he coolly dismisses the idea that "we are going to get out of this war what we went in for," David, the self-described fatalist of Cather's *One of Ours*, cannot help thinking that "something must come of the war. . . . Nothing we expect, but something unforeseen." "You remember in the old mythology tales," he asks Claude, the novel's young protagonist who will, like Tom Outland, die in the war, "how, when the sons of the gods were born, the mothers always died in agony? Maybe it's only Semêle I'm thinking of. At any rate, I've sometimes wondered whether the young men of our time had to die young to bring a new idea into the world . . . something Olympian."[8]

The desire to bring forth a new idea into the world, something epochal, if not Olympian, takes concrete form and specific direction in novels by women appalled by the moral and economic deterioration of the postwar world and exasperated with stalled initiatives for democratic reform. The great and remarkably patient Victorian novelists wrote of political and industrial unrest with an equanimity that itself seemed a solution to the festering resentment and latent violence that threatened to rend communities, and even the nation, apart. But their successors were less willing to write narratives featuring stalwart heroines, brave struggles, and sanguine outcomes. They wrote with often shocking candor about sexually liberated women who had casual affairs, made terrible marriages, and had abortions, even as they worked to bring about a revolution they didn't really believe in and sometimes may not have wanted.

Nor did these women writers behave themselves, even when writing about those who shared their political views about what should and needed to be done. This was especially apparent during the 1930s and '40s, when an energized democratic Left was under pressure to conform to the dictates of socialist realism mandating an idealized depiction of the working classes, a blanket indictment of the bourgeoisie, and an uncritical embrace of collectivist ideology, especially in its Soviet form. Tess Slesinger and Mary McCarthy defied the orthodoxies of socialist realism by writing personal narratives about contemporary life and refusing to pretend that gender was not as important as class in determining who has and wields power. They helped consolidate a tradition formally dedicated to a clear-eyed, often pitiless realism, sparing readers none of the shameful particulars of the disintegrating social and economic scene. But it was also a tradition as concerned with envisioning new social forms as in denouncing the old democratic alliances. The titles of Grace Paley's short story collections—*Enormous Changes at the Last Minute* and *Later the Same Day*—are witty reminders of the tenacity of this tradition, hardy enough to survive transplantation in the ethnic ghettos of midcentury New York. We call these keen-eyed political visionaries the Exaltadas, after Margaret Fuller's vision of a new breed of principled, self-sufficient women whose devotion to truth would herald, and indeed beget, a new world order. The most politically aware and active of the peripatetics whose work and legacy we celebrate in these pages, they attest to a talent, disciplined into a vocation, for political prophecy that is at once utopian and pragmatic, self-dependent and disinterested.

This dream of a new world persists with surprising tenacity in the work of contemporary writers, whom we discuss in chapter 6 as the "multinationals." These women complicate the already fraught equation between home and world, self and country. They come from diverse cultures and often contending traditions, but they share a common aspiration: to open up routes into territories where the rival claims of the new and the old country, the new habits and old ways, the new and the "native" self might be equitably resolved. In their fictional universes emigration is sometimes forced and sometimes sought, and it often produces painful dislocation and cultural estrangement. But, surprisingly at times, their narratives move beyond national identity and division to imagine spiritual and political possibilities that transcend geographical boundaries and rigid definitions of self. Writers like Nadine Gordimer, Anita and Kiran Desai, Jhumpa Lahiri, and Edwidge Danticat contemplate a new relationship between home and abroad, and imagine the possibility of living "in between." These contemporary women writers show, in radically different ways, styles, and forms, how the female tradition has continued to address modern social, political, and ideological realities. They expose the inequities and prejudices of non-Western cultures, especially with regard to the treatment of women, but in so doing, they also reveal the distortions and liabilities of our own and point to the unfinished business of women's quest for emancipation across the globe.

At Home in the World acknowledges and champions this public-spirited tradition of female writing as an epic undertaking in need of greater acknowledgment and fuller assessment. Our title is meant to conjure the image of those dauntless women writers who ventured across the threshold that leads from home into the public thoroughfares of thought and action where history is made, the world reformed and reimagined. The peripatetics whose work and tradition we chronicle in these pages are determinedly and inventively moving toward a promised land—for so many called it that—where they hope to feel, at last, at home in the great world.

CHAPTER 1

Adventure

IN A HAUNTING PASSAGE IN VIRGINIA WOOLF'S *To the Lighthouse* (1927), Mrs. Ramsay, one of the last great literary avatars of Victorian womanhood, settles in for a few precious moments of calm and reverie after an exhausting day of tending to children and houseguests and meals and plans to visit the lighthouse. She sits by herself, knitting, relishing the moment in which she "need not think about anybody":

> To be silent; to be alone. All the being and the doing, expansive, glittering, vocal, evaporated; and one shrunk with a sense of solemnity to being oneself, a wedge-shaped core of darkness, something invisible to others. . . . it was thus that she felt herself; and this self having shed its attachments was free for the strangest adventures . . . Her horizon seemed to her limitless. There were all the places she had not seen; the Indian plains; she felt herself pushing aside the thick leather curtain of a church in Rome. This core of darkness could go anywhere, for no one saw it.[1]

In this novel, framed by plans for a journey and its delayed realization some ten years later, travel, adventure, and limitless horizons are pleasures out of reach for the profoundly domestic Mrs. Ramsay, save in fantasy. The circumscribed life of even this comfortable, well-off woman on the eve of the First World War renders travel an almost illicit mental pleasure, something undertaken when the family is asleep and chores are finished. And even then, Mrs. Ramsay does not imagine herself venturing into Rome or onto the Indian plains in the form of her physical self—in her own body—but rather in the invisible form of a "wedge-shaped core of darkness." Invisibility lends her the freedom to roam and shields her from public exposure. To see and yet be unseen is the utmost she can conjure. Mrs. Ramsay will plan the expedition to the lighthouse, knit a long brown sock for the lighthouse keeper's tubercular son, and try to cajole her husband and son into believing that the wind might change and the day become fine enough for a sail. She will not, however, live to see the plans come to fruition, let alone live to enjoy such a journey—and all that it stands for—herself.

For Woolf's protagonist, as for the nineteenth-century heroines who came before her, home and travel, domesticity and adventure, private and public, represent the inevitable antitheses that framed their lives. Indeed, women's writing was shaped by these oppositions and, more specifically, by a particularly charged dialectic of home and abroad. The pull of home generated both attraction and repulsion in women's writing; the draw of public realms— whether in the form of adventure, travel, political debate, social engagement, wandering, or even exile—excited the imagination and helped to produce narrative energy, innovation, and sometimes impasse.

We know that many nineteenth-century women left travel memoirs—records of journeys to the Continent, Africa, or the Middle East—and that missionary work, exploration, scientific research, and projects of empire took women abroad in greater numbers than we often imagine. Mary Kingsley and Isabella Bird are well known for their intrepid travels and the texts in which they recorded their journeys, but other women travelers also left astonishing documents of adventure across the globe. The botanical illustrator Marianne North's *Recollections of a Happy Life*, published in 1892, told the tale of her numerous journeys abroad—to Jamaica, Turkey, Egypt, Syria, Canada, and the United States—in pursuit of plant species to collect and draw. Mary Seacole, a Creole woman from Kingston, Jamaica, grew up "tracing upon an old map the route to England" and thought of herself as "quite a female Ulysses."[2] Her wanderlust, coupled with the skills of tending the sick, which she learned from her "admirable doctress mother," set her on a course to the Crimea in 1854. In *Wonderful*

Adventures of Mrs. Seacole in Many Lands, published in 1857, she recounts her determination to reach Scutari, her unsuccessful struggle to persuade the War Office to accept her as a hospital nurse, and her eventual establishment of the "British Hotel" in Balaclava—a place where she welcomed, housed, healed, and provided supplies for soldiers. Anna Leonowens, born in India in 1831, sailed for Singapore and then Siam, where she tutored the king's children and acted as his amanuensis. Her *English Governess at the Siamese Court: Being Recollections of Six Years at the Royal Palace in Bangkok* (1870) influenced a biography, *Anna and the King of Siam*, which in turn spawned a play and then a musical. The travels of Anna Jameson, Mary Shelley, Lady Eastlake, Harriet Martineau, and Frances Trollope may seem tame by comparison, but no voyages to Italy, America, and the Middle East in the early and middle decades of the nineteenth century were for the faint of heart.

If we are aware of these extraordinary journeys, we tend to bracket them in our notions of Victorian culture and to imagine such women as highly exceptional, to separate their experiences from the stuff of the nineteenth-century novel, in which women writers and characters are understood to have hewed closely to the subjects of domestic life, the bourgeois family, and private emotions. But the novel also reflected powerful impulses to escape the private realm of home and claim the wide world as woman's turf. We can trace in the fictional narratives of writers like Jane Austen, Charlotte Brontë, and George Eliot the emergence of an iconoclastic strain that defied the social and literary expectations of their day and, in doing so, imagined a variety of departures from home ground. Consideration of these moments of departure—of setting sail—might prompt us to reconsider whether "domestic fiction" is a term that adequately describes women's narratives. We offer here a portrait of women writers not as housebound, in either a literal or a figurative sense, but as authors of stories that are resolutely *anti-domestic*—stories of restlessness, wandering, adventure, and homelessness.

A number of phenomena have stood in the way of our seeing this body of literature as anti-domestic: some of these impediments are rooted in nineteenth-century bourgeois life and ideology, some in the pressures of the literary marketplace, and some in mythologies of the nineteenth-century woman writer and her presumed antithesis—the male adventurer. Middle-class women were constrained by the ideology of separate spheres, the notion, articulated by John Ruskin in his 1865 manifesto *Sesame and Lilies*, that woman was for the Home (the "place of Peace . . . the shelter . . . from all injury") and man for the World (the place of "peril and trial"), woman for the hearth and man for business, governance, and the wide, if tainted, realm beyond domestic life.[3] Social historians have demonstrated in recent years that the middle-class doctrine of separate spheres was just that—a doctrine, an ideology, a prescription—rather than a description of historical reality. That such prescriptions were effective and the social pressures they exerted powerful, we can't deny (consider Mrs. Ramsay), but this is not the whole story. We now recognize that this fiercely articulated doctrine was as much an anxious response to the participation of women in public life as it was an accurate reflection of social patterns.

In salient mythological, literary, and critical traditions, woman is habitually associated with the subject of home, man with the enterprise of travel and adventure; woman perennially imagined as Penelope, man as Ulysses (Karen Lawrence gives the insistent title *Penelope Voyages* to her important study of women's travel in the British literary tradition); and the woman who dares to venture forth understood as both dangerous and endangered.[4] Paul Zweig's suggestive meditation, called *The Adventurer* (1974), on the literary history and meaning of adventure stories, from the *Odyssey* to T. E. Lawrence's *Seven Pillars of Wisdom*, makes the following claims:

> The adventurer's essential triumph is masculine. His gift is to bind the binder, to outwit and defeat the mysterious identities of woman. The woman he defeats expresses the bewitching domesticity of the house, the space of the community—which is immobile, predictable, fenced off against the amoral potencies of the extra-human world. She presides over the safe

breathing-space of human—that is, social—needs. Woman rules the home, and home is where the arts of man are nourished.[5]

Drawing on Ruskinian rhetoric, Zweig suggests that woman is precluded from taking the role of adventurer in myth and literature and that, furthermore, she is the very thing—the "binder," in his term—man wishes to escape when *he* becomes one. And it is not woman as individual or even lover that the adventurer seeks to escape but rather woman as she expresses the "bewitching domesticity of the house": woman, that is, as mother.

The generic division Zweig points to here lays out the longstanding association between the sexes and their respective literary ventures. Homer, the "Gawain poet," Cervantes, Henry Fielding, Walter Scott, Robert Louis Stevenson, Joseph Conrad, and T. E. Lawrence all wrote adventure stories in which their heroes are engaged in "extraordinary" exploits at the margins of culture, in flight, in one way or another, from the spirit of home—and women. By contrast, the bourgeois novel, a product of eighteenth- and nineteenth-century female and male authors, gives us individuals, placed within "the framework of the ordinary," who are "essentially conservative" and "move, not too energetically, in a solid world of relationships."[6] The extraordinary world of adventure and the ordinary "world of relationships" are contiguous but don't overlap; the true bourgeois novel cannot be an adventure story; and women are irrevocably tied to home as both authors and characters.

Zweig has an interesting psychoanalytic reading of the adventure paradigm that might help explain certain persistent misrepresentations of women's writing. If woman *is* home for the male adventurer, the spirit that presides over, protects, and personifies home, she is both to be desired—or idealized—and to be rejected or escaped. She is permanent, immobile, "fenced off." This form of projection onto woman—the need to imagine her as propelling men and offspring outward and yet also drawing them back home—extends as well to the literary forms women have historically favored. In our collective imaginations, woman cannot be uncoupled from "domestic fiction," for it defines the sensibility and form of writing that men eschew when they adopt the mode of adventure, and that subsequent generations of writers, whether male or female, seek to overturn when they separate themselves from the weight of the literary past.

One such rebel against the maternal past was Virginia Woolf, who sought to "think back through [her] mothers," to reconstruct and celebrate the often eclipsed literary traditions they had built so heroically and with so few resources but also to throw off the inheritance that might not suit a new way of being and writing. Perhaps the most influential source for understanding the nineteenth-century woman writer as domestic novelist is Virginia Woolf's *A Room of One's Own*. Woolf's indispensable text, which inaugurated the enterprise of feminist literary criticism in the 1920s, uses a number of fictions and fictional figures—Mary Seton, Judith Shakespeare, Mary Carmichael—in order to make the argument that women had historically been denied the material and psychological conditions necessary to becoming a writer. Another of Woolf's fictions is the nineteenth-century woman writer herself: schooled narrowly in the ways and emotions of the middle-class sitting room, confined to the domestic sphere, sheltered from and ignorant of "the world," denied the freedom to travel, and, as a consequence of all this, wedded to the novel as a form of writing that could be undertaken—actually written—in the common sitting room and could also use to advantage women's "training in the observation of character" and "the analysis of emotion." Some of us know the passages by heart: Jane Austen never got to ride in an omnibus through London or lunch by herself in a shop; "experience and intercourse and travel" were not granted Charlotte Brontë, and so her books would be "deformed and twisted," her genius never expressed "whole and entire"; and the extraordinary works *Villette*, *Emma*, *Wuthering Heights*, and *Middlemarch* were "written by women without more experience of life than could enter the house of a respectable clergyman."[7]

At this last point the mind boggles just a bit, and Woolf, to her credit, anticipates our reaction: yes, she adds, George Eliot did live in sin with a married man for decades, but she lived in seclusion, "cut off from what is called the world," in Eliot's own phrase.[8] When we consider that Charlotte Brontë, an unmarried clergyman's daughter from Yorkshire, twice lived abroad in Brussels and traveled numerous times to London, especially after the deaths of her sisters, and that Eliot journeyed to the Continent almost yearly between 1854, when she began living with George Henry Lewes, and 1880, when she died, and had a more cosmopolitan frame of reference—both intellectually and socially—than any other major Victorian novelist, we know that Woolf is up to something. That something, as we've already said, is fiction making, expressly for the purpose of defining her predecessors as a phenomenon against which to define herself and her own modernist work. For *A Room of One's Own* is, among other things, a manifesto for new kinds of women's writing, in which, according to Woolf, the writer has forgotten that she is a woman and so writes without grievance or consciousness of her sex.

Woolf seeks to both reconstruct a tradition and mark that tradition as limited and constraining, and in so doing she creates a myth about the nineteenth-century woman writer that has almost indelibly distorted our view of her. To portray her predecessors as sheltered and housebound creatures and to overlook, whether deliberately or not, the heroic and public-facing impulses of their fiction is to set the stage for Woolf's own literary project. Lily Briscoe, the "new woman" artist of *To the Lighthouse*, represents the generation that will succeed Mrs. Ramsay, adoring and mourning her but also rebelling against Victorian imperatives of marriage and realist aesthetic practices alike. Lily's painting of Mrs. Ramsay, completed as the novel ends and Mr. Ramsay, James, and Cam finally reach the lighthouse, takes the form of abstraction—a bold line in the center of her canvas, a shape akin, perhaps, to the dark wedge of Mrs. Ramsay's reveries. Lily, like Mrs. Ramsay's daughters, who sit at their mother's table brewing "infidel ideas . . . of a life different from hers; in Paris perhaps; a wilder life; not always taking care of some man or other," thinks back through but also effaces her "mothers."[9] Lily and the Ramsay girls appear as less murderous versions of the hypothetical journalist in Woolf's essay "Professions for Women," who feels the need to kill off the phantom that looks over her shoulder as she sits down to write a review of a novel by a "famous man." This maternal phantom, the "Angel in the House," interferes with the journalist's critical task because the older woman exemplifies sympathy and unselfishness: "She excelled in the difficult arts of family life. She sacrificed herself daily." This matricidal imperative, Woolf tells us, "was found to befall all women writers at that time. Killing the Angel in the House was part of the occupation of a woman writer."[10] Though Woolf, who was among the most acute critics of her predecessors' writing, especially in her essays and reviews, could separate the Angel from the woman novelist, she cast them both as sister members of a generation that needed to be—and would be—superseded.

Of course, the Angel in the House hovered over the nineteenth-century woman writer herself, sometimes in the form of advisers and reviewers, sometimes as an internalized voice counseling self-effacement and calculated obscurity. Reviewers tended to judge a woman's work by moral rather than aesthetic or literary standards and, as Elaine Showalter puts it, to "focus on her femininity and rank her with the other women writers of her day, no matter how diverse their subjects or styles."[11] Patterns of moralistic reading and public squeamishness about ethical infractions against feminine propriety in women's writing helped to make women novelists vigilant about protecting their privacy and preserving their images as genteel and unworldly creatures. One author of the domestic image of the nineteenth-century woman writer was, then, the nineteenth-century woman writer herself. Minimizing the scope and ambition of her work, Austen referred to herself as a miniaturist, painting on a piece of ivory just two inches wide. In *A Room of One's Own* Woolf remarks that Eliot asked not to have any visitors at the Priory unless she invited them herself, as if to suggest that she saw few people and preferred to see even fewer. In her "Notice" to new editions of *Agnes Grey* and *Wuthering Heights* in 1850, Charlotte Brontë insisted that their authors, her sisters Anne and Emily, were reclusive, retiring, refined, and, by extension, chaste, implicitly ignorant of the sensational experiences about which they wrote: adultery, physical cruelty, emotional brutality, and alcoholism.[12] The Angel in the House, Woolf reminds us, was, above all things, pure. Just as the Victorian woman novelist relied on pseudonymous publication to protect her privacy and the fact of her sex, so too did she continue to block and sanitize the public's knowledge of her real life after her works were in circulation. The Brontë sisters and George Eliot had to negotiate with care the desired separation between private self and public author when they ventured into the public sphere, whether attending London literary gatherings or hazarding opinions on women's rights. The detestation of publicity, about which Woolf wrote so perceptively in *A Room of One's Own*, prompted the Victorian woman novelist to participate in the creation of her own myth as a profoundly and inescapably domestic creature, attached to hearth and hesitant to offend, however distant that image was from the truth of her life.

Of all the women writers who understood the connections between the form of the novel, the phenomenon of travel, and the struggle for women's emancipation, Mary Wollstonecraft was the most important and incisive. Author of political treatises on the rights of "men" and "woman," one finished and one unfinished novel, and a travel memoir in the form of letters, she stands as a barely acknowledged forerunner of the nineteenth-century women novelists who returned again and again to tropes of travel as expressions of the desire for liberty from constraining and unjust domestic arrangements. Her most famous work, *Vindication of the Rights of Woman* (1792), inspired by the principles of the French Revolution, depicted women's lives as a form of slavery: not the kind enforced by shackles and the lash but an insidious and easily disguised type dependent on the praise of women's weakness, passivity, and beauty for its own sake. Confined to their "gilt cages," women had come to love their "prisons," and only through the "invigorating air of freedom" would women be revived and redeemed.[13] She encourages women to pursue the virtues of friendship, exercise, knowledge, reason, and the "cultivation of the understanding" to lift them out of their indolence and "overweening sensuality."[14] Marriage and a wholly domestic existence prove an impediment to true liberty (widows, she mused, might be the ideal independent

women); novel reading stunts young women's intellects; and a belief in the "state of nature" lulls them into complacency. Through
education and the proper cultivation of self (Wollstonecraft used
the botanical metaphor of plants rooted in too-rich soil to evoke
enervated womanhood), women might become rational and productive beings.[15]

Wollstonecraft regarded travel as one such form of self-
cultivation—the "completion of a liberal education," she called it
in *Letters Written during a Short Residence in Sweden, Norway,
and Denmark* (1796)—and as an opportunity to understand the
relationship between the social and the natural in another context.[16] The dramatic coasts and waterways of Scandinavia gave
her a chance to meditate on the sublime and on the role of human
resourcefulness in taming or refining the unruly seascapes she
glimpsed from one small boat after another. "Nature resumed an
aspect ruder and ruder," she writes, "or rather seemed the bones
of the world waiting to be clothed with everything necessary to
give life and beauty" (42). If Nature itself was rude, skeletal, it had
also "bastilled" the inhabitants of the coast of Norway, "shut[ting]
them out from all that opens the understanding, or enlarges the
heart" (102). She speculates that discussions of "politics" and the
spirit of the French Revolution itself would open up the sympathies and intellects of the people of this region. At present, she
laments, the scope of their concerns is limited, and they care "only
for their families" (64). Time and again in the course of her letters,
she advocates inquiry, observation ("I was a woman of observation, for I asked . . . men's questions"), curiosity, and "mixing with
mankind" as antidotes for prejudice, fanaticism, and what she calls
"Rousseau's golden age of stupidity" (15, 89). Travel and the circulation of ideas provide such antidotes and move individual concerns out of the private and into the public sphere.

In the structure of thought that marks Wollstonecraft's writings, unredeemed nature, political tyranny, and the oppression of
women all produce prisons of the body and mind. She was the first
and perhaps most militant exponent of the notion that there was no
absolute distinction between public despotism and the despotism
of the home, and her use of metaphors bears this out. "Marriage

had bastilled me for life," the character Maria writes in a memoir for her daughter in Wollstonecraft's unfinished novel *Maria, or The Wrongs of Woman*.[17] This heroine inhabits a horrific space of confinement as the novel begins: a madhouse as bastille or Gothic prison, where she is incarcerated by order of her husband and bereft of the child she has borne. In this problematic and fragmentary text, women are hunted "from hole to hole" like "beast[s] of prey" or creatures "infected with a moral plague"; they are "buried alive," locked up, secluded, hidden, held captive.[18] The images that dominate this truncated narrative appear in stark contrast to the images of open space, sea travel, and perpetual inquiry that characterize the *Letters*, though she sees both the woman isolated in her home and the Norwegians hemmed in by their rugged coast as prisoners of a metaphoric bastille.

The problem for Wollstonecraft here was to plot a novel that hinges on the relationship between Maria, her heroine, and Darnford, the man she loves, while moving toward the sense of openness and liberty she associates with the "self-cultivation" of travel. Would this narrative trace Maria's escape from literal and symbolic incarceration into a sustaining love affair with Darnford, thereby conforming to the conventions of sentimental fiction? Or would this escape be an illusory one, not into the light and free air of liberty and independence of thought but into another prison—a bastille—of romantic love and its inevitable betrayals? If the latter, would Maria's life end in tragic, premature death, following the path of Richardson's *Clarissa*, or would she, as some of Wollstonecraft's notes suggest, "live for [her] child" within a small female community?[19] *The Wrongs of Woman*, as it stands, never sorts out how to reconcile inherited novelistic conventions with a vision of independent womanhood and the emancipatory ethos of the travel narrative. That Wollstonecraft strove for such reconciliation, however, seems all but certain.

Although not descended in a direct line of inheritance from Mary Wollstonecraft, the great women novelists of the nineteenth century struggled in the course of their literary careers to insert a critique of women's domestic confinement into their novels of courtship and marriage—or death. In ways both predictable and not, they exploited and subverted novelistic convention to express the impulse to reject, even revile, the domestic sphere and to venture forth into uncharted waters. It has been said, most eloquently by Ellen Moers, that the Gothic novel became a "feminine substitute for the picaresque," the form in which heroines could embark on adventures, undertake journeys, and conquer adversity, in short, a form that allowed them to be travelers without leaving the proper and ultimately safe space of indoors.[20] In this view, the Gothic narrative becomes a pretext for travel and adventure: the same could be said of the nineteenth-century courtship plot.

In the works of Jane Austen and Charlotte Brontë, in particular, and, to a lesser extent, George Eliot, the search for a mate or soul mate often involves a departure, sometimes an escape, from some incommodious, uncongenial home and the discovery of what we might call Home with a capital "H": a site, though not necessarily a dwelling, of true belonging. This terminus of Home is not always a literal place or abode and, even when it is, it is virtually never imagined as a domestic space, the locus of conventional family life. Increasingly in the works of Austen, Brontë, and Eliot, this ideal place of dwelling is pictured as a non-place or imagined space and homecoming imagined, perhaps paradoxically, as leave-taking. These three novelists' final completed novels—*Persuasion*, *Villette*, and *Daniel Deronda*—are their most powerfully and overtly anti-domestic works, as well as their most inconclusive and experimental. If the literary conventions of what we call variously sentimental or domestic fiction operate as constraints on women writers, obscuring or deforming their own experience and perception of life, then a hard-won insistence on anti-domestic narrative—more possible at the peak of a career than at its outset—would also necessitate reinventing or at least modifying novelistic form. Each of these three novels culminates in the abandonment or dramatic reinvention of home.

The first chapter of *Pride and Prejudice*, associated most famously with its opening sentence ("It is a truth universally acknowledged, that a single man in possession of a good fortune, must be in want of a wife"), closes with an indictment of marriage, or at least of the most important marriage we are witness to in the novel—Mr. and Mrs. Bennet's. If the chapter begins with a sly, ironic announcement that this will be a narrative about courtship, it ends with a subtle warning about what courtship can lead to: a lack of understanding between badly matched husband and wife that cannot be overcome by twenty-three years of marriage. As the novel unfolds, it is clear that nearly dire consequences follow from the Bennet misalliance. As the result of Mrs. Bennet's witless obsession with marrying off her daughters and unchecked identification with the most wayward and foolish of them, and Mr. Bennet's passivity and uncensored contempt for his wife, Lydia Bennet comes dangerously close to becoming a ruined woman. After she runs off with Wickham and the novel is plunged into a dark subplot—a story of fallen sexuality that might destroy Lydia and, by association, all of her sisters—Elizabeth understands the full force of her parents' mismatch:

> Had Elizabeth's opinion been all drawn from her own family, she could not have formed a very pleasing picture of conjugal felicity or domestic comfort. Her father captivated by youth and beauty, and that appearance of good humor . . . had married a woman whose weak understanding and illiberal mind, had very early in their marriage put an end to all real affection for her. Respect, esteem, and confidence, had vanished forever; and all his views of domestic happiness were overthrown.[21]

The phrases "conjugal felicity," "domestic comfort," and "domestic happiness" stand out in this passage as markers of an ideal familiar to Austen's readers from fiction, if not from life. Elizabeth's image of all of these has been undermined by the example of her family; and the anti-domestic thrust of Austen's narrative begins with and is propelled by the Bennet's mismatch and the home it has built.

Elizabeth's grasp of the regrettable consequences of her parents' marriage intensifies, and her view of her family ultimately conforms to the nasty and humiliating things that Darcy, a man ostensibly guilty of both pride and prejudice, thinks about them. Even before she knows the worst, however, Elizabeth's sense of the Bennets' marriage produces in her an antipathy to domestic life that fuels her restlessness and keeps her in almost constant motion, striving, as much as possible, to be away from home. At the drop of a hat she is off to tend to an ailing Jane by hiking three miles to Netherfield, "crossing field after field at a quick pace, jumping over stiles and springing over puddles with impatient activity" and exercising, in Bingley's sisters' view, "an abominable sort of conceited independence" (P&P, 33, 36). She visits her friend Charlotte Lucas's new "establishment" in Hunsford, where the advantage of being absent from her own home will make even a stay with the offensive Mr. Collins bearable, at least for a while. She stops at her aunt and uncle Gardiners' in London and then travels with them to Derbyshire, where she sees Darcy's estate, Pemberley, for the first time, and where the news of Lydia and Wickham's elopement aborts a greatly anticipated journey to the Lake District.

The suspicion the novel casts on the realm of home is fed not only by the disarray, emotional and otherwise, of the Bennet marriage but also by the sense, indeed, the fact, that the home, or at least the house, is a male possession and preserve. Each country estate in the novel, with one exception, is identified with a man. Although Rosings is clearly the domain of Lady Catherine de Bourgh, Netherfield is Bingley's, although he does not own it; Pemberley is Darcy's—indeed, Pemberley *is* Darcy; the parsonage at Hunsford is Mr. Collins's; and Longbourne, the Bennets' home, is also Mr. Collins's. The law of entail, which dictates that Longbourne be inherited not by any of the Bennet daughters but by their male relative, Collins, plays an important role in the narrative, not least in helping to make absolutely clear that the home, like the women who inhabit it, is the property of men. Elizabeth is both a restless inhabitant of Longbourne and a temporary one, a transient. Houses, as Pemberley makes clear more than any other residence, are extensions and expressions of the male self. When Lady Catherine says that Darcy and her daughter are destined for each other "by the voice of every member of their respective houses," she makes use of the aristocratic understanding that a house stands as a metonym for pedigree, the lineage of wealth, property, and position that descends through the male line (P&P, 337).

There is one residence in *Pride and Prejudice* that stands outside of the patriarchal model, whether aristocratic or gentry, and that is the Gardiners' house in Cheapside, a district of London associated with trade. From his home in this odd- and vulgar-sounding quarter of the capital, Mr. Gardiner can see his own warehouses—a fact that earns him the opprobrium of people like the Bingley sisters, who are anxious about their own status. The Gardiners' home is the site of as egalitarian a marriage as exists in the novel. The aunt and uncle's intimacy, like-mindedness, lack of pretension, and shared good judgment make them the perfect guides for Elizabeth in her quest for a place of belonging. The house in Cheapside reflects this: here, their children strike the right balance between ebullience and reticence; here, the urban dwelling opens out into an easy exchange with the public sphere. Elizabeth, Jane, and their aunt spend the mornings in "bustle and shopping," the evenings at "one of the theatres" (*P&P*, 150).

Appropriately, then, the Gardiners accompany Elizabeth when she first visits Pemberley. Together the three are equipped to read the house, to take its measure as the perfect blend of nature and human art, to understand the tasteful furnishings of the house as an expression of its owner's discernment in weightier things, and, most important, to gauge the contentment of those in his domestic employ as signs of Darcy's charity and good mastership. In the end, the house Darcy has built becomes a magnet, not just for Elizabeth but for her aunt and uncle, her father, her sister Kitty, and Jane and Bingley, who vacate Netherfield and move to Derbyshire after a year of marriage, expressly to get away from Mrs. Bennet. Mr. Darcy, all perceive, is a superb homemaker and ideal parent to his sister. After all, he had saved her from the very fate from which Mr. Bennet did not manage to save Lydia. The true spirit of home in *Pride and Prejudice* turns out to be a man, an ideal paternal figure that protects the interests of young women, and not the maternal force that sends Elizabeth running from domesticity.

Home as a masculine province takes a number of forms in Austen's novels. In *Pride and Prejudice*, as we have seen, Pemberley is both an idyllic spot and a reflection of Darcy's benign and responsible governance. In *Emma* the eponymous heroine hesitates to leave the protection and privilege of her widower father's home after she marries Mr. Knightley. Faced with the choice of living under her husband's roof or her father's, she chooses the latter, in part because Mr. Woodhouse claims he cannot do without her and in part, we infer, because she might not need to accede to Knightley's authority in what is essentially her own home to the degree she might have had she moved into his. On the face of it, however, Emma's choice vividly reminds the reader that in Austen's world, women are passed from father to husband and, ordinarily, from father's to husband's dwelling. In *Mansfield Park* the centrality of the Bertrams' estate to the story Austen wants to tell is signaled, of course, in the novel's title. Not only is this property firmly associated with patriarchal inheritance, a possession to be bequeathed by father to oldest son, it is also linked to the spoils of colonialism and the slave trade. However equivocally Austen regards the economic underpinnings of Mansfield Park, she ends the novel by, as Susan Fraiman has pointed out, "settling her [heroine] firmly on its periphery."[22] Fanny Price and her husband, Edmund Bertram, keep their distance from this home built, or at least maintained, by Sir Thomas Bertram's investments in Antigua. In Austen's final novel, *Persuasion*, as we shall see, the family estate bespeaks not just the identity of the patriarch but his unbearable narcissism as well.

Persuasion is the Austen novel most explicitly engaged with historical, or public, events and the changes in British society these events helped to produce. The heroine's story is not only embedded in these but her relationship to home is shaped by them. If Elizabeth Bennet is a refugee from Longbourne, Anne Elliot, the heroine of *Persuasion*, is an exile from her natal home, the family seat Kellynch-hall. Both heroines are peripatetic—Anne travels to her sister Mary's home at Uppercross, to Captain Harville's home in Lyme Regis, to Uppercross a second time, and then to Bath, where her father and sister Elizabeth have taken up residence. And just as Mr. Bennet had never economized for the sake of his daughters because he assumed he would someday have a son to inherit Longbourne, Sir Walter Elliot is forced to vacate Kellynch-hall as the novel opens because he has been profligate and is now "distressed for money."[23] Although Mr. Bennet chooses not to leave Longbourne in the course of *Pride and Prejudice* until Elizabeth marries, his attachment to home pales in comparison to Sir Walter's narcissistic regard for his estate and vain preoccupation with the lineage that estate embodies. His entry in the Baronetage, which he pores over obsessively as the narrative opens, is "*Elliot of Kellynch-hall*," as if to underscore that the man's identity is inseparable from his dwelling. The family entry includes the Christian names used repeatedly over generations by the Elliots—numerous Walters, of course, and "all the Marys and Elizabeths they had married"—to underscore the unchangeable and, ultimately, cyclical nature of patriarchal succession (*P*, 5). Anne, not a recycled name in the Baronetage, will follow a different path and, in the end, reside in a very different kind of dwelling.

The portrait of Sir Walter is scathing, and, unlike Mr. Bennet, who dotes on Elizabeth, he dismisses and depreciates Anne as a "nobody," a person unworthy of any regard or attention. As the father of daughters, Sir Walter will be forced to leave his estate to a male relation, Mr. William Elliot, just as Mr. Bennet's property will go to Mr. Collins. Exiled from the home she loves for its connection to her beloved late mother, and in spite of her callous father and oldest sister, Anne Elliot will wander in search of congenial surroundings and sympathetic companions throughout the novel. Unlike the plucky Elizabeth Bennet, however, Anne feels herself barely entitled to happiness or a place of belonging—life has passed her by, she is a mere appendage to her relations, an all-but-invisible faded spinster. Strangely, she will be revived and reborn—and, not coincidentally, her first love rekindled—by becoming a wanderer, a woman without a home.

For Anne Elliot, then, a lack of station, house, and property comes as a true mark of liberation. The signs that this will be the case—that to be landless, quite literally, will mean true happiness—accrue throughout the narrative. Kellynch-hall, to Sir Walter's considerable chagrin, is rented not only to a naval man, made rich through the Napoleonic Wars, but to his wife, the sister of the very man of "obscure birth" Sir Walter and his friends and relations had "persuaded" Anne not to marry years before. And this brother, Captain Wentworth, has, through "merit and activity," reached as high in his profession as was possible and now has a substantial fortune of 25,000 pounds (*P*, 218). These new tenants of Kellynch-hall are understood by Anne, however, to be worthier occupants of the estate than her own kin: "she could not but in conscience feel that they were gone who deserved not to stay, and that Kellynch-hall had passed into better hands than its owners" (*P*, 113). These "better hands," Admiral and Mrs. Croft, present Anne with an example of conjugal happiness and loving companionship achieved within the context of public service and institutional life. Mrs. Croft stands before her as the model of womanhood she might have emulated had she married Wentworth long ago. Her face reddened and weathered by many years at sea with her husband, Mrs. Croft has been an intrepid traveler all over the globe—the East Indies, Cork, Lisbon, Gibraltar—and made five different ships her home. Although not a widespread practice and, strictly speaking, against naval regulations, it was not uncommon for ships to carry officers' wives to an overseas station. Austen's sister-in-law Fanny, for example, accompanied her husband Charles from Bermuda to Halifax.[24] For Mrs. Croft, domestic comfort is achieved in being with her husband, discomfort and inconvenience suffered when she is forced to separate from him. As is the case with the Gardiners in *Pride and Prejudice*, the Crofts' exemplary union is inseparable from the unconventionality of their habitual dwelling and from a sense of life beyond the strictly private realm, whether in the British Navy or the bustling commercial streets of the metropolis.

Other unconventional households in the novel serve to loosen Anne's attachment to the ideal of home that had been her mother's. The rooms in Bath of her loyal and ever-hopeful friend, Mrs. Smith, are humble and out-of-the-way. Captain Harville's home in Lyme Regis, where Anne goes with a congenial party of her sisters-in-law and Wentworth, has tiny rooms, inadequate furnishings, and the dingy air of a seaside dwelling; and it is rented rather than owned by its resident. Still, to Anne it is "the picture of repose and domestic happiness," a reminder, like Mrs. Croft's world travels, of what her life might have been had she married Wentworth—even the poor Wentworth, the man of no consequence (*P*, 89). Lyme, with its Cobb extending, as if suspended, out into the water, exists as a kind of halfway house between land and sea, a location closer to both Anne's lost life and ultimate fate than Kellynch-hall. The sea air, acting as a promise of things to come, revives Anne's youthfulness and brings color to her cheeks: if she is lucky, it will eventually redden and age her face to resemble Mrs. Croft's.

Unlike Elizabeth Bennet, who ends up in the perfect house, Pemberley, the embodiment of her husband's fine character and taste, Anne Elliot will end in a non-place, a true Home alongside Captain Wentworth but with an indefinite location, as likely to be on board a ship, or many ships, as anywhere else. In *Persuasion*, the critique of landed domesticity that appears in mild form in *Pride and Prejudice* becomes a full-scale assault. Here, in her last completed novel with its autumnal tones, Austen appears to be taking leave—of a permanent abode, of commodious country life, perhaps of life itself—without any apparent regret. As Virginia Woolf wrote of *Persuasion*, the novel makes us feel that Austen has "done this before [but] also that she is trying to do something which she has never yet attempted . . . discover[ing] that the world is larger, more mysterious."[25] The heroine's pilgrimage toward a perhaps literally unmoored and unrepresentable dwelling place works in tandem with the novel's embrace of new social structures, newly ascendant sources of wealth and influence, and a society that values "worth" over birth, character over lineage. *Persuasion* envisions a world that is determined not by repetition and replication, as Sir Walter's beloved Baronetage suggests, but by contingency, accident, change, and the forces of history. It imagines a world in which women are not pale, smooth-skinned, and passive but are, instead, intrepid and adventurous, in which women cross the Atlantic over and over again and do not cleave to home in its landed, stationary, or inherited form. Home, for Mrs. Croft and now for Anne Elliot, is not simply where the heart is—though it is clearly that. More a space of possibility than anything real or realized, this new incarnation of Home begins to take shape at the moment when these women set sail.

Some of Charlotte Brontë's anti-domestic and outward-bound impulses extend and deepen features we have seen in Austen: restless heroines, first and foremost, with a penchant for venturing out alone and wandering in search of true Home. *Jane Eyre* follows the paradigm of *Pilgrim's Progress*, tracing the peripatetic heroine's journey from Gateshead Hall to Lowood School to Thornfield to Marsh End and then, finally, to Ferndean and redemption. (It is worth remembering in this context that Jane also has the chance to sail to India as the missionary wife of St. John Rivers, a man she cannot love. Rather than offer adventure, vocation, or a place of belonging, this journey would entail sacrifice or, as one critic has shrewdly put it, "a martyrdom of heroic housekeeping."[26]) As in the Austen novels I have discussed, the grand estate in *Jane Eyre*, the place Jane believes might become her home, is distinctly the property of—indeed, the physical extension of—a man. Unlike Pemberley, however, Thornfield, with its madwoman incarcerated in the attic, atmosphere of a "Bluebeard's castle," and oriental boudoir fit for the sultan Rochester aspires to be, must finally be razed.[27] Its destruction follows from two potent anti-domestic forces that Brontë introduces into the fabric of her narrative: the protofeminist articulation of a desire for economic independence and equality with men and the potentially disruptive powers of sexual longing and fulfillment. Brontë's insistent rhetoric of slavery and servitude throughout the novel and the contest between dependence and independence work themselves out, somewhat uneasily, in the equilibrium of the home finally imagined at the novel's end—the home of Ferndean rather than Thornfield Hall. Homelessness and rebellion, which determine Jane's condition for much of the narrative, threaten nonetheless to override the domestic and domesticating pressures of the novel's denouement and have their lingering effects in Rochester's diminished circumstances and Jane's implicit power, the result of both economic and perhaps temporary physical dominance.

The formative Continental experiences of Brontë's life found their way into her fiction, from the settings of *The Professor* and *Villette* to the French language spoken in the midst of Yorkshire in *Shirley* and by the child, Adele, in *Jane Eyre*. The alienating and anti-domestic effects of such intrusions and dislocations are felt most powerfully in Brontë's last novel. In *Penelope Voyages*, Karen Lawrence writes that the first hundred pages or so of *Villette* "offer the domestic as a kind of annihilating setting, as the narrative increasingly robs Lucy Snowe of her ability to signify, to mark her place."[28] Increasingly, Lucy comes to "mark her place," not as wife or keeper of a household but as traveler, writer, and teacher, very quickly leaving behind the spaces of domestic fiction that fill the novel's first chapters. In both the content and form of *Villette*, Brontë does nothing less than offer a critique of the "domestic" novel, in part through a pattern of uncanny repetition, which continually undermines any idea of permanence or stability in the narrative, and in part by imagining a wholly new idea of home. Brontë creates, as well, a prickly narrator, Lucy Snowe, who withholds information from the reader, a strange duo of possible male lovers for the heroine, and an ending that leaves the reader hanging. We choose two strands of this complex novel to follow here: the unraveling of the idea of home as a stable and sheltering place, and the tropes of sea travel, storms at sea, and shipwreck that help to undermine the possibility of bourgeois domesticity even further.

Brontë begins to recast the relationship between home and abroad, domestic and foreign, in the first disorienting pages of her novel. The unnamed narrator begins her tale in a place called Bretton, in the home of her godmother, whose surname is also Bretton. The reader puzzles momentarily over whether this "clean and ancient town" is in the British Isles or on the Continent. Are we in England, Ireland, Brittany, or Belgium? We also wonder whether the heroine of the novel will be our narrator (is this book going to be about her?) or whether it will turn out to be the girl, Polly, with the significant surname of Home, whose story the narrator seems to be telling. And why are the godmother's surname and the name of the town the same? Lucy tells us she isn't sure. The female characters' names we do know at the outset—Louisa Bretton and Polly Home—encourage us, at the very least, to think about the deep connection between place, or home, and the identity of woman. We are also alerted to the possibility, however, that the surname Polly carries can have an ironic twist: her mother, Mrs. Home—"(Home it seems was the name)," the narrator tells us, repeating the word parenthetically—was a "giddy careless woman, who had neglected her child, and disappointed and disheartened her husband."[29] Home and family can be made by woman or, if she proves inadequate to the task, broken.

Her mother having died, Polly is left to her father, to whom she is deeply attached, and, temporarily at least, in the company of Mrs. Bretton, her petted son Graham, and the goddaughter, the narrator we come to know in the second chapter as the fourteen-year-old Lucy Snowe. Lucy, whose status as daughter, sister, or relation of any kind remains opaque throughout the entire novel, observes the drama of these two parent-and-child dyads as an outsider. What we do know about her is that she is closed out of these Oedipal couples, whose very intimacy seems to define the fact and the idea of home. The novel establishes, here in the first brief chapters, the inextricable connection between a particular form of domesticity, certain kinds of familial relations, gender roles, and the nature of the traditional novelistic heroine. In a flourish, Brontë joins the social, the psychological, and the literary, summing up—and ultimately dispensing with—fundamental paradigms of the bourgeois novel.

In the pattern that Karen Lawrence observes, Lucy loses the series of transitory homes she journeys through at the beginning of the narrative, as if Jane Eyre's entire pilgrimage were compressed into just a few opening chapters. The reader inserts Lucy tentatively into various domestic contexts, and then the vicissitudes of the plot quickly and repeatedly remove her. At the beginning of chapter 4, we encounter a complicated, not to say confusing, extended metaphor (or is it wholly a metaphor?) of shipwreck that appears to evoke Lucy's final separation from any family she may have had. The wreck of this "bark slumbering through halcyon weather" sends Lucy on to a position as a lady's companion and then, in the space of less than a chapter, the death of her employer and collapse of this particular home sends her off to London (V, 30). There she begins to enjoy an expansive sense of life and adventure until, abruptly and without adequate explanation, Lucy decides to take a steamer to the imaginary country of Labassecour. Though it is wholly reasonable to read Labassecour as Belgium, just as it makes sense to take Bretton for an English town, we might also consider that it is explicitly an unreal place and so adds to the vertiginous landscape of the novel. This journey is both an

adventurous "voyage out"—the ship she takes is called the *Vivid*—
and a gesture of utter self-estrangement, even self-obliteration, a
crossing, as she imagines it, of the River Styx to the Land of Shades.
"I had nothing to lose," she informs us, "If I died far away from—
home, I was going to say, but I had no home—from England, then,
who would weep?" (*V*, 44; emphasis added).

Homeless, Lucy Snowe makes her way to the town of Villette in
Labassecour and to a girls' school and *pensionnat* (formerly a convent) where she gains employment. An outsider again, this time by
nationality, religion, and language, the Protestant Englishwoman
takes masochistic refuge in her alienated and dissociated state of
being. At least, that is, until she breaks down completely, confesses
to a Catholic priest in near delirium, and collapses. At this moment,
the uncanny enters Lucy's narrative to dizzying effect. In a chapter
ironically titled "Auld Lang Syne," Lucy awakens in a place unknown but disorientingly familiar. Surrounded by objects "of past
days, and of a distant country" that may, on the other hand, be
"ghosts of such articles" ("phantoms of chairs, and . . . wraiths of
looking-glasses, tea-urns and teacups"), haunted by Bretton and
her fourteenth year, she knows not where she is or what year she
may have time-traveled back to: "Where was I? Not only in what
spot of the world, but in what year of our Lord? . . . Am I in
England? Am I in Bretton?" (*V*, 162, 165). The disorientation the
reader feels on the very first page of the novel here returns (in another instance of uncanny repetition) in the consciousness of our
narrator. The objects she fixes on—including her godmother's pil-
low with the initials "LLB" formed in gold beads—are the markers
of homely, respectable bourgeois clutter, and they comfort Lucy
even as they disturb her. Even Graham is present here, in the form
of a portrait on the wall that depicts him as an adult.

What is the promise of this return for Lucy Snowe? We wonder
if it will provide her with the home and homecoming that had
always eluded her: Will she be able to settle here in this comfortable and familiar place, cared for by the only kind of family the
novel has conjured for her? Will Graham, now identified for the
reader as the Dr. John who has frequented the text since Lucy's arrival in Labassecour, begin to return the romantic feelings she has

had for him? These possibilities, which the novel encourages us to contemplate, soon prove illusory. Lucy recognizes this as early as the beginning of her stay with Mrs. Bretton and expresses the inevitable distance between herself and her godmother through the by-now familiar figure of the seagoing vessel. The elder woman is "the stately ship cruising safe on smooth seas, with its full complement of crew," while the younger is a mere "life-boat, only putting to sea when the billows run high in rough weather, . . . when danger and death divide between them the rule of the deep" (V, 176–77). "No," Lucy concludes, "the *Louisa Bretton* never was out of harbour on such a night, and in such a scene" (V, 177). Lucy's lot is to be that storm-tossed raft, as we already know from the beginning of chapter 4, and will be reminded of again at the novel's end. Her godmother's is to voyage out only in the safest of conditions, bolstered by a capable crew.

Graham's fate is to marry Polly Home, who also reappears in Labassecour. The Oedipal dyads of Lucy's youth reconstitute themselves there, only this time the child bond of Polly and Graham is remade as a marriage bond. Closed out of the circle again, Lucy contemplates the plenitude of Polly's gifts, symbolized by the interwoven plaits of hair, one from a lover and one from her father, she places in a locket around her neck. A phantasmagoric outing into the nighttime streets of Villette culminates in Lucy's vision of the Homes and Brettons celebrating the union of their families, with Polly "compassed by the triple halo of her beauty, her youth, and her happiness" (V, 449). The idea of Home that eludes Lucy over and over again is constituted by certain relations between parents and children and the replication of those relations in the field of heterosexual romance.

Displaced again by Polly, that feminine avatar of the patriarchal idea of Home, Lucy retreats from the idea that she will find repose in bourgeois domesticity and begins to envision another kind of place of her own. Her vision is quite specific: a home as schoolroom, a "tenement with one large room and three smaller ones . . . with a few benches and desks, a black tableau, an *estrade* [platform] for myself, upon it a chair and table, with a sponge and some white chalks" (V, 357). This version of home is inevitably and intimately tied to a love object quite different from Graham: the grouchy, saturnine M. Paul Emanuel. When, later in the narrative, M. Paul brings Lucy to the school and "neat abode" he has acquired for her before he leaves for Guadaloupe, it has an uncanny air, for Lucy has imagined it precisely before. Here are the benches and desks, here the teacher's *estrade* with table and chair, there behind them the tableau. A new model of Home had taken shape in Lucy's imagination and is now realized, as if by magic, in the flat before her: a place where work and home merge, where home is all but stripped of its domestic associations, where a family or even a romantic partnership is not essential and may indeed be superfluous, where a woman can live and thrive alone.

The notorious ending of *Villette* tries not to tell the reader whether M. Paul, who has been abroad for three years, will ever return to share this flat with Lucy Snowe. Her "wonderfully changed life [and] relieved heart" have sustained her to the point of the novel's conclusion, which abruptly suspends time and action. "My *school* flourishes, my *house* is ready," she tells us, staying with the present tense as she underscores the inseparability of home and work in this new life she leads (V, 490; emphasis added). Lucy challenges the reader to picture happiness if she so chooses, to imagine a future for Lucy Snowe beyond the ending. But the reader's inclination to "picture union and a happy succeeding life" is blocked by mention of the "south-west storm" in the Atlantic that may or may not have stopped M. Paul in his journey home. Even had Lucy not told us that she knew the "signs of the sky; . . . noted . . . ever since childhood," we would recognize the return of a deadly image (V, 491). By the novel's end we have learned to read these repetitions, this return of the repressed, the cyclical pattern of Lucy's life, and we have also learned the meaning of threatened, metaphorical, or real shipwrecks. Home as the place of companionship and warm familial relations will elude Lucy permanently; the unhomely rhythm of loss will continue to determine the shape of her life; and home will inhere only in the sphere of work and authorship.

The unconventional ending of *Villette* is a far cry from the joyous if tentative conclusion of *Persuasion*. Lucy remains alone though happily employed, the death of her beloved hovers, and, we are told in the brief final paragraph of the novel, her enemies prosper. The ship at sea, whose image dominates the ending of Brontë's novel, is bound for shipwreck and, in that regard, doesn't resemble the place of conjugal contentment that Mrs. Croft promises Anne Elliot. Yet Austen closes her story of Anne and Captain Wentworth with an allusion to the "quick alarm" of war and a note of caution about the anxieties involved in marrying a naval man during wartime (*P*, 221). The hint of death is here, too, as it is in so many narratives of journeying out, not least Virginia Woolf's aptly named first novel, *The Voyage Out* (1915), in which the youthful Rachel Vinrace sets sail for South America and dies before her return to England. Departure and oblivion are difficult to separate in narratives of adventure, and *Villette* makes this abundantly clear when Lucy Snowe sails from London as if crossing the River Styx to the Land of Shades. We need only think of Tennyson's Ulysses—"my purpose holds / To sail beyond the sunset, and the baths / Of all the western stars, until I die"—a Victorian variant of the adventurer whose life, as Zweig puts it, "is a flight into danger."[30] The more threatening danger in all of these cases, however, is domestic imprisonment: a form of being "buried alive" that haunts the Gothic *pensionnat* where Lucy first lands in the town of Villette. Like Wollstonecraft's Maria before her, Lucy escapes this living death but, unlike Maria, she also escapes the grip of subservience to male power and her own desire. She will not, as she tells Polly Home, share anyone's life "in this world, as you understand sharing" (*V*, 421). And she will survive, the elderly woman with white hair beneath a white cap—a sign of her permanent virginity, perhaps—to write the book of *Villette*.

What then of George Eliot? The anti-domestic strain of Victorian women's writing takes a strange twist in her hands. Put simply, Eliot sends her heroines out, bound for travel, elopement, itinerant preaching, or a life devoted to social reform and, one by one, she brings them back again. Dinah, the woman preacher of *Adam Bede*, gives up the itinerant life, now outlawed for women by the Methodists, to stay home as Adam's wife. In *Middlemarch*, the idealistic Dorothea Brooke ultimately trades the life of a social reformer for the life of a reformer's wife. Not satisfied with condemning Dorothea to a "hidden life," Eliot's narrator buries her finally in an "unvisited tomb."[31] Maggie Tulliver, the doomed heroine of *The Mill on the Floss*, in an aqueous tradition that links her to Anne Elliot and Lucy Snowe, ventures forth on the water, sailing out on a tide of sexual, anti-domestic desire only to be brought back again, conscience stricken, to her provincial home. Her disgrace dictates that she will be a "lonely wanderer," unmarriageable and homeless.[32] But before she can leave again in search of a life elsewhere, a flood claims her, the waters closing over her head rather than carrying her out to adventure, love, or a new life. Our last glimpse of Maggie, like our last of Dorothea, is a grave.

Are the fates of these Eliot heroines a matter of realism or punishment? Does Eliot share Virginia Woolf's impulse to represent the life of the unexceptional Victorian woman, always stymied by social convention, enshrined in the domestic realm? Or is she determined to block the route of any heroine who starts to get away? In partial answer to these questions, we offer Eliot's experimental final novel, *Daniel Deronda*, with its split narrative and dual protagonists: one, Gwendolen Harleth, who remains an unattached young widow about to return to her mother's home as the novel concludes; and the other, the eponymous hero Deronda, who, having been raised an Englishman in an aristocratic home, discovers that he is a Jew and ends the novel looking for a Home of another kind—a Jewish homeland and republican polity in the Levant.

Deronda is the only one of Eliot's novels set in the present and, though it is also the only one set in contemporary London, it travels the Continent and imagines a voyage to the Middle East. At the novel's opening, Gwendolen Harleth appears at the gambling table in Baden; Deronda will wander on the Continent to a variety of unnamed places, as well as to Frankfurt; Mirah, the woman Daniel will eventually marry, has lately come from Prague and the United States; Gwendolen and her husband, Grandcourt, cross paths with Deronda in Genoa, where Daniel also encounters his mother; and, ultimately, Deronda and Mirah will leave England, we assume for good. The musician Klesmer, a hybrid of German, Slav, and Semite, refers to himself as "the Wandering Jew," and Deronda, even before he discovers the nature of his identity, feels a kinship with the Hagars and Ishmaels of this earth, that is, with its outcasts and wanderers.

The novel also features a number of voyages and water journeys, most of them associated with death or the possibility of drowning. Daniel, with his "old love of boating," rows down the Thames until after dark, singing the gondolier's song from Rossini's *Otello*, and contemplates whether he should risk "tak[ing] part in the battle of the world."[33] His answer seems to appear in the form of Mirah, who stands at the river's edge wetting her cloak in the water, about to drown herself. He rescues her, thereby initiating the chain of events and discoveries that will lead to the knowledge of his birth and commitment to Jewish nationalism: she is his first link to the "battle of the world." Toward the end of the novel, in a scene that is in some ways the companion episode to Mirah's rescue by Daniel, Gwendolen Harleth sails out once and then twice from Genoa with Grandcourt. She goes unwillingly because she dreads being alone, isolated, with her husband, and also, perhaps, because vastness, a sense of unlimited spaces, has been a source of terror to her since girlhood. The second sortie ends in Grandcourt's death—he is struck by the sail and falls overboard—and by the specter of Gwendolen's. Though unable, and likely unwilling, to save him, as Daniel had saved Mirah, she jumps in after her husband nonetheless and watches him drown, helpless. Like Mirah, however, she survives.

The account of the incident she later offers Deronda is telling:

> I was full of rage at being obliged to go—full of rage—and I could do nothing but sit there like a galley-slave. And then we got away . . . into the deep . . . and we never looked at each other, only he spoke to order me—and the very light about me seemed to hold me a prisoner and force me to sit as I did. It came over me that when I was a child I used to fancy sailing away into a world where people were not forced to live with any one they did not like—I did not like my [stepfather] to come home. And now, I thought, just the opposite had come to me. I had stept into a boat, and my life was a

sailing and a sailing away—gliding on and no help—always into solitude with *him*, away from deliverance. (*DD*, 695; emphasis in original)

Though Gwendolen's ultimate purpose here is to tell Daniel that she had really wanted her husband to die, the language and sentiment of her confession touch on the themes and terms of women's relation to travel, liberty, and its opposite—imprisonment—that, beginning with Wollstonecraft, we have been thinking about in this chapter. Not a journey of emancipation, like the fantasies of escape she harbored as a child, this trip with Grandcourt is a voyage of enslavement (similar, perhaps, to what Jane Eyre's voyage with St. John Rivers might have been like had she consented to go to India with him). There can be no deliverance from this journey, for it ends in death and crippling guilt or perpetual captivity in an intimate and detested bond. In this voyage out, neither Grandcourt nor Gwendolen is saved or freed, and Gwendolen also misses her chance to save others, the mission Deronda prefers and advises her later to follow.

While Daniel's rescue of Mirah prefigures the sea voyage they will take together at the novel's end, the catastrophe of Grandcourt's drowning presages only the continuation of Gwendolen's paralysis. Not only does Gwendolen mistake relations with men as the means to escape her own psychic confinement, but she also suffers from rootlessness, an inadequate connection to the idea or place of Home. Eliot's novel is, perhaps above all, about home and homelessness, on the level of the individual life in the story of Gwendolen and on the level of the collective life—the community—in the case of Daniel. We know from early on in the novel that the former lacks the psychic health and ability to love that derive from being "well rooted in some spot of native land" (*DD*, 22). Though a dweller in many homes (with a small "h"), she experiences an insidious form of Homelessness and, as a consequence, the novel implies, a fear of vastness, of the wide world beyond her limited ken. Without rootedness, Eliot's novel proposes, there can be no true sympathy for others or for the "great movements of the world, the larger destinies of mankind" (*DD*, 803).

As the novel closes, Gwendolen is forced to confront the "vast mysterious movement" that Daniel's Jewishness has introduced into his life and, as a result, begins to see that her own "horizon" "was but a dipping onward of an existence with which her own was revolving" (*DD*, 804). Perhaps as important for Gwendolen as this lesson in world geography and history is her return to her mother's home, where she may lay down roots for future restoration. Eliot's gift to Gwendolen is that she will neither die nor remarry before the narrative ends. She represents Eliot's attempt to leave a heroine suspended, neither married nor dead, the denouement of her life's story not yet conclusively written or known. Purely a daughter again, Gwendolen is sent back to the beginning, but she is also alerted to the historical vision that Eliot's novel, a meditation on rootedness, embodies.

Daniel, once a deracinated man who identified with Caliban and sang the gondolier's part in a drama about a Moor, will set sail to a distant place to find true Home in its deepest and widest sense. In this respect, he is more like Anne Elliot or Lucy Snowe than are any of Eliot's heroines. We might, then, regard him as a stand-in for the stymied Eliot heroine, homeless and disillusioned, in search of a congenial community and place of belonging, but this time voyaging out with a sense of mission in search of freedom, citizenship, and a new manifestation of Home. As Deronda, Mirah, and Mirah's brother Mordecai, the ailing visionary who has been Deronda's mentor and guide, are about to leave England, it becomes clear that Mordecai will, like Moses and other travelers bound for death, never glimpse the promised land. But he cheers Daniel by reminding him that the two of them are joined and so go forward together in soul if not in body. "Where thou goest, Daniel," Mordecai says, quoting the biblical Ruth to her mother-in-law Naomi, "I shall go" (*DD*, 811). The bond between two women—mother-in-law and her Gentile daughter-in-law Ruth, one of the Bible's great converts—has been rewritten as that between two men: an ailing Jewish sage and his new brother-in-law, who is both a Jew and a convert. The trapped Eliot heroine has likewise been remade as a man, feminized, perhaps, through his religion, beautiful black curls, and "thrilling" voice but, in Eliot's mind, a more convincing candidate for voyaging out and surviving the journey than any woman.

Constrained by literary convention, the narrow and moralistic expectations of some reviewers and readers, and their own desire to remain anonymous and undefined in the eyes of the public, nineteenth-century women writers trod a narrative path that stretched between home and abroad. Their novels, especially those they produced in the late phases of their careers, did not represent a safe, domestic world that was "immobile, predictable, [and] fenced off" but rather a space of aspiration, adventure, and public engagement. They sought to dismantle the idea of home as a confining and male-dominated place and to reinvent it as a realm of self-cultivation and liberty. True Home might be created on shipboard, in a school, or in a nation conceived only in the mind. But did the departure matter more, perhaps, than the destination? Was it a moment of Homecoming in itself? "Today," Anna Jameson writes in *Diary of an Ennuyée*, "for the first time in my life, I saw the shores of England fade away in the distance."[34] Mary Seacole declares at the beginning of her *Adventures* that she always longed to be aboard the "stately ships homeward bound [to England]" and to "see the blue hills of Jamaica fade into the distance."[35] Leaving England aboard the *Vivid*, Lucy Snowe asks herself if she is "wretched or terrified" and, feeling herself neither, wonders why: "'Methinks I am animated and alert, instead of being depressed and apprehensive!' I could not tell how it was" (*V*, 45). Adventure inheres not just in setting sail but also in seeing one's own home in retreat.

CHAPTER 2

Emancipation

IN THE WAKE OF THE PUBLICATION OF Harriet Beecher Stowe's
Uncle Tom's Cabin in 1852, Elizabeth Barrett Browning admon-
ished Anna Jameson for registering a certain amount of shock at the
incendiary subject of Stowe's novel. By this time Barrett Browning
herself had published one antislavery poem, "The Runaway Slave
at Pilgrim's Point," which first appeared in the American abolitionist journal the *Liberty Bell* in 1847, and would contribute a second,
"A Curse for the Nation," to the same publication a few years later.
"Is it possible," she responded to Jameson with indignation, "that
you think a woman has no business with questions like the question of slavery? . . . Then she had better use a pen no more. She had
better subside into slavery and concubinage herself, I think, as in
the times of old, shut herself up with the Penelopes in the 'women's
apartment,' and take no rank among the thinkers and speakers."[1]
Barrett Browning's response to Jameson is significant for at least
two reasons: first, it is emblematic of a transatlantic, indeed international, network of women who asserted their right to an active role in political life in the middle decades of the nineteenth
century, and, second, it proposes an analogy between travel—or
adventure, as we have called it in chapter 1—and "think[ing]" and
"speak[ing]" about pressing political issues of the day.

Not to speak out, not to enter into topical debates, would be
tantamount to accepting the position of a kept woman, an enslaved woman, or a woman who, like Penelope, waits patiently,
confined to home, for the husband who enters the fray. Taking
up the pen, Barrett Browning implies, is a politically engaged act,
a way to intervene in public life. For her and other women like

her, the domestic sphere was both spatial and intellectual, and she would not be confined in either sense, but especially in the latter. Four years later, she again wrote to Jameson about Stowe, praising the American above all for having "moved the world—and *for good*."[2] Like George Eliot, who famously wrote to Stowe after completing *Daniel Deronda* that she also wished to "rouse the imagination of men and women to a vision of human claims in those races of fellow-men who most differ from them," nineteenth-century women who wrote novels and poems about slavery, industrialism, the working class, Chartism, Jews, and Gypsies wished to evoke sympathy for the oppressed but also, and more radically, to "move the world" by having a public voice in debates about the most controversial and charged matters of their time.[3]

This chapter focuses on four figures whose writing was a form of political activism: Stowe, Harriet Jacobs, Harriet Martineau, and Elizabeth Gaskell. With Martineau as a kind of lynchpin between women who wrote about slavery in the United States and those who wrote about industrial life in Britain, these two American and two British, one black and three white women all fulfilled Eliot's aspiration of rousing the public's imagination against injustice and in favor of what we might call, broadly speaking, emancipation. This term, with its implications for women's own liberation from patriarchal law and custom, covered a wide spectrum of political causes and proved a catchword for the loosely but self-consciously bound group of women who devoted themselves to the freeing of slaves, the enfranchisement of workers and peasants, the unification of nations, and the political integration of Jews and Catholics in the period from 1830 to the mid-1850s.[4]

The link between the fictional texts these women produced and the trope of escape or sailing forth goes beyond the analogy in Barrett Browning's letter. Escape to freedom—to the American North, to Canada, or to Liberia—plays a major role in abolitionist fiction and slave narratives, and emigration plays an important, if equivocal, part in industrial fiction as well. The slaves and workers fleeing their homes in these works have far more at stake than the restless heroines of Austen, Brontë, and Eliot, and yet the flights of both groups of protagonists raise questions about the vexed meaning of home and the literary forms with which it is associated. How does the woman writer, whose literary métier is inevitably tied in this period to the forms of domestic and sentimental narratives, employ these forms for radical political purposes? And how do they expose aspects of conventional forms and tropes as bankrupt, barren of meaning relevant to the problems of the persecuted and oppressed? In a related way, we also ask what the domestic realm might signify to those whose homes are not their own, to those with no legal claim to familial bonds or even personhood, and to those whose dwellings deteriorate and decay under the strains of poverty. Are there utopian visions of home that serve as literary resolutions to homelessness? Does the possibility of sailing forth, of escape from subjugation, exist for those without rights?

When Elizabeth Gaskell completed her preface to *Mary Barton*, published anonymously and given the subtitle "A Tale of Manchester Life," she placed a date at the bottom: October 1848. Though not an uncommon practice—Dickens consistently dated his prefaces—Gaskell never repeated the gesture after this. *Mary Barton* was her first full-length work of fiction and widely regarded as the first major industrial novel, a work that helped to define the genre.[5] Her preface at once apologizes for and defends the working-class claims of suffering and maltreatment she would represent in her narrative, and the dateline that follows amounts to a silent admonition to her middle-class readers that they ought to take such claims seriously. The lines that conclude the preface suggest why: "the idea which I have formed of the state of feeling among too many of the factory-people in Manchester . . . has received some confirmation from the events which have so recently occurred among a similar class on the Continent."[6] In this momentous year of 1848, revolutions fueled by the miserable conditions shared by British and Continental workers alike had erupted all over Europe—in France, Italy, and Austria, just about everywhere except Great Britain. Gaskell, whose diffidence about accusing the middle classes of cruelty sometimes turns her prose into a frustrating knot of self-contradiction, says here, in effect, "I have given you fair warning."

This gesture of Gaskell's confirms for us the importance of the element of middle-class fear during this period, as well as its role in the formation of the industrial novel. But it also suggests the pivotal importance of 1848—as reality and symbol—in the literary imaginations and political impulses of women writers who took up a variety of causes in their novels, poems, and activism. Other events of that year, as apparently disparate as the large but peaceful Chartist demonstration in London and the first convention for women's rights in the United States at Seneca Falls, contributed to an intercontinental sense among women that the need for dramatic social change was urgent, ubiquitous, and, above all, within the scope of their own efforts.[7] Women writers who took up the subject of large-scale social transformation saw themselves as part of a unified, if diverse, movement, bound by an acute consciousness of their historical moment.

That English women writing about the working class saw 1848 as their loadstar is less surprising, perhaps, than the fact that Americans writing about slavery did so as well. On the final page of *Uncle Tom's Cabin*, in a warning to her readers that mirrors Gaskell's preface to *Mary Barton*, Harriet Beecher Stowe invokes the revolutionary spirit of the age: "This is an age of the world when nations are trembling and convulsed. A mighty influence is abroad, surging and heaving the world, as with an earthquake. And is America safe? Every nation that carries in its bosom great and unredressed injustice has in it the elements of this last convulsion."[8] The "mighty influence" generating uprisings abroad is a universal force, the same in Paris or London as it is in Virginia and South Carolina, and it might also wreak havoc on American shores if injustice goes unchecked. Stowe alludes to the events of 1848 at a number of other points in the novel. Augustine St. Clare, father of Eva and a languid, doomed, but enlightened Southerner who comes to oppose slavery, twice refers tellingly to the Continental rebellions of '48 as possible harbingers of American events (*UTC*, 234, 273). The narrator invokes Hungary's attempt to gain its freedom from Austria in 1848–49 in the context of a discussion of fugitive slaves. Americans greet Hungarian refugees—fugitives from Austria in the wake of their failed rebellion—with open arms, despite their unlawful status in their own country, but fail to welcome "despairing African fugitives [who] do the same thing" (*UTC*, 172). The former are celebrated, the latter hunted down and captured.

In *Dred*, published in 1856, Stowe again cites the upheavals on the Continent. Slave rebels are prominent actors in this second slavery novel of Stowe's, and the idea of a slave insurrection like Nat Turner's or Denmark Vesey's is an ever-present though ultimately unrealized possibility. A woman with abolitionist tendencies defends the idea of educating slaves against an opponent who claims this will only lead to rebellion and disaster. "How do you account for it?" the proponent of literacy argues, "that the best-developed and finest specimens of men have been those that have got up insurrections in Italy, Austria, and Hungary?"[9] Later on, in a discussion of the slave rebel Dred, the novel compares the Bible, as a text that celebrates the overthrow of tyrants, to the lyrics of the French revolutionary anthem "La Marseillaise."[10] There is a suggestion in many of these references that Americans should, by their nature and history, endorse the attempted revolutions in Europe and, if so, extend this endorsement to American slave rebellions at home. Writing from Italy in 1847 in one of her dispatches to the *New York Tribune*, Margaret Fuller, whose magisterial *Woman in the Nineteenth Century* had appeared just two years before, saw the struggles for freedom across the Continent and in the Americas as indistinguishable. "I find the cause of tyranny and wrong everywhere the same," she wrote, "I listen to the same arguments against the emancipation of Italy, that are used against the emancipation of our blacks; the same arguments for the spoliation of Poland as for the conquest of Mexico."[11]

This consciousness of a common cause among women activists on either side of the Atlantic had been building since the early 1830s. Crosscurrents among women novelists and poets were numerous during these years and, from the vantage point of a critical tradition that tends to separate American, British, and Continental writing, the affinities appear unlikely. Eliot corresponded with Stowe and reviewed *Dred* with enthusiasm. Critics with carping objections to this powerful novel, Eliot wrote, were like "men pursuing a prairie fire with desultory watering cans," and she wished that English women novelists could portray "religious life among the industrial classes" with as much seriousness and interest as Stowe had done.[12] Eliot saw Stowe's work as a model and pretext for her own, a literary and ethical standard that she would strive to emulate. Charlotte Brontë, having recently finished writing *Villette*, declared to her publisher that she simply could not sustain a book on the "topics of the day" (though she had tried in *Shirley*) but "sincerely veil[ed her] face before such a mighty subject as that handled in . . . *Uncle Tom's Cabin*."[13] Martineau, Barrett Browning, and Gaskell all met Stowe and corresponded with her. In France, George Sand, who herself was an important model for women writers across the English-speaking world, reviewed a French translation of *Uncle Tom's Cabin* in 1852. Barrett Browning devoted two sonnets to Sand, and George Eliot judged the prolific French novelist to have combined "tragic depth of passion" with Rousseau's "eloquence and deep sense of external nature."[14] Sand praised Stowe as one of the "saints [who] also have their claw! . . . She buries it deep in the conscience."[15] Of Elizabeth Gaskell, a writer less dramatic in her impact on contemporaries than either Sand or Stowe, Sand wrote that she had "done what neither I nor other female authors in France can accomplish—she has written novels which excite the deepest interest in men of the world and yet which every girl will be the better for reading."[16] Throughout these evocations of peers across the water, we hear a constant strain: admiration for serious ethical and political subjects and for an ostensibly female sensibility combined with what would then have been considered masculine knowledge, astuteness, and daring.

Many who agitated for the emancipation of slaves and industrial laborers regarded themselves as engaged in twin enterprises. Mary Howitt, English Quaker turned Unitarian, who took up abolitionist and suffrage causes and was known on both sides of the Atlantic, published a literary weekly, *Howitt's Journal*, with her husband, William, beginning in 1847. Directed at a working-class audience, it was devoted to the abolition of slavery and "popular progress" generally. The Howitts included poems written in honor of William Lloyd Garrison and Frederick Douglass, translations of stories by George Sand, and the first industrial tales of Elizabeth Gaskell, published under the American-indebted pseudonym Cotton Mather Mills. Gaskell and Stowe use the same phrase, "masters and men," to refer to two different vexed relationships, one based on class and the other on race. In *Uncle Tom's Cabin* Augustine St. Clare discusses the similarities between these relationships with his skeptical cousin Ophelia, an antislavery Northerner. He describes them as forms of appropriation: planters and capitalists "*appropriat*[e]" slaves and workers "body and bone, soul and spirit, to their use and convenience" (*UTC*, 199). When Ophelia rejects the comparison, arguing that the "English laborer is not sold, traded, parted from his family, whipped," St. Clair responds: "He is as much at the will of his employer as if he were sold to him. The slave-owner can whip his refractory slave to death,—the capitalist can starve him to death. As to family security, it is hard to say which is the worst,—to have one's children sold, or see them starve to death at home" (*UTC*, 200). Though St. Clair concedes that the American system of slavery amounts to the crueler and more dehumanizing infringement of rights, he continues to maintain that the two forms of deadly exploitation are "in [their] nature" the same.

Years before Stowe signaled this alliance of American and British reformers and radicals, Harriet Martineau, the woman writer who first and perhaps most prominently embodied transatlantic abolitionism, drew social and especially economic parallels between the conditions of slavery and those of industrial labor. "We have a population in our manufacturing towns," she wrote to the American Abby Kelley in 1838, "almost as oppressed . . . as your Negroes. These must be redeemed."[17] Martineau traveled to the United States in 1834, already known as a writer who had stood against slavery in her work. Though she was anxious to convey a dispassionate and impartial attitude toward American society, the events of her visit compelled her to express a clear public identification with militant abolitionism. She toured the slave states of the South and saw the radical abolitionist William Lloyd Garrison dragged by a vicious proslavery mob through the streets of Boston with a noose around his neck. The growing intensity of her views reached its peak in the delivery of a fervent denunciation of slavery before the Boston Female Anti-Slavery Society in 1835. Thinking particularly of the events in Boston, Martineau declared that the 1830s marked a turning point in women's activism: "We have arrived at the most remarkable period of the great struggle, when an equal share of its responsibility and suffering came to press upon women" (*WS*, 57). After the American trip Martineau published two books about her travels—*Society in America* (1837) and *Retrospect of Western Travel* (1838)—and wrote a series of articles, "The Martyr Age of the United States," for a British periodical.

In these pages Martineau offers astute sociological and psychological observation about the corrosive effects of slavery on both white and black Americans. Repeatedly and in different ways, she describes the degraded state of blacks and then concludes that this has resulted from the conditions of their enslavement and not from anything like "negro nature" (*WS*, 23). As she says later in a striking formulation, the majority of slaves are "living under a mask," and the traits, such as a childlike demeanor, attributed to them are merely adaptations or acts (*WS*, 301). She writes of slave suicides, attempts to escape to the North and Canada, liaisons—what she calls "connexions"—between the "Quadroon girls" of New Orleans and married white gentlemen, and the planters who "sell their own offspring to fill their purses" (*WS*, 33, 34, 16–17). She continued to write about the United States for British periodicals throughout the 1850s and '60s. Reporting on Stowe's visit to England in 1853, she declared that the author of *Uncle Tom's Cabin* was "no Corinne [Mme. de Staël's extraordinarily popular artist-heroine], crowned for intellectual triumphs" but rather "the apostle of the greatest cause now existing in the world" (*WS*, 92).

It was a story called "Demerara," about slavery on a plantation in British Guiana, that made Martineau's reputation in the United States and established her as an opponent of slavery there even before her visit. The story was one of the first in her *Illustrations of Political Economy* and appeared in 1832, the year of the Reform Bill, a year before slavery was abolished in Britain, and two years before Martineau sailed for America. In *Illustrations*, which proved to be enormously popular across a number of continents, Martineau dramatized abstruse economic principles so that readers of both sexes and all classes could grasp them easily. She set out to promote reform by educating her audience about law, economy, and morality, thereby changing their views of social life.[18] Each story focuses on one or more issues—Poor Law reform in "Cousin Marshall," overpopulation and birth control in "Weal and Woe in Garveloch," wages, unions, and factory labor in "A Manchester Strike"—and is followed by a "Summary" of points Martineau wishes to reinforce. The summaries amount to the bare bones of political economic principles, which Martineau clothes in the fiction of the tales. Deborah Logan argues that Martineau meant her stories for an audience that included middle-class women and working-class readers but also financiers, slave owners, manufacturers, and imperial adventurers.[19]

The central point of "Demerara" is that wage labor is more effective, more productive, and more salutary for both worker and employer than slave labor. Martineau's critique of slavery hewed to an economic rather than a strictly moral, humanitarian, religious, or political argument and allowed, on the surface at least, for a more ameliorative view of slavery than Stowe's and certainly than Harriet Jacobs's would do. In "Demerara" slavery is a liability to the plantation owners in Guiana, and capital acquired using the unrighteous and risky practice of slave owning is destined to dwindle. The tale's hero, Alfred Bruce, heir to a plantation in Demerara, returns home from England (where the slave trade had been abolished in 1807), having learned the best methods of business and cultivation. He is appalled by both the inhumane treatment of his father's slaves and by the economic decline his father's property has suffered. Alfred declares that, as a general principle, men have no right to hold other men as property and that, as a principle of labor economics, people must have a motive for hard and good work.[20] Martineau tries to make rationality and self-interest central to her argument against slavery and appeals to what she takes to be universal laws of economy and human behavior.

She illustrates these laws by showing how easily ruin comes to Alfred and his neighbors, but her story becomes most compelling when she focuses on the fates of two individual slaves. She imbues one of them, a slave named Cassius, with a canny ability to act on the basis of an economic calculus. Owned by a man named Mitchelson, Cassius has been tending his own garden plot (he grows plantains, maize, and vegetables but is forbidden to raise the more lucrative crops of his owners—sugarcane, coffee, and cotton) so that he can sell produce and save money toward purchasing his freedom through self-ransom. Alfred sees that Cassius's own garden flourishes and so wonders why the man is not a productive slave in Mitchelson's fields. The reason for this lies in Cassius's canniness: he wants to deflate his own value—the ransom he would have to pay his owner to be free—by appearing to be the proverbial lazy slave.

When Mitchelson's dam breaks and Alfred undertakes to rebuild it by paying the slaves actual wages, thereby proving the efficacy of wage labor and the profit motive, Cassius's value to his owner increases as a result of his excellent work. Now feeling trapped by his inability to provide an adequate ransom for himself, Cassius prays angrily to God, imploring him to send a hurricane Mitchelson's way. Cassius's Christianity is not the passive, self-martyring variety of Stowe's Uncle Tom, and Martineau lets it stand, more willing than Stowe to endorse the slave's anger. Alfred's promises to ensure Cassius's ultimate freedom prove worthless. The tale leaves him in slavery, sold off by Mitchelson, who refuses to let Cassius purchase his own freedom lest this encourage other slaves to do the same. Neither Alfred's nor Cassius's economic calculus proves sufficient against the juggernaut of slavery.

The other slave whose story illustrates the intractable and vicious nature of the slave system is Willy, son of old Mark, patriarch of the Bruce slaves. Willy appears at first as a taciturn and mistrustful man, unwilling to put his faith even in Alfred, who used to ride on his shoulders as a child. His fatalism is borne out when the elder Bruce is forced to relinquish some of his slaves to creditors and old Mark's family is dispersed. The family marches off "in sullen despair, with drivers at their backs, they knew not whither, to become the property of they knew not whom" (114–15). Willy attempts an escape with his sister, Nell, but falls prey to slave hunters' dogs. The following passage stops the flow of the story and provides a chilling contrast to the abstract principles of political economy and the enlightened, measured rhetoric of self-interest:

> [A] fierce blood-hound had sprung at Willy's throat and brought him down. Once having tasted blood, the animal was not to be restrained by whistle, shouts, or blows, till the long death-grapple was over. When the mangled negro had ceased to struggle, and lay extended in his blood, the hound slunk back into the bushes, licking his chops, and growling at Nell as if he would make another spring if he dared.
>
> The remaining fugitive had no power to resist, even if she had had the will. But her will was annihilated. . . . she could not stand. She did not speak when they took up the body of her brother from its bloody bed, nor start when they tossed it into the stream. . . . She was asleep or in a stupor when brought back to her hut, a circumstance which was pointed out by a white as conclusive of the fact that negroes have no feeling. (128–29)

This account, shocking and horrific without being lurid or sensational, represents the second nail in the coffin of hope in Martineau's story, and it has nothing to do with the principles of political economy. Cassius cannot escape the degradation of slavery through hard work, cleverness, and thrift, and Willy cannot escape by running away. The mild, teacherly prose of the story, which never explicitly drives home the idea that slavery equates human beings with beasts of burden, is replaced by the stark description of an animal allowed, probably trained, to make a meal of the blood of a man. The family feeling among slaves, already established by Martineau to show their fundamental, recognizable humanity, and the cruelty of the system that divides children from parents, here deepen the devastation. Not only is Willy a sentient and thoughtful being, for whom the reader feels sympathy, but his murder has a witness in the person of his sister. The annihilation of her will and the misreading of her catatonia by white people complete the portrait of human catastrophe that Martineau mainly refrains from presenting or naming as such.

Martineau concludes her tale with Alfred's decision to join the American Colonization Society, which helps to settle free blacks in Liberia so that they can "make their own laws, guard their own rights, and be . . . men and citizens" (139). He answers his father's skepticism by declaring that the slaves they know in Guiana are, as Martineau would later say, living under masks and consequently unknown and unknowable. Just as Nell is unreadable in the moments after her brother's death, so are all slaves at virtually all times. We cannot know what the slave will become, Alfred says, when "there is no white man to fear and hate, and where he may reap whatever he has sown" (140). Martineau ends, then, with a reminder about the power of self-possession, self-interest, and ownership of the fruits of one's labor. However, what she manages to impress upon her readers, though she neglects to include the point in her "Summary," is that individual agency means nothing in the face of an entrenched, brutal system. Cassius can try to use economic logic to gain freedom for himself, but his efforts will be foiled. Willy can try to resist the destruction of his family, but he will be crushed. And, most important, Alfred Bruce can try to save individual slaves through his humane and British-inspired ideals, but he is ultimately impotent to improve their lot in any meaningful way under the terms of British slavery. The overwhelming conclusion to be drawn here is that there is no way out while the system of slavery still exists. Economic rationality, the very cornerstone of Martineau's critique of slavery, fails utterly to solve the problems that her own story exposes.

Martineau uses fictional narrative to make her economic principles more digestible and to make traditionally masculine forms of knowledge more acceptable in the work of a woman writer. In the end, however, the narrative escapes her control and leaves an air of defeat and loss hovering over the hopeful, or at least forward-looking, dicta of political economy. To the extent that Martineau gives her slave characters individual personalities and stories, she defeats her own efforts at dispassion and abstraction. She has to negotiate two daring forms of suasion: the presumptuous wielding of scientific authority, associated with the male pen, and the iconoclastic power of rousing deep feeling, in which women writers were thought to excel.

Unlike Harriet Martineau, who made a point of arguing for political and social change on the basis of hard-edged ideas of political economy, Elizabeth Gaskell, Harriet Beecher Stowe, and Harriet Jacobs all made use of what we might call "maternal economy" in the strategies and substance of their fiction. Drawing on the common experience of parenthood to form the connective tissue of sympathy between disparate peoples, and mining the persuasive power of maternal sentiment and domestic drama, they took up large and controversial issues—slavery and the oppression of industrial workers by the manufacturing class—and so entered the public square of debate.

Martineau was known and often caricatured as the quintessential Victorian spinster-intellectual, surrounded by cats and piles of paper at her desk. Stowe and Gaskell, on the other hand, both projected an image of conventional femininity, their surnames often preceded by "Mrs." during the nineteenth century and beyond, and their visions of social change sometimes regarded by subsequent generations of readers and critics as cautious, if not conservative. Both of their husbands were clergymen, and each woman drew on the rhetoric and symbolism of Christian belief to promote the cause of social reform. The only scandal with which they were ever associated involved the discrepancy between this domestic image and the provocative nature of their views. This paradoxical combination of tendentious subject matter and maternal economy in Gaskell and Stowe is reflected in more radical form in Jacobs's *Incidents in the Life of a Slave Girl*. Jacobs's slave narrative pivots in large part on her identity as a mother of two children and uses the traditional plot of threatened female virtue to tell the horror story of slavery. All three writers take the domestic realm as their stage and use the private sphere to argue, sometimes to militate, for difficult and sweeping public change. They all make use of sentimental tropes and forms for the purposes of suasion, but they also ultimately question the value of maternal love, chastity, and the shelter of home as adequate solutions to the devastation of slavery and exploitation.

Gaskell and Stowe both lost children, not an uncommon experience in the mid-nineteenth century, and both used the trope of the dead child to create bonds between characters in their fictions and between readers and fictional characters these readers might otherwise have shunned. In *Mary Barton*, written by Gaskell three years after the death of William, her infant son, an unusually large number of characters suffer the deaths of children, parents, wives, and friends, many to diseases that affected the urban poor. The most salient deaths for Gaskell's purposes of fostering understanding between classes are those of the sons of John Barton and his erstwhile employer, Mr. Carson. Barton, the aggrieved millworker, murders the arrogant, callous son of the mill owner Carson as an anonymous act on behalf of his union. But Barton and Carson Sr. are reconciled at the end of the novel, in part because the worker too has lost a child (through starvation) and recalls the pain of this death and its role in his growing desperation as he lies dying in Carson's home. Witnessing Barton's death moves the elder Carson to some feeling of sympathy and identification, and Gaskell goes so far as to imbue this experience of parental loss with Christian meaning through the iconography of the pietà. The image of Carson cradling Barton's dying body in his arms—"He raised up the powerless frame"—recalls the ultimate loss of a son and the potentially redemptive power of that loss (*MB*, 441). That the body of the worker-assassin Barton takes the pose of Christ suggests something of the iconoclasm involved in Gaskell's use of this conventional but sacred image.

Stowe's task, more daunting than Gaskell's, was to transcend the difference of race by using the deep feelings of parenthood, especially those of wrenching parental bereavement. At the beginning of *Uncle Tom's Cabin*, when Tom and Eliza learn that their master, Mr. Shelby, intends to sell both Eliza's young son and Tom himself, the older slave urges the young woman to flee with her child but declares that he will stay behind to meet his fate. Looking at his wife Chloe and their children—a "trundle-bed full of little woolly heads"—Tom breaks down:

> Sobs, heavy, hoarse and loud, shook the chair, and great tears fell through his fingers on the floor: just tears, sir, as you dropped into the coffin where lay your first-born son; such tears, woman, as you shed when you heard the cries of your

dying babe. For, sir, he was a man,—and you are but another man. And, woman, though dressed in silk and jewels, you are but a woman, and, in life's great straits and mighty griefs, ye feel but one sorrow! (*UTC*, 34)

Continuing with this motif of the bond of parenthood, Stowe suggests that Eliza gains the help of Senator Bird and his wife as she flees principally because they have lost a son. Mrs. Bird goes to the drawer where she has kept the dead child's small clothes, shoes, and toys, and takes them out to give to Eliza's Harry. Again, the narrator turns to the readers and asks the mothers among them if they possess such a drawer, the opening of which is like the reopening of a grave (*UTC*, 75). From early in the nineteenth century, women abolitionists used the separation of female slaves from their children as an image to rally support for their cause.[21] Stowe's version of this humanizes the slave father and adds the crux of infant mortality as the grounds for identification.

Though Harriet Jacobs writes in her preface that she seeks to appeal to the "women of the North" on behalf of "two millions of women at the South," her direct addresses to the reader are few.[22] She does not use Stowe's technique of turning to her audience or interrupt the flow of her retrospective narrative to comment on the relevance of her experience to those who are hearing it. But two easily recognizable female plots, both likely to draw the sympathy of women readers, structure her story: the drama of threatened sexual virtue and the plight of tortured motherhood. Like Richardson's Pamela fending off the predatory Mr. B____, Jacobs's protagonist and alter ego Linda Brent struggles for many years to keep her master, Dr. Flint, from raping her and establishing her as his mistress. She calls this "the war of my life" (*ILS*, 18). Dr. Flint's diabolical persistence and viciousness, and his enervated, jealous wife's taunting, make Brent's existence an uninterrupted misery. Though Linda is a slave and a black woman, her battle against ruin offers white middle-class readers a core of feminine virtue to admire and approve.

This constant threat is compounded by Brent's anxiety over her daughter and son, who are also the property of her master. If Linda runs away, as she longs to do, she leaves her children behind in slavery. Dr. Flint repeatedly balks at selling the children to sympathetic buyers who want to give the children their freedom. Finally, after Linda does escape, Flint imprisons the children and then sells them: they are bought and freed by their father, a white man, and left safely with their grandmother, a freed slave. Jacobs recalls that at that instant, in hiding at a friend's, she saw the forms of her children in a streak of moonlight, either in a vision or a dream (*ILS*, 107–8). Though the grueling struggle for her own freedom will continue, she lets her readers know that this is a blessed moment. "It was the first time since my childhood," she writes, "that I had experienced any real happiness. . . . The darkest cloud that hung over my life had rolled away. Whatever slavery might do to me, it could not shackle my children" (*ILS*, 109). The private story of woman's vulnerability, apparent powerlessness, and maternal love enable her to make her case against slavery by establishing common ground with white readers.[23]

The strategies of maternal economy help these writers to cushion the impact of controversial claims. Both Gaskell and Stowe struggle to come to terms with the anger and rebelliousness of the oppressed peoples they champion. In *Mary Barton* Gaskell often hedges when she tries to justify the worker's wrath—"I know that this is not really the case; and I know what is the truth in such matters: but what I wish to impress is *what the workman feels and thinks*"—or to explain why John Barton joins a union and becomes a Chartist (*MB*, 60; emphasis added). As many critics have observed, she shifts the emphasis of her plot away from political rebellion to a love triangle and romantic melodrama, from public to private matters. But Gaskell risked—and won—the disapprobation of numerous middle-class readers by indicting the callousness of manufacturers, implying that workers and their families starve to death at the masters' hands, pleading for understanding for the murderous desperation of men like Barton, and allowing the class murder Barton commits to go unpunished. At a number of emblematic moments in her fiction, Gaskell represents the determination and fear attendant on the private woman's public acts: when Mary Barton withstands shame and collapse to bear witness in court; when Margaret Hale, in *North and South*, puts herself in bodily danger to shield Mr. Thornton from the anger of aggrieved workers; and when the eponymous heroine of *Ruth* defies those who fear her own powers of contamination by going forth to tend the bodies of the sick and dying. These distinctly nondomestic, unacceptably public gestures, which stand in for the writer's own forays into contested public matters, extend beyond the current of parental sympathy and encourage the reader to contemplate other, riskier modes of political engagement.

One of the ways these writers signal the muted audacity of their narratives and their departure from comforting domestic or maternal narratives is by staging episodes of travesty and inversion. In *Mary Barton*, the prostitute Esther dresses herself as a mechanic's wife to appear at the door of her still respectable niece, Mary. This disguise hints at the artificiality of certain class and moral distinctions and invites speculation about the superficial nature of sexual respectability. In Jacobs and Stowe, runaway slaves of light complexion disguise themselves as black people. Linda Brent darkens her face with charcoal in order to run away undetected from Dr. Flint, and George Harris disguises himself as a Spaniard by dying his hair black and making his "yellow skin a genteel brown."[24] If female virtue can be a costume—or, as Martineau might say, a mask—so too can race, and both can be understood at the very least as elusive categories. Otherwise, how can a slave be disguised as a black person? Linda Brent changes her sex when she runs away, making herself into a black-skinned sailor, and Gaskell also uses gender inversion to call into question the nature of the maternal principle that presides over her novel and to challenge the presumed connection between sex and domestic or public roles.

In chapter 9 of *Mary Barton*, the worker Job Legh tries to console John Barton after his failed Chartist appeal in London by telling the story of another journey to London, this one to fetch Job's orphaned granddaughter, Margaret, with her other grandfather. Unable to get the baby to sleep or feed, one of them dresses up in a woman's nightcap and climbs into bed to lie with the child in his arms. The baby roots around, looking for the breast, and eventually cries itself to sleep. "My heart were very sore for th' little one," Job recalls, "as it groped about wi' its mouth; but for a' that I could scarce keep fra' smiling at th' thought o' us two oud chaps, th' one wi' a woman's night-cap on, sitting on our hinder ends for half th' night, hushabying a baby that wouldn't be husha-bied" (*MB*, 149). Though a comic interlude and diversion for the dejected Barton, Job's account of trying to keep the infant com-forted and alive on the trip back to Manchester offers a portrait of what Lisa Surridge calls "manly nurturance" and, further, allows Gaskell to disguise herself in the character of a working-class man, who in turn disguises himself as a woman.[25] The novel is filled with motherly men who raise children on their own, just as Stowe gives us the maternal Tom and Tiff, the consummate male mother in *Dred* who rigs a bit of salt pork on a cradle for one of his mother-less charges to suck.[26] Men can handle, however awkwardly, even the most fundamental of motherly functions.

Gaskell and Stowe replace the loss of a child, which they experi-enced in their own lives, with an infant's loss of its parents, but they also conjure male nurturers who save small children from death, something neither managed to do but surely must have dreamed of doing. One could argue that these writers imbue only femi-nized, powerless men—workers and black slaves—with maternal natures, yet they also use these gender travesties to challenge the distinction between women's and men's roles and to suggest that domestic care (nursing a baby) and political acts (being a Char-tist or abolitionist, or writing a novel with political implications) can be carried out by the same person, male or female. Through comedy, Gaskell and Stowe want to suggest that the lines between private and public acts, and between maternalist and political so-lutions, are faint and eradicable.

Stowe's reluctance to represent or endorse the anger of her slave characters in *Uncle Tom's Cabin* and her insistence on Tom's martyrdom in the face of humiliation and suffering often form the basis for readers' impatience (and worse) with the novel. Part of the Christian catharsis Stowe uses to move and mollify her readers—the death of Uncle Tom—is, however, only one element in her assault on slavery. The radical power of this novel by the woman Elaine Showalter rightly calls "the most important figure in the history of women's writing" inheres in large part in Stowe's challenge to legal and religious authority.[27] She repeatedly makes the point that the law upholds slavery—that slavery *is* the law—and that the established order sanctions brutality, murder, and the separation of wives from husbands and children from parents. George Harris, Eliza's husband, rails against his master for dividing him from his wife and expecting him to live with another woman—and "all this [he cries] your law gives him the power to do, in spite of God or man" (*UTC*, 97). Even the repugnant slave catchers who pursue those, like Eliza, who have escaped to the North work within the law. "This catching business," the narrator reminds especially her Northern readers with sarcasm, "is rising to the dignity of a lawful and patriotic profession," and traders and catchers are destined to "be among our aristocracy" (*UTC*, 62). Morality and the law do not coincide and, as in the case of Martineau's "Demerara," no well-meaning individual, whether Mrs. Shelby, St. Clare, or the angelic Eva, can countermand the law of the land.

The sentimental Christian narrative of Tom's suffering and death is artfully coupled with the novel's attack on religious hypocrisy and its insistence on the fundamental uselessness of institutionalized Christianity to solve the problem of slavery. When St. Clare, who had intended to give Tom his freedom, dies prematurely and his slaves must be sold at auction, Stowe inserts a chilling chapter called "The Slave Warehouse." After a description of the women's quarters and the variety of slaves waiting there, like animals, to be appraised and sold, the narrator concludes: "and the gentleman to whom they belong, and to whom the money for their sale is to be transmitted, is a member of the Christian church in New York, who will receive the money, and go thereafter to the sacrament of his Lord and theirs, and think no more of it" (*UTC*, 285). Here, as in the instance of the remark about slave catchers, Stowe makes clear that Northerners are implicated in the slave system, benefit from it, and function under an unethical set of laws. Christian hypocrisy is not confined to Southerners: "The country," St. Clare warns, "is almost ruined with pious white people" (*UTC*, 130).

Stowe also has the temerity to suggest that white people resent and mistreat their slaves because of their own feelings of inferiority.

George Harris is a worker-engineer, very much like Gaskell's Job Legh, the worker-scientist in *Mary Barton*. Because of Harris's talent, his master has farmed him out to a factory that makes bags to carry cotton. Harris, with as much "mechanical genius" as the inventor of the cotton gin, has created a machine to clean hemp. When his master sees George walking proudly around the factory, speaking so articulately and looking "so handsome and manly," he "begins to feel *an uneasy consciousness of inferiority*" and shortly thereafter punishes the slave for his accomplishments by deciding to sell him away from his wife and child (*UTC*, 10; emphasis added). Like Martineau's Cassius, whose skill as a farmer can bring him a good income, sufficient perhaps to help him buy his freedom, George can be imagined as a successful wage earner, capable of financial independence outside of the context of slavery and possessed of a kind of talent and resourcefulness that dwarfs those of his bosses and masters.

The conventional qualities of Harriet Jacobs's plot of maternal vigilance and defended virtue are counterbalanced by a number of powerful and controversial currents in her text. Like Gaskell and Stowe, she confronts her readers with their own complicity in the system she exposes, and she provokes them into acknowledging the repressed truths upon which this system depends. Like the many mixed-race characters in Stowe's fiction (Eliza and George Harris, Harry Carson in *Dred*), Jacobs's alter ego, Linda Brent, and her family tell the story of intimate ties between white owners and the slaves they traffic in. In the first pages of her memoir, Jacobs talks of her father's intelligence and skill as a carpenter, the literacy that many of her relatives enjoyed, her grandmother's free and independent life, and the disjunction between skin color and legal status. Her parents were "a light shade of brownish yellow," her uncle "nearly white" (for he "inherited the complexion my grandmother had derived from her Anglo-Saxon ancestors"), and her mother's mistress and sometime foster sister only just minimally "whiter" than Jacobs's mother (*ILS*, 5–7).

When Dr. Flint begins to pursue and then torment her, the likely outcome of his pursuit (one that Jacobs miraculously avoids) reflects back on the history of her family and of slavery in general.

"The secrets of slavery," she declares, "are concealed like those of the Inquisition. My master was, to my knowledge, the father of eleven slaves. But did the mothers dare to tell who was the father of their children? Did the other slaves dare to allude to it, except in whispers among themselves? No, indeed! They knew too well the terrible consequences" (*ILS*, 35). The "flowery" Southern home, she concludes, is "ravaged of its loveliness" and the senses of white Southern wives "deadened" by keeping the secrets that constitute their family histories (*ILS*, 36). The sensational sexual drama of her own life is, in other words, at the very heart of slavery, and there are no women and no families, either white or black, that have not been "ravaged" by this perverse institution. And what exists in plain sight—the various skin colors that result from mixed couplings, whether forced or not—is denied as a reality that reflects the true experience of slave and slave owner alike.

The sexual liaisons that make up the "secrets of slavery" appear in Jacobs's memoir in another form, one that threatens to destabilize the narrative of preserved chastity she tells. As Dr. Flint builds a small home for Jacobs and prepares to install her in it as his mistress, she places an obstacle between herself and this fate in the form of a freely chosen, unmarried white lover, Mr. Sands. He becomes the father—and later the emancipator—of her two children, but when he first appears in the narrative, in the midst of Jacobs's account of her fierce struggle to elude the sexual predations of her master, he presents something of a problem. How is she to defend this relationship while making herself the sentimental heroine of her own life and securing her place in the economy of heroic motherhood and undefiled womanhood? How does this part of her life square with the "codes and conventions of white-authored anti-slavery fiction" to which slave authors had to accommodate themselves when they bore witness to the evils of slavery?[28] Jacobs tries apologizing and asking for sympathy—"Pity me, and pardon me, O virtuous reader!"—but this rhetoric of contrition seems to be borrowed from sentimental fiction and never quite rings true in Jacobs's almost consistently unrepentant and uncompromising voice (*ILS*, 55). More convincing is Jacobs's admission that she entered into the affair with Sand partly out of a desire for revenge against Flint—"it was something to triumph over my tyrant"—and hoped, out of "calculated interest," that it would convince him to sell her (ibid.). Indeed, when Flint comes to tell her that the cottage he was building is ready for her to occupy, she is able to tell him that she is already pregnant and will never do so. But most convincing of all, as well as potentially most unsettling to her white female readers, is her assertion that she took pleasure in choosing a lover who could not control her and seemed bound to her by "kindness and attachment" rather than power (*ILS*, 54–55). This last explanation for entering into a sexual relationship with Sand is the most provocative because it confirms Jacobs as just that— sexual. She defends herself as a chaste woman, thereby laying claim to the sympathies of her readers, and a protective mother, and she turns out to be unchaste, capable of desiring a white man to whom she is not married—of *choosing* him—and the mother of two illicitly conceived mixed-race children. As Deborah Garfield writes, Jacobs appears to disqualify herself as a "sentimental 'Heroine.'"[29]

Finally, the liaison with Sand reinforces Jacobs's intimations that the "secrets of slavery" are ubiquitous and unavoidable, concealed but fundamental, coerced but also willed, and, in the end perhaps, of a piece, regardless of their genesis. There is a sense in Jacobs's narrative that motherhood can never be unproblematic for a slave, that it brings with it tragedy, shame, and scandal, even as it brings attachment, joy, and pride. When her daughter is born, she gives the child her own father's surname, which is, of course, also the surname of her father's owner. "What tangled skeins are the genealogies of slavery!" Jacobs declares, "I loved my father; but it mortified me to be obliged to bestow his name on my children" (*ILS*, 78). The name hints at illegitimacy, incest, and the obliteration of the slave's identity and personhood. It proves far easier for slave memoirists to praise and celebrate their mothers and grandmothers than to dwell on their own motherhood. To be a grateful and protected daughter is more unequivocally admirable than to be the mother of children who are the products of rape, coercion, or illicit sex.

Among the many hints in these texts that maternal economy is insufficient to solve the problems of oppression, hunger, and enslavement are brief but telling allusions to infanticide. Like Linda Brent's sexuality, infanticide introduces a taboo that threatens to sever the reader's sympathy for the victims in these narratives. In *Uncle Tom's Cabin*, Cassy, the onetime concubine of Simon Legree who tends to Tom after he has been brutally whipped, tells the story of her miserable life. Hers is the story of a beautiful and educated "New Orleans quadroon," whose fall begins with a white man who kept her in lavish style, showed her off in carriage rides on city streets, and then sold their two children into slavery. Abandoned by him and involved with a kind plantation owner, she gives birth to another child. This one, she vows, will never meet the fate of her first two:

> I would never again let a child live to grow up! I took the little fellow in my arms, when he was two weeks old, and kissed him, and cried over him; and then I gave him laudanum, and held him close to my bosom, while he slept to death. How I mourned and cried over it! And who ever dreamed that it was anything but a mistake, that had made me give it the laudanum? but it's one of the few things that I'm glad of, now. I am not sorry, to this day; he, at least, is out of pain. (*UTC*, 318)

In *Dred*, Stowe repeats the scenario of the slave mother who lives in relative freedom with her children but wants to ensure that they will never be enslaved. The mulatto slave Harry Gordon's sister, Cora, also the child of a white man, kills her two children rather than allow them to become slaves. "Born to liberty . . . brought up to liberty," they are dead because, their mother says, she loved them.[30] Before a judge she claims she was not in a frenzied or altered state when she committed these acts and was willing to lose her soul in order to save her children's. Whether Stowe was influenced by Elizabeth Barrett Browning's "Runaway Slave at Pilgrim's Point," which tells the story of a black woman who smothers her baby, the result of rape by her master, or by true stories of slave infanticide, she does not sensationalize or condemn these acts and leaves them, without editorializing, for the reader to try to comprehend. As we know, the story of infanticide is at the center of Toni Morrison's *Beloved* (1987) and accounts for much of its disturbing power.

Morrison draws on the history of slave families, as well as on the literature of slavery and abolition, to tell her tale, though she does so without the reticence of her predecessors.

The notion that women wrote "domestic fiction," a form that embodies and promotes the repressive ideology of bourgeois domesticity, is sorely challenged by a careful look at the domestic spaces—the homes—of industrial novels, antislavery fiction, and slave narratives. The vexed, equivocal meaning of these spaces suggests that for the impoverished laborer and the slave, home is always in the process of being destroyed or corrupted, and that Home as a place of belonging and independence—or emancipation—remains a virtual impossibility and an ever-deferred dream. Although we might understand Gaskell, Stowe, and even Jacobs to be holding out the bourgeois paradigm of home as a longed-for ideal, out of reach but still cherished, it seems equally clear—and more fundamental to their literary and political purposes—that entrenched social, economic, and legal structures prohibit the fulfillment of this dream for the worker and the slave. In these writers' hands, the idea of home becomes a vehicle for social criticism, a private symbol of public injustice.

Two homes are at the center of the heart-wrenching class contrast Gaskell uses to move her readers in *Mary Barton*. The below-ground dwelling where the impoverished, ailing Davenport family barely subsists is dark, damp, cold, and fetid enough to "knock . . . two men down." The narrator introduces this place, as seen through the eyes of John Barton, as a "cellar in which a family of human beings lived," as if to underscore its fitness for only nonhuman creatures (*MB*, 98). Indeed, the back cellar next to it is a receptacle for the moisture and "worse abominations" dropped from a pigsty (*MB*, 102). The unsettling effect on the reader is heightened a few pages later when another worker, Wilson, enters the home of the mill owner Carson at breakfast time to try to get an infirmary order for medication to treat the Davenports' typhus. Coming in through the kitchen, he sees "glittering tins," a "roaring fire," coffee steaming on the stove, and an abundance of food—steak, toasted bread, eggs. The cooking smells, warmth, and visual display offer a contrast to the sensory impact of the Davenports' cellar that requires no commentary or elaboration. Not only do these descriptions impress on the reader the injustice and inequities of life in Manchester, but they also serve to empty out the idea of home.

A subtler indication that Gaskell uses the working-class home to tell the story of immiseration appears in the novel in the form of periodic descriptions of the deteriorating Barton household. Here, too, contrast plays a role, though the disparity in this case does not have to do only with class but also with John Barton's economic and psychological decline over the course of the narrative. In chapter 2 we find a careful and detailed account of the way the Barton home looks when times are flush, before the deaths of Mrs. Barton and the Bartons' young son and Barton's loss of employment. Mrs. Barton enters the house and sees the "one bright spot" of the "red-hot fire smouldering under a large piece of coal," which Barton immediately stirs into a "warm and glowing light in every corner of the room" (*MB*, 49). The main room of the house is large, filled with "conveniences" and colorful household items, and the source of great pride to the family:

> On each side of [the window], hung blue-and-white check curtains, which were now drawn, to shut in the friends met to enjoy themselves. Two geraniums, unpruned and leafy . . . stood on the sill. . . . In the corner between the window and the fire-side was a cupboard, apparently full of plates and dishes, cups and saucers, and some more nondescript articles. . . . [I]t was evident that Mrs. Barton was proud of her crockery and glass, for she left the cupboard door open, with a glance round of satisfaction and pleasure. . . . The place seemed almost crammed with furniture (sure sign of good times among the mills). . . . [R]esting against the wall was a bright green japanned tea tray, having a couple of scarlet lovers embracing in the middle. The fire-light danced merrily on this. (*MB*, 49–50)

Light, warmth, and the clutter of bright and decorative objects signal a state of contentment and pleasure, comfort and belonging. Aesthetic detail, along with hospitality and good fellowship, reflect a delicacy of taste and feeling that Gaskell portrays as human rather than class-bound.

As "good times" fade for the working people, their homes suffer, even as the masters move from grand house to grander. "Large houses," the narrator tells us, "are still occupied, while spinners' and weavers' cottages stand empty, because the families that once occupied them are obliged to live in rooms or cellars" (*MB*, 59). The unemployed worker thinks of his "uncomplaining" wife and crying, hungry children at home and of the "dying life" of those closest to him (*MB*, 60). Overwhelmed by death, Barton enters into a pact with the union that undoes him and is transformed into a wraithlike and guilt-ridden man. Mary tries to tend to him and, by the end of the novel, approaches "the house that from habit she still called home, but which *possessed the holiness of home no longer*" (*MB*, 421; emphasis added). What is called home and what truly feels like home are no longer the same. She sees her father sitting "still and motionless," and the following brief description reminds the reader, by contrast, of the colorful, welcoming Barton home of chapter 2: "He sat by the fire; the grate I should say, for fire there was none. Some dull, grey ashes, negligently left, long days ago, coldly choked up the bars. He had taken the accustomed seat from mere force of habit, which ruled his automaton-body" (*MB*, 422). Bereft of wife, friends, health, sustenance, employment, and guiltless conscience, Barton's state is reflected in the fireless hearth and the gray, colorless dwelling that is no longer a home. He has been reduced to the state not of an animal but rather of a machine.

That the idea of home is very much on Stowe's mind in *Uncle Tom's Cabin* is obvious from its title. In an essay titled "What Is a Home?," written for the *Atlantic Monthly* in March 1864, Stowe offered thoughts on the meaning of home for women, especially in relation to their husbands. Though a "work of art peculiar to the genius of women," home was not simply a matter of male ownership and female housekeeping (as it is in Austen) but rather a place of spiritual partnership between husband and wife.[31] She observes that, in European countries, where marriages are "commercial partnerships" only, there is no word equivalent to "home" (as distinct from house: *maison, casa, haus*). "There can be no home," she writes, thinking of the position of women but also of the American ideal, "without liberty."[32] *Uncle Tom's Cabin* meditates upon this inextricable association between liberty and home in the case of the slave. When George Harris reaches the safety of the Quaker settlement and the hospitable dwelling of the Hallidays, the narrator declares that he had "never yet [until that time] known a meaning" for home (*UTC*, 122). When, later on, he and Eliza are about to cross the border into liberty in Canada, the narrator turns to the reader again and, using the rhetoric of the Founding Fathers, declares that for George freedom is not the right of a nation to be a nation but rather the right of a man to be a man and to "have a home of his own" (*UTC*, 332). The novel sounds this note yet again in its description of the slave warehouse in New Orleans, with its facade of propriety and ordinariness and its interior of dehumanizing commerce and brutality. The warehouse is "a house externally not much unlike others, kept with neatness" but betrays its grotesqueness by the rows of men and women standing along its side "as a sign of the property sold within" (*UTC*, 283). Conventional domestic spaces can contain within them the most hideous creations of man's social existence. True home for the slave is not simply a naive ideal but something unimaginable under the system of slavery, a concept to be grasped only with the coming of liberty.

The dwelling that gives Stowe's novel its title is a site that at first belies the notion that the slave cannot know home and then confirms its truth. Like Barton's deteriorating home, Uncle Tom's cabin is gradually emptied of its "homeness" and ultimately evacuated of its inhabitants. It begins in chapter 4 of the novel as an apparently idyllic cabin, a place of learning, worship, prodigious amounts of cooking, and patriotism. The master's son, young George Shelby, teaches Tom to make his letters, fellow slaves gather to sing spirituals and hear George read from Revelation, Aunt Chloe tends her flourishing garden and makes fragrant chicken pie, and a portrait of George Washington hangs on the wall. Stowe wants to establish the fundamental and recognizable humanity of these slaves, and yet she also wants to suggest the fragility of this scene, one unprotected by law and wholly subject to the whim of others. Perhaps the only signal of this in chapter 4 is a mention in the first paragraph of the location of Tom's cabin right next to "the house"—the quotation marks are Stowe's—the place where Tom and Chloe's owners reside. Tom and his family may think they have a home, but there is only one secure home on this property, only one home possessed by its inhabitants, and it belongs to the Shelbys.

As the novel proceeds, this fact becomes clear. Tom is sold away, and Chloe eventually leaves for Louisville to earn wages as a confectioner's assistant so that she can pay for her husband's freedom. Wage earning (as Harriet Martineau and others have claimed) meant a kind of liberty unavailable to slaves, even if it meant leaving what had once seemed to be home. Tom's cabin is shut up "for the present," the Shelbys mistakenly believing that it will once again be reopened and revived when the family is reunited. The wages Chloe proudly earns and the efforts of George Shelby to buy Tom back prove useless, and Tom dies, a victim of Simon Legree. The slave's family is never reconstituted and the homecoming meal Chloe prepares for her husband in the master's house is left uneaten. The cabin ceases to be a home at all and becomes instead a kind of mausoleum. George frees all the Shelby slaves so that none will ever again "run the risk of being parted from home" and declares to them: "think of your freedom, every time you see UNCLE TOM'S CABIN; and let it be a memorial" (*UTC*, 380). Only because it marks the antithesis of freedom can the cabin serve as its symbol. There is no Home without liberty and self-possession.

If Barton's and Uncle Tom's dwellings illustrate the fragility and elusiveness of Home for the worker and the slave, Harriet Jacobs's account of her experience of enslavement and escape challenges the notion that Home can ever exist for the black person, whether slave or free, Southern or Northern, as long as slavery exists as the law of the land. It is not that Jacobs dismisses the dream of home but rather that she sees it as something out of reach. At the end of *Incidents* she declares that the endpoint of her story is "freedom" and not, as in the case of other women's narratives, marriage. She addresses us with "Reader, my story ends in freedom; not in the usual way," as if to underscore her deviation from the literary paradigms of novels like *Jane Eyre*, with their declarations of

"Reader, I married him!" The terminus of freedom is not, however, the limit of her aspirations. "The dream of my life," she continues, "is not yet realized. I do not sit with my children in a home of my own, however humble" (*ILS*, 201). This remark indicates both how problematic the achievement of Home continues to be for the slave and how radically its meaning for this black woman might diverge from the ideal held by the white heroines who typically populate literary texts.

As Jacobs's narrative proceeds, it disqualifies a succession of dwellings as possible models of home. Dr. Flint's household, typical of the slave owner's domestic arrangements everywhere, conceals the "secrets of slavery," as we have seen. His sexual relations with numerous female slaves, a slew of mixed-race offspring, his bizarrely behaved wife, and his sadistic pursuit of Linda all expose his domestic life as corrupt and bankrupt—a "cage of obscene birds," Jacobs calls it (*ILS*, 52). She assures us that she draws "no imaginary pictures of southern homes," as if hoping to dispel the notion that the system of slavery is compatible with the existence of true Home for either white or black (*ILS*, 35).

Brent is repelled by the idea of living in Dr. Flint's household, and the news that he wishes to "build a small house for me . . . to give me a home of my own" fills her with dread (*ILS*, 53). She would rather "drudge out [her] life on a plantation"—work in the fields—than occupy either the main house or the "lonely cottage" some distance away (*ILS*, 31). The words "house" and "home," heavily freighted with irony for Jacobs, also reflect on the terms "house negro" and "master's house" (as in "the house" adjacent to Uncle Tom's cabin) and on the multiple distortions of reality they convey. The ostensible privilege of being a house slave turns out to be a curse, the "home" of her own a travesty. Even the Bruce household in Brooklyn, where Brent lives comfortably after escaping the South, fails as a home for her, both because she is still a dependent and because the Fugitive Slave Law makes her vulnerable to recapture. "I was . . . a slave in New York," she writes, "as subject to slave laws as I had been in a Slave State. Strange incongruity in a State called free!" (*ILS*, 193). Jacobs discredits even the flight to freedom as a possible homecoming.

In the abolitionist fictions of Stowe and in Gaskell's *Mary Barton*, flight appears as the imagined answer to enslavement and oppression. Mary Barton and her lover and future husband, Jem Wilson, emigrate and settle in Canada after both have been disgraced in Manchester, not by virtue of any offense they have committed but only because the taint of mere accusation has irreparably and unjustifiably tarnished their reputations. Gaskell's Canada has the air of an Edenic paradise, a pastoral refuge from civilization, full of "primeval trees," gardens, orchards, and the luscious beauty of "Indian summer" (*MB*, 465). Canada is also, of course, the temporary home for Eliza and George Harris in *Uncle Tom's Cabin*, though in the end they leave North America for Liberia. George dreams of "a republic formed of picked men . . . an acknowledged nation . . . a people . . . an African nationality" (*UTC*, 374–75). These words may well have influenced George Eliot in her vision of national independence, emancipation, and homecoming in both *The Spanish Gypsy* and *Daniel Deronda*. In the former work a group of Gypsies leaves Spain to seek a homeland on the coast of Africa, a nationalist project not typically associated with the Romany people. In *Deronda*, conceived well before the Zionist mission had been launched, Daniel and Mirah leave for the Middle East, hoping to find freedom and a nation-home of their own, but one that will be, in the words of Mirah's brother, the visionary Mordecai, "a new Jewish polity . . . a republic, where there is equality of protection . . . an organic centre . . . a community" (*DD*, 594–95).

At the end of *Dred*, after the slave rebellion fails to materialize and Dred has been killed, a group of slaves that includes Harry Carson escapes by boat to New York, setting sail on a harrowing but emancipatory journey. Harry continues on to Canada. By this point Stowe has abandoned the idea of Liberia (a controversy that divided the abolitionist cause) and makes Canada into the place of desired settlement and community, a pastoral haven of wheat fields and forests. It replaces and fulfills the strange and transitory "common settlement" of the Dismal Swamp, where Dred and other fugitives hide from masters and slave hunters. The anti-plantation of the Swamp is likened to the "wilderness" where the Jews wandered before entering the Promised Land in the Old Testament, as well as to Egypt, where they fled from the "murder of the innocents" in the New.[33] The first biblical flight prefigures the second, and both presage the slaves' escape to the limbo of freedom in the Swamp and then the Eden or Promised Land north of the US border.

Jacobs departs from this pattern of idyllic escape not just in the way she ends her narrative—still in search of home—but also in her earlier account of the "escape" that turns into a strangely freeing captivity. Jacobs's story is not the typical runaway-slave narrative: her flight from Dr. Flint ends in self-confinement rather than in release. The most astonishing, if not incredible, aspect of *Incidents* remains Linda Brent's decision to hide in the attic space of a shed attached to her grandmother's house in the very North Carolina town where she had resided since birth. Hiding not in plain sight but in the heart of slavery, Brent eludes her master and those he employs to find her, who believe she has escaped to the North. She accepts her confinement in this "hole," not more than three feet at its highest point and with a slope so steep that she cannot turn over in a prone position without hitting her head, in order to be near her children and continue to work for their emancipation. Deprived of air and light, and warned by her friends that she will be crippled for life after this period of agonizing bodily constraint, Linda continues to live this way for nearly seven years. Her unfathomable incarceration is preferable to her "lot as a slave" and is not, she tells us, without consolations: "I heard the voices of my children" (*ILS*, 114). She hears, too, stories about other female slaves running from their owners, one who is sold away with her baby to a trader once her mistress sees a resemblance to the master in the child's face, and another who jumps in the river and drowns rather than be stripped and beaten by her irate mistress (*ILS*, 122). Better to be enclosed in a cramped attic, unable to move and yet free of persecution, than to meet with the fates of these women. Able to create a "loophole"—three rows of holes in the side of the shed—after she discovers a gimlet in her compartment, she progresses from only hearing her children to seeing them too. Now her literary model shifts from Pamela, the chaste heroine defending her virtue, to Robinson Crusoe, a stranded isolate who "rejoice[s] . . . at finding such a treasure" as the tool that enables her to peer at her son and daughter (*ILS*, 115).

This attic home that is not a home, a tiny place of concealment and precarious safety, also links Jacobs's narrative with the historical and literary phenomenon of hiding in dramatically confined spaces. In *Uncle Tom's Cabin*, published before *Incidents* but likely influenced by the events of Jacobs's life that were known to Stowe, the runaway slaves Cassy and Emmeline hide briefly in a large box in the garret of their master Simon Legree's house.[34] The box, supplied with pillows, clothing, and candles, serves, as Cassy says, as their "home for the present" (*UTC*, 353). Complete with knothole, which the women use to track Legree's movements, this box is a version of Jacobs's attic but almost certainly draws on other instances of miraculous confinement as well. The most notorious of these was the case of Henry Box Brown, who in 1849 sent himself from slavery in Virginia to freedom in Philadelphia in a box and whose story was widely known through his frequent lecturing for the Anti-Slavery Society and his autobiography, a success in both America and Britain. In the *Story of Mattie Jackson*, a dictated slave narrative published in 1866, Jackson tells of her family's escape from slavery through running and "secreting themselves."[35] Her little brother, only two years old and incapable of keeping silent, was "confined in a box" by their mother, who didn't know how else to hide him. The child, who became paralyzed, died before the family could make it to freedom in Indianapolis.

These temporary, sometimes lifesaving spaces of confinement emerge as complicated images of escape, emancipation, and home. For the slave, to escape is to hide and, perhaps, to have the power of vision, of seeing without being seen. Box Brown, Cassy, Emmeline, and Mattie Jackson's brother are only transients, tentative sojourners in impossibly cramped places; Linda Brent is a semipermanent resident, a seven-year occupant of a hole. It is more home to her than the cottage Dr. Flint builds for her or, in some sense, the house in Brooklyn where she lives as an ostensibly free woman. The attic is, after all, part of her grandmother's own home, a dwelling possessed by a former slave who is now a freewoman. It also renders Linda invisible and therefore untouchable and so able to oversee her son and daughter's existence.[36] Jacobs seems to suggest that the only true emancipation comes in being invisible, for being visible makes her vulnerable not just to capture, whether in the South or in the North, but also to irrevocable separation from her children. At narrative's end, to repeat, she "do[es] not sit with [her] children in a home of [her] own" (*ILS*, 201).

When Toni Morrison wrote her own slave narrative in *Beloved*, she chose to focus not only on the impossible, soul-crushing choices of motherhood in slavery but also on the links between slavery and the idea of home, rewriting Stowe and Jacobs, perhaps, in meditating on this always vexed, never fulfilled connection. Precisely because the condition of slavery involves being "moved around like checkers," all loved ones and acquaintances "run off or . . . hanged, got rented out, loaned out, bought up, brought back, stored up, mortgaged, won, stolen or seized," the dream of permanence and a residence that is true Home remains powerful, tantalizing.[37] The novel offers us two homes: the ironically named Sweet Home, the Kentucky plantation where Baby Suggs, Sethe, and Paul D lived as slaves; and "124," the house on Bluestone Road in Cincinnati where Sethe tries to live as a freewoman. The plantation is the home that makes Sethe shudder and scream, even in retrospect. When Sethe thinks of Sweet Home, she sees its "shameless beauty" in her mind's eye, but its evil makes her wonder if hell, too, is a pretty place (29). The plain numerical tag 124 suggests this dwelling's difference from Sweet Home and begins each of the three sections of the novel, a refrain that marks its importance as a framing place and idea, and in each beginning sentence the house is personified. "Spiteful," "loved," then "quiet," it pulsates with the emotions of its inhabitants and perhaps with the anger of a ghostly child. The house, haunted by "some dead Negro's grief," as Baby Suggs understands all such houses to be, expels and disburses its inhabitants (6). They run from it, while Sethe, its one obdurate, immovable resident, tries to hold it together and make it a home.

The novel makes clear what might constitute such a home. When Sethe first arrives at 124 after escaping from Sweet Home with her children, she sees a "buzzing, cheerful house" and is greeted by

Baby Suggs, her mother-in-law, with "wide arms." What follows is the cherished twenty-eight-day period of Sethe's "unslaved life":

> Days of healing, ease and real-talk. Days of company: know-ing the names of forty, fifty other Negroes, their views, habits; where they had been and done; of feeling their fun and sorrow along with her own. . . . One taught her the alphabet; another a stitch. All taught her how it felt to wake up at dawn and *de-cide* what to do with the day. . . . Bit by bit, at 124 and in the Clearing [where Baby Suggs preaches], . . . she had claimed herself. *Freeing yourself was one thing; claiming ownership of that freed self was another.* (116; emphasis added)

A freed self, safe children, a community that teaches and comforts, time within one's control, and ownership—and not in the twenty-first-century banal sense of the word but literally—of self: this makes for home. From the moment the "boys" from Sweet Home come to reclaim Sethe and her children, assaulting the mother with a brand of sexual violence directed at her maternity, and she kills her baby rather than allow it to be raised as a slave (she wanted to "outhunt the hunter"), 124 cannot retain its "homeness." Return-ing to it later with her daughter Denver and her sons, she finds it uninhabitable, aggressively haunted, so that she loses her living children one by one and takes besotted refuge in the enigmatic Beloved, who may or may not be the returned dead child. As the novel ends, with the chance that 124 could be shelter for the lov-ing pair of Sethe and Paul D but never replicate the cheer and buzz of truly "unslaved life," it reaffirms what *Incidents in the Life of a Slave Girl* had conveyed more than a century before: that without full emancipation, the survival and presence of kin, especially chil-dren, and possession of self, there is no possibility of true Home.

Incidents in the Life of a Slave Girl may be the ultimate anti-domestic woman's narrative. It characterizes the domestic world of Southern whites as hellholes and the homes of sympathetic North-ern whites as more commodious but still unsafe and estranging, and it represents a severely cramped hiding place as the nearest thing to home the female slave can inhabit. Like Linda Brent's white lover, this hiding place is deliberately, perhaps even freely, chosen.

We began this chapter with Elizabeth Barrett Browning's revulsion at the idea of "Penelopes" shut up in the "women's apartment," an image of sequestration very different from that of Linda Brent in her attic hiding place. Brent's confinement is a form of rebellion, Penelope's of acquiescence. Brent's defiance of slavery and evasion of her master are prologues to the public, political act of Harriet Jacobs's memoir. Penelope's captivity amounts to a rejection of public life and independent action and an acceptance of what Barrett Browning calls, with deliberateness, "slavery." Barrett Browning, Jacobs, Martineau, Gaskell, and Stowe all reject the "slavery and concubinage" that would have them restrict their pens to safe subjects and tame, domestic plots. Better not to write, better to relinquish the pen, than to accept the role of a Penelope who never ventures forth, even in imagination. Some of these women entered public debates by way of sentimental strains of writing and drew on maternal economy as a means of suasion, but their aim was to "take [their] rank among thinkers and speakers," their cause emancipation, and their ardor the spirit of 1848.

CHAPTER 3

Pioneers

FOR CHARLOTTE BRONTË'S LUCY SNOWE, "To walk in London alone seemed in itself an adventure." So it very well might, given that walking alone in a strange—or even familiar—metropolis was beyond the expectation of most nineteenth-century women. Nonetheless, Lucy's excitement should not be dismissed as the overreaction of a sheltered provincial with little, if any, knowledge of the greater world. For all the idiosyncrasies that distinguish her manner and her narration, Lucy belongs to, and indeed helped to consolidate, the novelistic tradition of adventuring heroines. These female adventurers, eager, sometimes driven, to escape the restricted life that seemed their appointed social fate, formed the vanguard of an emerging social type in women's fiction, the peripatetics, we have christened them, women who departed the home and class-bound precincts of the domestic novel in search of less fettered existences. Ellen Moers, impressed by their courage and resourcefulness when confronted by the vicissitudes and assorted villainies that can make life away from home as dangerous as it is exciting, credited them with bringing a singular moral energy to the novel—traveling heroism, she called it.[1]

Moers fretted, however, that traveling heroism found its most formidable expression in the Gothic, notably in the fictions of Ann Radcliffe, a novelist who personally never ventured beyond London and Bath but whose imagination, heedless of plausibility, transported her heroines to exotic locales not to be found anywhere but in the annals of romance. As Moers herself mordantly, if regretfully, observed, it was only within the labyrinthine interiors of the Gothic castle or ruined mansion that the traveling heroine could "travel brave and free and still remain respectable."[2]

Unless, that is, she went to America, a land of sprawling coast-
lines, broad waterways, dense backwoods, open prairies, and
mountainous expanses where the female peripatetic could travel
brave and free without ending up in disgrace or in prison. Within
the confines of the English novel, emigration is generally involun-
tary, a form of social or legal banishment rather than a personal
adventure. Such is the pitiable lot of David Copperfield's childhood friend, Little Em'ly, who emigrates to Australia to escape
the stigma of being seduced and abandoned by Steerforth, or the
even sadder fate of Hetty Sorrell, the strongly sensual but morally
infirm beauty of *Adam Bede* who is spared the gallows and transported to Australia for killing the illegitimate child fathered by her
aristocratic seducer, Arthur Donnithorne.

How different is the wayward life of Ántonia, the eponymous
heroine of Willa Cather's "pioneer woman's story," who bears a
child out of wedlock yet eventually marries (a good man, too),
oversees a prosperous farm, and nurtures a brood of sons. Ántonia's childhood friends, Lina Lingard and Tiny Soderball, herald
even more pronounced social freedoms for women. Cather goes
so far as to hail them as a "race apart"—women "early awakened
and made observant by coming at a tender age from an old country to a new."[3] Starting life as immigrant country girls with "rough
and mannish" ways, they take up a new, salaried life as "hired
girls" in the prairie town of Black Hawk, Nebraska, where their
"positive carriage and freedom of movement" make them "con-
spicuous among Black Hawk women" of more delicate constitu-
tion and sedentary ways (*MÁ*, 198). While their wages are initially
earmarked to help discharge paternal debts and send their younger
siblings to school, they soon begin to invest in themselves: they
buy more fashionable clothes, refine their manners, and then, surer
now of their talents and prospects, venture out into the world, Lina
to Lincoln, where she sets up her own dressmaking shop, Tiny to
the goldfields of Alaska. When we last hear of them, they have
reunited and settled in San Francisco, entrepreneurial business-
women answerable to no one but themselves.

The fictional lives we summarize here do not, needless to say,
unfold along one untroubled and triumphant arc, but they do confirm that female protagonists with an appetite for unfamiliar places

and uncommon experiences were no longer routinely herded into the phantasmagoric territories of Gothic or sensationalist fiction. History, for once, conspired with the aspirations of adventurous women intent on remaking rather than escaping reality. The opening of the American frontier to pioneering homesteaders offered women an unprecedented opportunity to explore social and geographical latitudes undreamed of by their forebears. In the rough and ready ways of the frontier, gender codes, while not abolished, became more relaxed. Women had freer rein in managing the family homestead or running the family business. They might, like the "hired girls" Lina and Tina and the trio of Bohemian Marys, celebrated "heroines of a cycle of scandalous stories" (*MÁ*, 202), become prominent and beloved fixtures in the communities their presence enlivened and which their labor helped mold, enrich, and sustain.

Eventually and inevitably, the pioneer era transformed the dialectic that had traditionally determined the scope and the itinerary of the peripatetic woman's travels. Home and abroad, native and foreign lands became interpenetrating rather than diametrically opposed terms in a new geopolitical equation. It was an equation devised to register and calculate the social and personal costs of a historic exodus: the large-scale migrations of peoples to the New World of America at a time when undeveloped federal land was being opened up to homesteaders. In the socioeconomic and cultural transformations that ensued, the pioneering heroine joined forces and often mingled indistinguishably with the impoverished, disenfranchised, and persecuted peoples who came to America in search of a new life. Economic betterment and social freedoms were the enticements, but, as we shall see, so was the lure of grander spiritual horizons.

If the female pioneer evinced the same intrepid character of the adventuring heroines of fiction who helped prepare the way for her, her heroism was, if anything, more pronounced. She battled the elements, rather than dastardly mustachioed villains, and was assaulted by both fatigue and fear in her attempts to tame the wilderness. She was indomitable in defending something more impersonal than female honor or even her own existence—her vision of the country's as well as her own future. This last claim may strike some readers as so much jingoistic sloganeering, but it expresses something concretely imagined by the pioneer woman and is celebrated as such in Cather's homesteading sagas, *O Pioneers!* and *My Ántonia*. In working to reclaim and soften the "somber wastes" and "vast hardness" of the American prairies for human settlement,[4] Cather's pioneering heroines secure and reinforce the link between a woman's private experience and the epic phase of America's nation building—the development of the Great Plains and the settling of the American West. They are not passive instruments or incidental casualties but forceful agents of America's self-proclaimed "manifest destiny." Although keenly aware of the patent injustices ignored or suppressed in such idealizations of the collective political will, Cather appreciated and to a degree subscribed to the ideal terms of this national myth, in which the development of America was inextricably tied to the prospects of a new personal beginning. "The history of every country begins in the heart of a man or a woman," is the assumption, verging on empowering belief, that inspirits Cather's *O Pioneers!*

It is an assumption that could, of course, be challenged on many grounds. Theologians and philosophers might counter that history does not begin in the human heart but outside of it, in God's providential will, or, as Hegel proposed, in the strivings of Spirit, or, as Marx contended, in the dialectics of economic production. Historians might insist that we look to the materially concrete and historically unique conditions that give birth to a nation. Cather's novels can accommodate most if not all of these theories of historical development, but that is not what is most remarkable about them. Nor do these objections, principled as they might be, respond to what is truly original and provocative about Cather's assertion: that it recognizes the origins of a country in a woman's as much as a man's feeling for the future.

Alexandra Bergson, who presides over *O Pioneers!* like a guiding spirit, deserves a special place in the female literary tradition for keeping faith with this feeling against all the inducements to return it to the protective custody of men. In her long struggle to tame the wild lands of the Nebraska prairie, we can see how the peripatetic is transfigured into the pioneering heroine who blazes, rather than obediently follows, historic trails. Alexandra moves through a world without traditional landmarks or basic comforts, but it is a world that entirely suits, even attracts her, promising as it does to yield, though not easily, to the transforming labor of her own hands. She dedicates herself to working the rich but resistant earth without interfering thoughts of love, sex, or social convention—the typical preoccupations of novelistic heroines from Elizabeth Bennet to Bridget Jones.

Cather is aware of how strange, even unappealing, such a heroine will seem to readers who like their heroines to be made of more emotional stuff:

> Most of Alexandra's happy memories were . . . impersonal . . . yet to her they were very personal. Her mind was a white book with clear writing about weather and beasts and growing things. Not many people would have cared to read it; only a happy few. She had never been in love, she had never indulged in sentimental reveries. Even as a girl she had looked upon men as work-fellows. She had grown up in a serious time. (*OP*, 119)

All times may be serious, but Cather, whose novels are invariably set in foundational or transitional times, regards some times as more serious than others in determining the character and historic fate of a culture or of a nation. Such epochal times produce not only serious but exceptional and frequently *anomalous* heroines like Alexandra, whose relation to the world of Nature—the weather, the beasts of the field, all things that grow according to their appointed season—seems impervious to, or uncompromised by, any romantic emotion. Hence the image of her mind as "a white book," betokening a virginal consciousness yet to be inscribed by the personalizing force of sexual desire.

Yet as much as Cather is intent on exploring a female consciousness more aroused by impersonal ideals than personal desires, she is careful not to picture her heroine working in dreamy isolation. She places Alexandra securely within the bustling heart of ordinary (indeed humdrum) community and not only sets but judges

her story against the traditions and tales of more conventional female longing. Alexandra, the anomalous heroine whose great and
impersonal love is reserved for the land she labors to make fertile,
yields the opening and many of the novel's concluding pages to
Marie Shabata, whose sensuality and emotional warmth give the
novel its surging current of erotic feeling. This current, running
invisibly but inexorably beneath the episodic recounting of Alexandra's gradual conquest of the land, finally surfaces in Marie's
illicit love for Emil, Alexandra's adored, restless, and passionate
younger brother. They will both die at the hand of the husband
Marie understands, but does not love.

This story of adulterous love is not even conceivable, much less
tellable, in Alexandra's white book, and yet it, too, Cather insinu-
ates, is part of the larger narrative of what civilization costs us,
not in physical toil but in moral pain. Alexandra may have the will
and vigor to tame the wild land, but Marie and Emil's death con-
secrates it. Alexandra will look upon their murdered bodies with
a kind of awe, a sign of Cather's deep respect for passionate Eros
as "an acceleration of life" that, as in high romantic myth, hurtles
toward death. Thus, even as Marie and Emil's deaths blacken the
pages of her white book, they also humanize and personalize it
by admitting into its pages the records of irresistible desire. After
Marie's death Alexandra becomes increasingly haunted by a recurrent dream in which she feels herself "being lifted and carried
lightly by some one very strong," a dream (Cather calls it an illusion) of being lifted by "the mightiest of all lovers," whose shoulders "seemed as strong as the foundations of the world" (OP, 165).
This unconscious fantasy of erotic surrender marks the moment
when Alexandra subsides, we might more accurately say relapses,
into a more conventional womanhood. She will conclude the novel
as a more traditional heroine, awaiting marriage.

So, too, the last pages of My Ántonia will enshrine Ántonia
as a figure of radiantly traditional motherhood, raising a family
to work and inherit the land she works and fructifies. Only the
last-minute decision of the narrator, Jim Burden, to affix the word
"My" to his title before he surrenders his narrative recollections of
the woman who epitomized his boyhood, suggests a resistance to a

fecundity that overwhelms her distinct individuality. This claim to her is attended by many emotional and historical ironies, however, perhaps the most telling being the disappearance of her name in the novel's last chapter title, "Cuzak's Boys." The boys are hers, but it is the father's name they bear, an illustration of how women's achievements are often hidden behind patriarchal habits of designating relation and possession.

The conflict between the pioneer woman's erotic desire to be transported beyond the toiling self into rapturous unions, and the more impersonal but equally compulsive drive to subdue and bring civilization (in the form of homesteads and the towns that grow out of them) to the wilderness, is the great, epic theme of Cather's fiction. She explores the varying forms and outcomes of this conflict in greater depth, although hardly with more poignancy, in the novels that followed: *The Song of the Lark*, *A Lost Lady*, and *The Professor's House*. But in *O Pioneers!* and *My Ántonia*, Cather is more concerned with identifying the impersonal aspirations that drive men and women to tame the wild land, no matter what the personal cost. For Cather's pioneering heroines, these aspirations are not rationally thought out or even consciously understood but emotionally inherited, a bequest of large-spirited but weak-willed fathers unequal to the hard terms imposed by the unreclaimed lands of the New World. Women do not always think back through their mothers, as Virginia Woolf proposed,[5] at least not in Cather's novels, many of whose heroines are strongly male-identified. We shall encounter other women novelists in the course of this book who trace their lineage through a male precursor and dramatize questions of inheritance (of money, guilt, and literary and cultural tradition) in the father-daughter relation. These relations do not preclude, but are also not limited by, erotically charged cross-gender identification.

Both Alexandra and Ántonia exemplify this characterological identification with the wider outlook and executive authority traditionally associated with men. They are daughters of fathers who possessed the vision but finally lacked the strength and the heart to tame the wilderness. In this they seem morally close, if culturally distant cousins, to Elizabeth Bennet, who inherits her father's intelligence but is strong—or prejudiced—where he is weak and feebly opinionated. Both Cather heroines have fathers who die, one a suicide, each a victim of stalled hopes and his own irredeemable loneliness. Each death promotes the daughter to the position of head of the family, where she is now entrusted with realizing the father's hope for a better life in the New World.

In *A Lost Lady*, Cather gives these aspirations the name and status of dreams, with all the vulnerability of dreams to adverse and intransigent reality. The potency of such dreams is vouched for by Captain Forrester, a successful dreamer who is credited with helping lay the first railroad ties across the plains. While acknowledging that "there are people who get nothing in this world," Forrester, a sort of instinctive prairie transcendentalist, holds to the belief that "what you think of and plan for day by day, in spite of yourself, so to speak—you will get," and that "a thing dreamed of in the way I mean, is already an accomplished fact." "All our great West," he insists, "has been developed from such dreams: the homesteader's and the prospector's and the contractor's." The dream that opens up the future, however, also brings sorrow and destruction to the people or cultures it (often violently) supplants, a reality Forrester himself tacitly acknowledges in allowing "something forbidding to come into his voice: the lonely defiant note that is so often heard in the voices of old Indians."[6]

Cather is a scrupulous historian of such accomplished facts and the lonely defiance they never fully subdue, the cultural wrongs they can never justify or make right. But she is also the first and still unrivaled novelist to make the dreamer of such historic facts a woman. This is a notable departure from the novelistic tradition that tends to chastise, thwart, or defeat the female dreamer for the audacity and persistence of her yearning for—she hardly knows what. Such is the plight of George Eliot's restless heroine, Dorothea Brooke, a woman who longs for "some unattained goodness" but is destined, as Eliot warns in her prelude to *Middlemarch*, to a "life of mistakes, the offspring of spiritual grandeur ill-matched with the meanness of opportunity."[7] Cather, who shares Eliot's fascination with spiritual grandeur wherever it manifests itself, also shares her preoccupation with what Eliot called "the various experiments of time," of which the American experiment is the most radical, as it is the most recent. Her heroines tend to be women of spiritual grandeur who find a ground for "far-resonant action" in the vast expanses of the Great Plains and the majestic landscapes of the Southwest.

Her image for this momentous conjunction of female idealism and a natural environment favorable to its expression is Alexandra's face as she looks upon the Nebraska land, which claims all her strength and most of her feelings: "For the first time, perhaps, since that land emerged from the waters of geologic ages, a human face was set towards it with love and yearning" (*OP*, 37). A face set with love and yearning would not strike us as an unusual subject for novelistic or painterly treatment, unless what is being represented is, as it indisputably is here, a love so impersonal as to confound traditional notions of what women want. They want, it now appears, to gratify their procreative urge by not only bearing children but by making the land teem with crops. Thus, we might say that Alexandra's yearning constitutes Cather's idea of an accomplished fact: her gaze does not just foresee but also encompasses the future transformation of the wild land into productive fields, a fact whose historic significance is signaled by its being recorded as a "first," not only in the annals of American history but in the history of the world as it is measured in geological ages.

This rather grand rhetoric of first times is not unwarranted. It is meant to register the accomplished fact of a new cultural dispensation: the opening and freeing up of spaces, and hence of possibilities, for innovation and expansion previously debarred or unknown to women. Cather is responding to the ideological but also the pragmatic appeal of America as a land of unprecedented and seemingly limitless opportunity. The phrase may seem commonplace or worse, an ideological ruse, but it spoke to the longings and attracted the ambitions of people, especially women, as no other country ever did or yet has.

Cather, the foremost novelist of the American settlement, nonetheless never fails to remind us that this first time is but one in a series of first times—that is, it is part of a far older story of

the civilizing endeavor. *O Pioneers!* opens with immigrant settlers struggling to tame the Wild Land of the Nebraska Divide
and concludes with one pair of lovers slaughtered under a mulberry tree and another (Alexandra and her long-self-exiled suitor,
Carl) united over their graves. The tragedy confirms that Alexandra "belong[s] to the land" on whose surface she divines "the old
story writing itself over. Only it is we who write it, with the best
we have" (*OP*, 179). The white book of Alexandra's mind is now
shadowed, if not blackened, by her newfound understanding that
her story, the story of the land fructified and turned to human use,
is an old one, told over and over from time immemorial.

This is a moment of vision that seems to justify all that Alexandra has suffered and sacrificed for the land she loves perhaps
more than she ought or even wants. What she sees inscribed on the
land is an old story continually rewriting itself with the materials of
the present, of which she might include her own labor, her focused
will, and the blood of her father and brother. What consoles her in
the face of this exorbitant expense in lives and spirit is the belief
that the land has not only been written over but sanctified. It has
been infused and transfigured by a human history that can never be
really lost, however much of it may be forgotten. More important,
it is a history that is still to be made. Even in her grief, Alexandra
looks back to look forward. Pioneers never see the land without
seeing the future waiting to spring from it. The space they long to
conquer is not just territorial, or even cultural, but spiritual as well.

Sara Orne Jewett, whose unassuming but remarkably sophisticated chronicles of America's coastal settlements laid the foun-
dation for Cather's prairie epics, suggests as much in identifying
her narrative domain as the "the country of the pointed firs" and
representing it as both a naturalistic and a visionary terrain. The
nameless narrator, who is but a visitor to that country, is especially
struck by the rugged landscape, which is less the backdrop than
the backbone of her islanded tales:

> Through this piece of rough pasture ran a huge shape of stone
> like the great backbone of an enormous creature. At the end,
> near the woods, we could climb up on it and walk along to

the highest point; there above the circle of pointed firs we could look down over all the island, and could see the ocean that circled this and a hundred other bits of island ground, the mainland shore and all the far horizons. It gave a sudden sense of space, for nothing stopped the eye or hedged one in,—that sense of liberty in space and time which great prospects always give.[8]

Jewett does not so much depict a physical scene as envision a spiritual prospect. Unlike Mary Wollstonecraft, who feared that the isolated, if sublime, features of the Norwegian shoreline "bastilled" the understanding and shuttered the heart of those who made their homes there, Jewett extols the rugged, elevated coastal ranges for imparting a "sense of liberty in space and time." This liberating apprehension of a far, perhaps limitless horizon radically transforms not merely the perception but the very meaning of space, the primordial fact of the American continent, as the poet Charles Olson proclaimed in "Call Me Ishmael," his landmark essay on *Moby Dick*. "I take SPACE to be the central fact of man born in America from Folsom cave to now," Olson announced. "I spell it large because it comes large here. Large and without mercy."[9] Jewett may write in the contracted form of the tale, but capitalized, visually overwhelming SPACE, large and without mercy, is the central fact for her, as it is for any man born in America. And although her imagination, unlike the American Ishmael, was not instinctively nomadic, she also conversed with the sublime feelings afforded by far horizons glimpsed at the furthest verge of the country of pointed firs. The simple but imposing adjectives "huge," "great," and "far" are signifiers of this commanding oceanic vista, whose boundlessness encompasses, transcends, and will outlast the islanded communities huddled on its shoreline.

In Cather's *The Song of the Lark*, the sudden and enlarged sense of SPACE afforded by the open prairies engenders a similar feeling, tantamount now to a core belief, that the land is actually *awaiting* those who have come from far away to settle upon it. It is a belief handed down from an immigrant mother to her daughter, Thea, who inherits and interprets it as a spiritual bequest:

She had often heard Mrs. Kronborg say that she "believed in immigration" and so did Thea believe in it. This earth seemed to her young and fresh and kindly, a place where refugees from old, sad countries were given another chance. The mere absence of rocks gave the soil a kind of amiability and generosity, and the absence of natural boundaries gave the spirit a wider range. Wire fences might mark the end of a man's pasture, but they could not shut in his thoughts as mountains and forests can. It was over flat lands like this, stretching out to drink the sun, that the larks sang—and one's heart sang there, too. Thea was glad that this was her country, even if one did not learn to speak elegantly there. It was, somehow, an honest country and there was a new song in that blue air which had never been sung in the world before.[10]

Thea is a singer (she will eventually become a world-famous opera star), so we would expect the art of song to provide her with the metaphor for this new historical manifestation of spiritual energy and need. The Whitmanian theme of her song is America, the grand idea as well as the grand hopes that attach to it. It is foremost a song composed out of the new meanings that accrue to the word "country": as the physical lay and expanse of the land, as a symbolic possession ("my country") that confers a sense of identity and belonging within a larger and often abstract polity, and as a place imbued with a moral as well as ecological character—a place, that is, marked by an honesty not found in the more civilized but less candid environs of the Old World.

"My country" inspires a feeling, as it does a song, that will undergo many permutations as it makes its way into the hearts and fiction of those women writers who "sing"—but not, as we shall see, always in such sweet voices—America. It is a leitmotif that reverberates as a chant in many immigrant chronicles, most notably in Mary Antin's *The Promised Land*, an autobiographical account of the "making" of an American. In keeping with Antin's belief that "a proper autobiography is a death-bed confession," *The Promised Land* is structured as a kind of postmortem immigrant's bildungsroman. The person who has died is "Mashka, the granddaughter of Raphael the Russian," a young woman who made her way to America and was so "made over" by the experience that she now speaks about herself in the third person. "*She* and not *I*," Antin writes, "is my real heroine. My life I have still to live; her life ended when mine began."[11] To credit this you must believe Antin's claim that as a self-chronicler, she "is absolutely other than the person whose story I have to tell." What makes her feel so absolutely other is her having found a place in the world, something she never felt in the land of her first birth.

Land, but never country. That is Antin's initial, abiding, and painful point throughout her autobiography, and the moral and psychological key to her transformation into the heroine of her own life. The excitement she describes in embarking "on a double voyage of discovery," her "zest" in exploring both her increasingly complex inner life and "a new outer universe" (*PL*, 3), is shadowed by a "more poignant sense of disinheritance" that predates her arrival in the New World. Hers is an Exodus before it is an Adventure; whatever possessions or unhappy memories she leaves behind, she always carries with her the knowledge that as a Jew, she and her family and fellow immigrants are "a people without a country." "Polotzk," she writes, "was not my country. It was *goluth*—exile" (*PL*, 178). Yet if *goluth* signifies the pain and indignities of exile, it also entails diaspora, the new life and tribal settlements apart from ancestral homelands. Leaving the land of her birth is what makes possible her second birth and the beginning of her real life in America, where she can finally experience and enjoy the native sense of *feeling* as well as being at home: "The people all desiring noble things, and striving for them together, defying their oppressors, giving their lives for each other—all this it was that made *my country* . . . I knew one could say 'my country' and *feel* it, as one felt 'God' or 'myself'" (*PL*, 177; emphasis in original). For Antin the very act of saying "my country" does not so much report a newly accomplished fact as communicate a feeling whose reality is as incontestable and unimpeachable as her feeling for God and her sense of being fully and distinctly herself.

Antin's old life as an outcast and exile ends and her new life begins when she feels her country to be as central a fact as self or God.

But this feeling is personal, and as such is especially susceptible to the assaults of time, prejudice, or outright discrimination. Cather's feeling for "her country" is, as we might expect, more impersonal but equally exalted. It is also sturdier, fortified as it is by the weight of tradition. The "country" that inspires a song never yet heard in the world in *The Song of the Lark* (1915) is the thematic burden of her historical narrative. Three years later Cather personified this burden in *My Ántonia*, whose narrator, Jim Burden, celebrates the pioneers who turned a wilderness into a country. This is disclosed in a famous scene in the novel in which Jim, an avid classicist, is instructed in the finer points of Virgil's declared ambition in the *Georgics*: "Primus ego in patrium mecum . . . deducam Musas; for I shall be the first, if I live, to bring the Muses into my country." Cather, being as fastidious as she is ambitious, is careful to have Jim recount how his teacher, a Latinist named Gaston Cleric (a name that anticipates the French sacerdotal hero of *Death Comes for the Archbishop*), explained to him "that '*patria*' here meant, not a nation nor even a province but a little rural neighborhood on the Mincio where the poet was born" (*MÁ*, 264).

This semantic lesson is not a gratuitous bit of pedantry. It instructs us in Cather's determination to bring the Muses to her *patria* within whose modest precincts the destiny of her country is being made. The poet who sought to bring the Muses to his patria would later invoke them to sing the destined course of Empire. Indeed, the seeds of empire are sown and germinate in the patria, the neighborhoods, country towns, and byways of home; what is the Mediterranean to the Romans but their neighborhood extended beyond native shores? The word "country" translates this more inclusive—and less innocent—idea of the patria, including its incipient imperialist drive to annex and control more territory, into a more modern American idiom. This translation is noteworthy for avoiding the patriarchal ideology embedded in the patria (literally of the fathers) while absorbing the Virgilian respect for what is grounded in local traditions. Others, of course, shared Cather's ambition to bring the Muses to their patria: Jewett to Dunnet Landing, Sherwood Anderson to Winesburg, Ohio, and, unsurpassed in the lurid grandeur only encountered in decaying small towns that history has bypassed or defeated, Faulkner to the towns and environs of Yoknapatawpha County. No need to quarrel over precedence here, as long as one concedes to Cather an inaugural voice in establishing and ennobling this tradition of the American literary *patriae*.

The Virgilian model translates well into the American tradition devoted to chronicling the life of rural, frontier America, since it allows writers like Cather to work in full confidence that their neighborhood *is* a country. Country becomes an especially privileged, almost numinous word for American women writers to designate the subject and the sweep of their art. Gertrude Stein, a writer of radically different imagination, was as invested as Cather in advancing an unmistakably modern and decidedly American sense of what a country is and where it can be found: "After all," she imperturbably wrote in and about her adopted country, Paris, France, "everybody, that is, everybody who writes is interested in living inside themselves in order to tell what is inside themselves. That is why writers have to have two countries, the one where they belong and the one in which they live really. The second one is romantic, it is separate from themselves, it is not real but it is really there."[12] The woman who advanced this witty distinction between the "country" where one lives and the inner country where one mentally and spiritually dwells is a woman, above all else, who identified with something both within and larger than herself. Her habit of inhabiting double worlds is contagious if not syntactically imitable. By midcentury, Flannery O'Connor can speak of "some other country," and most, if not all, of her readers eventually understand that it is the unbounded and uncharted territories of the spirit, not to be found on any map, to which she alludes.

Indeed, the American continent was so large and so varied in its physical and moral topographies that it gave birth to as many notions and feelings about one's country as there were artistic temperaments to memorialize or criticize, even repudiate them. Katherine Anne Porter in her Texas panhandle stories; Tillie Olsen in *Yonnondio: From the Thirties*, which pioneered what we might call the rural proletarian novel; Flannery O'Connor's and Eudora Welty's often grotesque and spiritually impatient stories recounting the commonplace evils and slight, if tender, mercies of small-town Southern life; and Marilynne Robinson in her *Gilead* trilogy, the last volume of which, *Lila*, is actually dedicated to a place—Iowa—rather than a person, are among the most singular voices upholding, diversifying, and extending an American tradition that seeks to bring the Muses to their patriae.

This tradition is at once amplified and complicated in the fiction of African American novelists like Zora Neale Hurston and Toni Morrison, who must wrest the idea of a soul-enriching patria from the tenacious clutches of a lamentable history of slavery, segregation, and all the forms of legal and economic inequity that follow in their wake. Against these realities of dehumanization, discrimination, and dispossession, the need and feeling for a patria nonetheless endures as a locus and ideal of belonging, keeping alive the aspiration to possess a stake in a country where one feels, finally, at home. This aspiration is embraced with an idiomatic comic zest in Zora Neale Hurston's *Their Eyes Were Watching God*, a novel structured around the successive marriages of Janie Crawford, its passionate and increasingly peripatetic heroine, each of which she is either told or hopes will give her a secure place in the world.

But a secure place is not a synonym for a patria, nor is it an antidote for isolation and loneliness, as Janie discovers after her grandmother virtually sells her into marriage to a prosperous but emotionally stingy older man. After his death she finds herself spiritually, if not sexually, drawn to Joe Starks because he "spoke for far horizon."[13] Starks does not so much betray the promise of far horizon as fail to locate its human meaning. He does, in fact, take Janie to a town that is "nothing but a raw spot in de woods" (*TE*, 56), which, with a pioneer's entrepreneurial acumen, he cultivates until it blossoms into a thriving town, Eatonville, of which he becomes mayor. Yet under his governance, the town never becomes more than a sorry simulacrum of a patria. Cowed by the "bow-down command in his face" (*TE*, 75), the townspeople accede more and more to his autocratic rule, which replicates the oppressive civic and social structures of the white capitalist enclaves they had come to Eatonville to escape. More dispiriting, at least for Janie, the very prosperity of the town not only deepens the divisions between rich and poor but alters its fundamental values. Things become more important than people and power more valuable than a shared "native" culture, especially as expressed in the untranslatable idioms and idiosyncratic humor that distinguish one patria from another. Once Starks's death releases Janie from the oppressive regime of domestic servitude and material pursuits to which he had confined her, Janie resolves to resume "her great journey to the horizons in search of *people*; it was important to all the world that she should find them and they find her" (*TE*, 138; emphasis in original).

Janie's resolve is expressed so idiomatically that it is easy to overlook the historical importance she attaches to her great journey in search of the people whose future, like hers, depends on her finding and settling among them. This claim is made in the spirit of comic hyperbole, which Hurston champions as one of social solvents and moral ballasts of African American folk culture. But Janie's great journey is also very much in keeping, as we have seen and will see again, with a transcultural and transhistorical tradition of epic voyages undertaken in search of a homeland, one's "true" country. Janie's last and greatest journey takes her to what surely must qualify as the most droll promised land in world literature—the land of "muck," where, according to Tea Cake, the young drifter who courts and wins her love, "dey raise all dat cane and string beans and tomatuhs." The sodden but fertile "muck," located in the Florida Everglades, offers itself as a comic alternative to the Great Dismal Swamp that Harriet Beecher Stowe decried as a national and indeed human disgrace. "Folks don't do nothin' down dere but make money and fun and foolishness" (*TE*, 192), Tea Cake assures Janie, echoing the exaggerated tales of fertile land and easy money that lured many a credulous pioneer into even more unpromising territory than the "muck" of Florida.

For a people historically deprived of liberty, of livelihoods, and often of their lives, the land of promise is a land of plenty—plenty of goods, plenty of fun, but mostly plenty of one's own "people." At the mere prospect, however slim, of a place filled with so much fun and foolishness, Janie's "soul crawled out of its hiding place" (*TE*, 192). She sets out, like many an adventuring heroine before and after her, on a "great journey to the horizons in search of *people*." The journey undertaken by Sethe, the ravaged heroine of Toni Morrison's *Beloved*, is much darker and her losses more grievous than Janie's, yet she too clings to the hope of finding the people in whose company she might find and be at home. For what else is Sethe's dream of "days of company: knowing the names of forty, fifty other Negroes, their views, habits; where they had been and done; of feeling their fun and sorrow along with her own" but a detailed blueprint for a patria that history has denied her—the names of those who reside there, their view and habits, their activities both at home and away, the feelings of fun and sorrow they share?

However much they differ in matters of style, form, historical outlook, and spiritual beliefs—whatever their class, race, or ethnic identity—all female writers in this tradition write in the shared conviction that in writing about their patria, they are writing about characters whose lives, as Cather remarks of the simple, often uncouth "old faces" of Moonstone (a fictionalized Denver) can be "as full of meaning, as mysteriously marked by Destiny, as the people who danced the mazurka under the elegant Korsunsky" (the aristocratic guests and host of the fateful ball where Count Vronsky begins his active pursuit of Anna Karenina) [*SL*, 118]). Hurston could make the same claim for the people of Eatonville as they sit on the porch in early morning, "passing around the pictures of their thoughts for others to look at and see," pictures that "were always crayon enlargements of life" and so "nicer to listen to" (*TE*, 81). Perhaps only a new country seeking direction and respect for its native literature would feel the need to proclaim the representativeness of its people and their stories.

The historic opportunity that the word "country" absorbs and in turn contributes to the modern lexicon is memorably registered in the advice Sarah Orne Jewett offered to the young Willa Cather: "Of course, one day you will write about your own country. In the meantime, get all you can. One must know the world so well before one can know the parish."[14] This was not easy advice to take, nor even, frankly, to understand, involving as it does a seemingly contradictory injunction to take in as much of the wide and richly appointed world as possible, only to return to the restricted moral scope and pinched economy of the backwater parish (Jewett's image for Cather's patria). George Eliot, who subtitled her great novel *Middlemarch* "A Study of Provincial Life," would have understood the advice, although she might have blanched at the thought of indulging such a ravenous and seemingly indiscriminate appetite for experience. "Get all you can" indeed sounds quite crude, almost feral next to Lambert Strether's more measured and diplomatic counsel to Little Bilham in Henry James's *The Ambassadors*: "Live all you can. It's a mistake not to."[15] James, of course, could never conceive of such advice leading the aspiring artist, Little Bilham, back to the parish (assuming he ever was associated with one). And neither, for that matter, did Jewett. She was encouraging Cather to acquire the knowledge that would be indispensable for a writer who aspired to become the chronicler and prose poet of a country whose destiny was still unfolding. Jewett may have confined the setting of her stories to the environs of Dunnet Landing, a quaint village cherished for "its elaborate conventionalities" and for its "mixture of remoteness, and childish certainty of being the centre of civilization," but her patria encompassed the moral and civic idea of her "own country," for which the parish is, as in Trollope's Barchester novels, for instance, not a sheltered section of the country but its synecdoche.

Jewett is an inaugural figure in the tradition of American women's writing committed to bringing the Muses to their country, a sophisticated project often realized with what may seem the least promising material—the life of quaint, provincial, often literal backwoods communities, the life, that is, of the patria. Like many women writers, she was doubly handicapped in making representative claims. Not only her sex but the literary trappings of regionalism often worked to disguise the scope and character of her rendering of the social and moral life of her "country." The well-traveled daughter of a cosmopolitan Boston doctor, Jewett is routinely characterized as a writer of tales of village life. Cather, her ardent disciple and still her most comprehending and appreciative reader, felt differently and ranked *The Country of the Pointed Firs* with *The Scarlet Letter* and *Huckleberry Finn* as "American books, which have the possibility of long, long life," claiming that she could "think of no others that confront time and change so serenely."[16] Cather not only places Jewett's work among the founding texts of a uniquely American literature but does so in a way that calls attention to the large public and great historic themes that distinguish Jewett's fiction: the imperceptible but decisive and irresistible advance—the costs and the benefits—of change. Her fiction served Cather and her successors as a prototype for the pioneer consciousness in its first, most modest, and yet undeniably world-historical expression. Her fictions are as busy watching God at work in the backwoods of Maine as Hurston's are in the muck of the Florida Everglades.

Reporting, though not always serenely, on how time and change manifest themselves in the small Maine community of Dunnet Landing is a nameless narrator, a sporadic visitor to the village whose reasons for coming are never divulged yet who appears to be in retreat from some unspecified trouble or anxiety. From her special vantage point as an outsider, the people she encounters assume the guise of an impressive, even daunting naturalness. This view is more or less vindicated by the stories and vignettes that follow, with the singular and therefore telling exception of an early and surreal tale that alerts us to how far Jewett's narrative country extends beyond its naturalistic boundaries. It is a tale recounted by Captain Littlepage, whose name suggests Jewett's willingness to joke at her own expense (an unexpected injection of self-irony not typical of her narrative manner elsewhere in the volume of stories). Under its allegorical cover, she sports with the way her unrushed and anecdotal tales might appear to all but the happy few (like Cather) who knew how to read them—little pages on quaint figures abiding in a country remote in time, place, and manners from us, her more worldly readers.

The pages, though short, and the tale, though tall, credibly transport us far from the settled shores of Dunnet Landing to an uncanny realm where one of the genuine mysteries of the world makes its home and, as it turns out, its last stand. Edgar Allan Poe hovers like an encouraging but anxious mentor over Captain Littlepage's recounting of a story told to him about an expedition that took its seasoned crew two degrees "farther north than ships had ever been." Striking a "coast that wasn't laid down or charted" (*CPF*, 395), the ship alights on the shore of a great town that seems to be inhabited by semitransparent creatures of human semblance formed, so it appears to the naked eye, of fog and cobweb. These spectral beings initially tolerate, then assail the crew like bats intent on driving these flesh-and-blood interlopers from their shores. The crew tries to escape but eventually perishes, with the exception of one who survived, like Melville's Ishmael, to tell the tale of this encounter with the demonic forces of the world.

One can't help wondering what this sea yarn is doing in a volume of tales devoted to relating the rather humdrum, all-too-solid, fleshly existence of the plain folks of Dunnet Landing. Indeed, the narrator herself seems taken aback and suggests that what the sailors saw was a mirage brought on by hunger or, as the ship's surgeon had initially thought, by the interplay of light and magnetic currents peculiar to northern climes. But Captain Littlepage is more open to the mystery uncovered on this ill-fated "voyage of discovery," seconding the doomed crew's opinion that the land they had come upon was "a kind of waiting-place between this world an' the next" (*CPF*, 397). Then, as if willing to cede some ground to the skeptics: "'T wa'n't a right-feeling part of the world, anyway" (ibid.).

There are undoubtedly other wrong-feeling parts of the world, but it takes a well-seasoned traveler from the right-feeling part to recognize the wrongness. Captain Littlepage is Jewett's surrogate in making these determinations and so helping extend her otherwise placid narrative into the most wrong-feeling reaches of human experience. How else could she write convincingly about polar expeditions that would likely bring discredit to her as a reliable chronicler of country life? More important, why would she want to, unless the risk was worth taking in light of what she might bring back from such an unlikely adventure—in this case, not so much a story but an idea about Space not reachable or expressible through any other means? The idea is embodied in a metaphor—the waiting place, a phrase that gives the chapter its title. The waiting place is a limit to the known world but also the threshold to another. As such, it does not so much designate a physical—or in this case preternatural—setting as denote a narrative juncture in which Space is perceived as a transit point in Time.

It is at this juncture that the Present reveals itself as a kind of waiting place, an antechamber, as it were, where the past impatiently awaits its passage to the future. This is just the kind of space that attracts pioneering spirits, eager to make off to unknown and uncharted territories. Jewett reminds us, in a historical footnote of great ethnological and literary interest, that this pioneering spirit survives, like the inhabitants of the waiting place, in somewhat spectral but still potent forms. Remarking on the prevalence of the "curiously French type of face" in the seacoast community, the narrator reflects on "how large a proportion of the early settlers on this northern coast of New England were of Huguenot blood, and that it is the Norman Englishman, not the Saxon, who goes adventuring to a new world" (*CPF*, 462). Jewett's narrative locale may be rustic, but it is precisely in these regions largely unvisited by modernity that the past might survive, both in the telltale features of otherwise nondescript rustics or, as we shall see, in more monumental forms. Cather's outsized claim for *The Country of the Pointed Firs*, which initially seems the skewed judgment of an enthusiast, increasingly seems an accurate reflection of Jewett's pioneering efforts to fashion a new way of understanding and writing history, sometimes on a surprisingly grand scale, out of the most homely materials.

Jewett's composure before the forces of time and change may be ascribed to the long historical reach of her narrative consciousness, against which disruptions and discontinuities in local and national traditions no longer appear as peak times but as undulations in human history. This composure is personified in *The Country of the Pointed Firs* in the tutelary figures of a mother and daughter, both bearing the name of Todd (an unsettling play on the German word for death) and both associated with sibylline powers. Mrs. Todd, remarkable for the height and massiveness of her physical presence, no sooner enters the narrative than she centers and stabilizes it, standing as she does "in the centre of a braided rug, [whose] rings of black and gray seemed to circle about her feet in the dim light" (*CPF*, 381). Perhaps Jewett's humor is greater than we first allowed, for surely there is something amusing and startling in this trick of light that transfigures a woman standing on a braided rug into a rustic icon enhaloed by rings of black and gray. Her auratic presence is confirmed rather than shrugged off in the sentence that follows: "Her height and massiveness in the low room gave her the look of a huge sibyl, while the strange fragrance of the mysterious herb blew in from the little garden" (ibid.).

Elaine Showalter has called attention to the weirdness but also the representativeness of this depiction of Mrs. Todd as an American sibyl. For Showalter the American sibyl, whose emergence she traces to Harriet Beecher Stowe's anointing the "the ex-slave Sojourner Truth . . . 'The Libyan Sibyl,'" encapsulated the prophetic ambitions of "the great woman writer as wise mother, high priestess, and oracle."[17] Mrs. Todd's sibylline character, propped up and supported by adjectives registering, above all else, her (huge) size and (massive) scale, certainly removes her from the realm of the rustic and folkloric, the "room" in which we first find her. In the narrator's eyes, she deserves to occupy an even larger semantic and historical Space, in which she would rightly appear, if possible, even more imposing: "In a wider sphere one might have called her a woman of the world, with her unexpected bits of modern knowledge, but Mrs. Todd's wisdom was an intimation of truth itself. She might belong to any age, like an idyll of Theocritus" (*CPF*, 424). Once again, Space, evoked here in the image of the wider sphere where women might appear in their true, though generally unperceived, historical character, is a large fact that opens up new perspectives on time. Mrs. Todd is at once a genius loci of the American seacoast settlements and a woman of all ages, an idyllic figure in both the formal and colloquial sense of the word.

Yet to see her as idyllic is somewhat misleading, given that Mrs. Todd cuts a physical figure that hardly seems native to the unprepossessing, intimate world of her backwater patria, Dunnet Landing. Her physical grandeur is brought into high relief against such idyllic backgrounds, but it is hardly confined to them. The grandeur intimated by our first glimpse of her standing still on a drawing room rug is registered with more clarity once her figure is seen atop a gray rock on a coastal promontory. Momentarily posed against this more open and decidedly majestic background, her body appears "grand and architectural, like a *caryatide* [*sic*]" (*CPF*, 401, emphasis in original). This impression of lurking grandeur begins to acquire iconographic solidity once the narrator becomes "well acquainted" with Mrs. Todd. The woman the narrator had initially come to know and esteem in her country role "as landlady, herb-gatherer, and rustic philosopher" (*CPF*, 403) increasingly assumes the look and stature of an icon of female indomitability, metamorphosing from caryatid into a "large figure of Victory" (*CPF*, 408). Victory of or over what? This question is never pursued, much less answered, by the narrator. She seems less preoccupied with the nature than with the classical precedents of Mrs. Todd's Victory. Caught in a certain attitude of body and spirit, Mrs. Todd, the village sibyl, suddenly sheds her rustic trappings and assumes the atavistic form, the monumentality, and the triumphant power of a Protector-Goddess carved in stone.

Her daughter, Joanna, is at once a less imposing and yet odder figure—a feminine incarnation of the isolato, that quintessentially American figure, like Melville's Bartleby the Scrivener, of disquieting moral apartness. The narrator notes "something medieval" in Joanna's "voluntary hermitage," which she learns stems from "a disappointment of the heart" (*CPF*, 433). Joanna's romantic plight may seem as dated as a plaintive medieval fable of disappointed love, yet her story couldn't be more American or more modern, concluding as it does as a parable of the sequestered consciousness that exists, often unacknowledged and unvisited, within each of us. This, at any rate, is how the narrator interprets Joanna's life in a meditation that would not be out of place, in fact, would be very much at home in that quintessentially American epic *Moby Dick*: "In the life of each of us, I said to myself, there is a place remote and islanded, and given to endless regret or secret happiness; we are each the unaccompanied hermit and recluse of an hour or a day; we understand our fellows of the cell to whatever age of history they may belong" (*CPF*, 444). The prose is so calm and accepting before the inalienable separateness and remoteness of human beings that it is easy to be lulled into a kind of quietism utterly opposed to the strenuous claims being made here for the universality and timelessness of Jewett's characters, precisely because of, rather than despite, their remoteness from modern life and contemporary concerns. The reclusive Joanna does not represent a renegade offshoot but a living reminder of a universal tradition that unites humankind through time and across cultures. The mother-sibyl and the daughter-hermit define and enclose that tradition. Although Jewett strings her tales together with the randomness of beads threaded onto a string, she is steadily shepherding her islanded narratives toward a point of culmination. The culmination, when it arrives, is social and historical rather than personal, albeit still defiantly tribal and idiosyncratic—a reunion of a local clan, the Bowdens:

> The plash of the water could be heard faintly, yet still be heard; we might have been a company of ancient Greeks going to celebrate a victory, or to worship the god of harvests in the grove above. It was strangely moving to see this and to make [sic] part of it. The sky, the sea, have watched poor humanity at its rite so long; we were no more a New England family celebrating its own existence and simple progress; we carried the tokens and inheritance of all such households from which this had descended, and were only the latest of our line. We possessed the instincts of a far, forgotten childhood. (CPF, 460–61)[18]

What had seemed a simple progress—of the pioneering advance upon the wildernesses of sea and land, of village tales to rural fables of personal, tribal, and, ultimately, national identity—is suddenly revealed as part of a more extensive and inclusive panorama of history: here is another example of Alexandra's "old story writing itself again and again." In the country rituals of a remote maritime community, Jewett refigures the relations between inherited instinct and social customs, between local and universal traditions that determine, and often plague, the life of human communities. These relations, always shifting and often obscured, complicate the notion, or even hope, of "simple progress."

These complications become the subject of Gertrude Stein's *The Making of Americans*, her thousand-page monumental novel

whose expansiveness is somewhat curtailed by its subtitle and declared historical theme: "Being a History of a Family's Progress."
One of the two families whose progress she chronicles bears the
semihumorous matrilineal name of Hersland, a very American
name in its preoccupation with occupying, ordering, and laying
claim to the land. The novelty, of course, consists in attaching this
preoccupation and dynastic ambition to a female line, the first of
Stein's many witty reworkings of novelistic and gender conventions. In fact, the novel opens with a semicomical rewriting of the
primal Oedipal assault on the father: a son drags his father along
the ground until the "groaning old man at last" yells "Stop I did
not drag my father beyond this tree."[19] This is the primordial event
that inaugurates a repetitive pattern of history and incremental
self-realization that Stein's style and her narrative tirelessly elaborate: insistent struggle, here associated with the Freudian mono-
myth of a universal Oedipal revolt against the father, is abruptly
and rather comically called to a halt, opening up a space for the
pacific and creative repetition that gives expression, but also a
distinctive charm, to what is recurrent and persistent in human
nature.

The "family progress" Stein recounts is thus, for all its formal
and stylistic innovations, very much in the tradition of pioneer fiction by women. Such fictions seldom wander far from the vicinity
of their chosen patria, remaining, as it were, within the borders
long ago marked out by the "family tree." At the same time, the
family's progress, whether chronicled in Stein's distended narrative
or in the more confined space of Jewett's "little pages," is, for all its
proud singularity, a representative one. With typically boundless
confidence in her own powers, Stein promises us that her family
progress encapsulates a universal history of humankind, one that
will account for "every man and every woman who ever were or
are or will be living and the kind of nature in them." We may be
amused (and are meant to be) by the extravagance of Stein's claim,
but we cannot entirely dismiss it as novelistic whimsy. If Jewett
can imagine Mrs. Todd at home in the idylls of Theocritus and
the Bowdens unconsciously reenacting some long-extinct Greek
ritual, then Stein can envisage her characters as embodiments of

"the kinds and ways of repeating, of attacking and resisting in different kinds of men and women, the practical, the emotional, the sensitive, the every kind of being in every one who ever was or is or will be living."[20]

Nonetheless, no progress, however simple it may appear and however attentive it may be to what Stein calls the "bottom natures" of "every kind of being in every one who ever was or is or will be living," is without its moments of impasse or outright stoppage. Pioneers setting off for the unclaimed territories are often burdened, but seldom deterred, by their awareness of the oblivion that is always threatening to annul what Cather called the "accomplished facts" of human enterprise. That may be because they already possess a strong appetite for destruction. This was the considered view of Frederick Jackson Turner, a pioneer in his own right as the historian who argued for the unexampled "Significance of the Frontier in American History" (the title of his groundbreaking essay). "The first ideal of the pioneer was that of conquest," Turner writes.[21] He then identifies the symbolic language and moral character that answers to that ideal: "The rifle and the ax are the symbols of the backwoods pioneer. They meant a training in aggressive courage, in domination, directness of action, in destruction." These meanings are characterological and can become the spring of violent, dramatic action, as they do in "Noon Wine," Katherine Anne Porter's feral tale of backwoods life, or any of Flannery O'Connor's blood-soaked stories of redemption in which, as the title of her most grisly prophetic novel announces, *The Violent Bear It Away*.

Sometimes the training in destruction can be seen as a necessary schooling in the universal history of humankind. This, at least, is how Ruth Stone, the narrator of Marilynne Robinson's *Housekeeping*, understands the catastrophes that decimate her family, which she, in the tradition of Alexandra, recognizes as "the old story writing itself again and again," a story written and consecrated in blood:

> Cain murdered Abel, and blood cried out from the earth; the house fell on Job's children, and a voice was induced or provoked

into speaking from a whirlwind; and Rachel mourned for her children; and King David for Absalom. The force behind the movement of time is a mourning that will not be comforted. That is why the first event is known to have been an expulsion and the last is hoped to be a reconciliation and return.[22]

This is Ruth in her more sibylline moods. She is so assured and calm in her prophetic declarations that it is easy to overlook how abject, even desperate, her own situation and prospects are. Like her biblical namesake, Ruth, she seems fated to make her home in a foreign land, which in her case are the precincts of Fingerbone, a town "chastened by an outsized landscape and extravagant weather, and chastened again by the awareness that the whole of human history had occurred elsewhere" (62).

For Ruth, Fingerbone is not so much a patria but the ground zero of time's devastating movement: it is where her grandfather dies in a spectacular train wreck; where her mother takes her own life; where she and her sister grow up but also part; where the family home breaks up, despite her aunt Sylvie's attempts, against the very instincts of her nature, to be a mother to her motherless nieces and accept the obligations of housekeeping. Sylvie's efforts prove too little, too late, and too misconceived to salvage what is doomed to destruction. Yet it is only when the family home becomes "Sylvie's house" that Ruth, despite the disorder that prevails, feels that "something I had lost, or might lose, could be found" (123).

The recovery of the lost and the restoration of perished things is not just the motive of Ruth's storytelling but the story itself. *Housekeeping* not only echoes the rhetoric but seems written from the vantage point of the book of Revelation, which foretells the Time when, in Ruth's local and personal imagining of it, "there would be a general reclaiming of fallen buttons and misplaced spectacles, of neighbors and kin, till time and error and accident were undone, and the world become comprehensible and whole" (92). In Ruth's apocalyptic vision, it is not enough that the world become comprehensible and whole; mourners must also be comforted, orphans restored to their mothers. This, Ruth assures us in her most ecstatic voice, is the ordained conclusion of the epic of expulsion, when we shall find "a garden where all of us as one child will sleep in our mother Eve, hooped in her ribs and staved by her spine" (192).

This vision of the "last event" when we will reenter the first garden of the world represents the farthest reaches of the pioneering imagination, schooled in violence yet emboldened, even cheered, by the hope that "wanderers will find a way home" (195). The poets of these prairie epics are, Ruth tells us, old women "who will make songs out of all these sorrows and sit in the porches and sing them on mild evenings": "Every sorrow suggests a thousand songs, and every song recalls a thousand sorrows, and so they are infinite in number, and all the same" (194). In contrast to these numberless songs made in the final days of the pioneer epoch is the single, triumphant song of first times that Thea Kronborg hears beneath and through the major chords of Antonín Dvořák's "Symphony No. 9 in E Minor," the so-called New World Symphony. The music and the association of ideas sparked by the program notes, "From the New World," vividly recall the beloved panoramas of her Western homeland—"that high tableland about Laramie; the grass-grown wagon-trails, the far-away peaks of the snowy range, the wind and the eagles, that old man and the first telegraph message" (SL, 181).

But it is not just the magnificent landscapes and epochal "first times" of the frontier that the New World Symphony calls up in Thea's imagination. She also has intimations of the primordial desire that animates "all the things that wakened and chirped in early morning; the reaching and reaching of high plains, the immeasurable yearning of all flat land" (ibid.). This mutual yearning and shared desire is what gives the pioneering heroine her most exalted sense of Home: "There was home in it too; first memories, first mornings long ago; the amazement of a new soul in a new world; a soul new and yet old, that had dreamed something despairing, something glorious, in the dark before it was born; a soul obsessed by what it did not know under the cloud of a past it could not recall" (ibid.).

If the pioneers' first ideal is conquest, symbolized by the rifle and the ax, their ultimate ideal is human settlement, symbolized by the Home. The home signifies more than a place of physical shelter, although it is certainly and fundamentally that. Home is also the place that shelters the first memories, glorious hopes and dark forebodings of the new soul in a new world, a place, as Cather sees it, for amazement.

The pioneer's amazement before the wild land survives to sustain and exalt the frontier souls who inhabit the latter-day fiction of Marilynne Robinson. Amazement is what lifts up the spirit of the dying preacher in *Gilead* as he makes his last confession and final bequest to the son he will leave behind:

> I love the prairie! So often I have seen the dawn come and the light flood over the land and everything turn radiant at once, the word "good" so profoundly affirmed in my soul that I am amazed that I should be allowed to witness such a thing. There may have been a more wonderful first moment "when the stars sang together and all the sons of God shouted for joy," but for all I know to the contrary, they still do sing and shout, and they certainly might well. Here on the prairie there is nothing to distract attention from the evening and the morning, nothing on the horizon to abbreviate or to delay. Mountains would seem impertinence from that point of view.[23]

This capacity for amazement before the "good" of the natural world is what distinguishes the pioneer spirit and recommends it to times like ours when there are fewer and fewer places for the spirit to retreat into, to be alone, and to think about the kind of Home it wants to build for itself.

In "My Western Roots," Robinson speaks eloquently of the radically individualist ethos of the frontier, champions the "lonesomeness" that allows one to experience "the sacred poetry in silence, strangeness and otherness," and bewails the conformism that society likes to impose on those who share its benefits (she wrote an entire essay on this theme, "The Tyranny of Petty Coercion"). But she then goes on to make a more telling admission:

> That said, I must say too how beautiful human society seems to me, especially in those attenuated forms so characteristic of the West—isolated towns and single houses which sometimes

offer only the merest, barest amenities: light, warmth, supper, familiarity. We have colonized a hostile planet, and we must staunch every opening where cold and dark might pour through and destroy the false climates we make, the tiny simulations of forgotten seasons beside the Euphrates, or in Eden. At a certain level housekeeping is a regime of small kindnesses, which together, make the world salubrious, savory, and warm. I think of the acts of comfort offered and received within a household as precisely sacramental. It is the sad tendency of domesticity—as of piety—to contract, and of grace to decay into rigor, and peace into tedium. Still it should be clear why I find the Homestead Act all in all the most poetical piece of legislation since Deuteronomy, which it resembles.[24]

In representing the homestead of the frontier as a numinous and material realm of human habitation, women writers like Robinson are investing the traditional sphere of women's activity with a uniquely spiritual, precisely sacramental, as well as historical meaning. The dream of the adventuring heroines of the nineteenth-century women writers to establish the home as a realm of self-cultivation and liberty seems to be nearing fulfillment in the pioneer homestead, whose regime of small kindnesses transfigure the domestic hearth as a scene where acts of comfort can take on a moral grandeur.

Yet even as she works to revive these pioneer traditions in homemaking and housekeeping, Robinson is acutely conscious of more contemporary alarms that the wilderness has all but disappeared and that the planet itself may be dying, precisely because we have lost the sense of the morning miracle and the primordial feeling of amazement it once inspired. In opposition to this dread, Robinson offers her own belief that the "Wilderness is not a single region, but a condition of being in the natural world."[25]

To this belief she appends an exhortation that might have been urged by any of our women novelists: "Perhaps it was a misfortune for us that so many interesting ideas were associated with access to a habitable wilderness. The real frontier need never close. Everything, for all purposes, still remains to be done."[26] Everything still remains to be done because, as Robinson says and Cather's novels attest, it is the "sad tendency of domesticity—as of piety—to contract." The lofty vistas of the Maine coasts, the "reaching and reaching of the high plains," the immeasurable yearning of the flat lands, and the limitless horizons of the prairies are offered as Nature's antidotes to this sad tendency. That is why open plains, soaring peaks, and lofty cliffs figure so prominently in the imaginations of women writers dedicated to expanding the sphere of women's activity and the reach of their spiritual life. But these same landscapes also impress those women writers who have looked at them with patient and grateful amazement with a new respect for the importance of Home, for its regime of small kindnesses and creature comforts.

Still, the idea of Home as both a human stronghold and a spiritual dwelling is, our writers tell us, in constant need of relocation, reinvention, and reconsecration. This is the larger but also more specific and ordinary meaning of Robinson's admonition that everything still remains to be done. The belief that everything still remains to be done liberated the pioneering heroines of women's fiction from the fetters of tradition and motivated them to reinvent the idea of home. It authorized them to take a public role in the making of a country and the forging of the national character. But with the closing of the American frontier, that feeling was harder to sustain. Or rather, that feeling began to translate itself to different realms of action, as the patria became less and less isolated from the political convulsions that were shaking the great world. The pioneering heroines' gaze may still have been fixed on the far horizon, but the moral summits and expanses they glimpsed were more and more obscured by gathering clouds of global war.

CHAPTER 4

War

PART I: THE GREAT WAR

Those women who left England to volunteer their services in the Great War also underwent a wrenching uprooting and pilgrimage, not to a new homestead or patria, as in the case of the pioneers of chapter 3, but as willing participants in a grim, morally vexed, and yet personally liberating national enterprise. Midway through her 1933 memoir of youth and the Great War, Vera Brittain recalls the moment of leaving home, sailing away from England toward the Mediterranean, where she was to be posted as a Voluntary Aid Detachments (VAD) nurse in Malta. Like a nineteenth-century heroine bound for adventure, escape, and possible danger abroad, Brittain greeted this journey with "mingled depression and exhilaration."[1] As her journey commenced, however, a sense of enchantment, excited energy, and "glamour"—a word Brittain often associates with her wartime experience in *Testament of Youth*—overshadowed the trepidation she felt, and she entered into one of the great phases of her life:

> The memory of my sunlit months in the Mediterranean during the War's worst period of miserable stagnation still causes a strange nostalgia to descend upon my spirit. For me, as for all the world, the War was a tragedy and a vast stupidity, a waste of youth and of time; it betrayed my faith, mocked my love, and irremediably spoiled my career—yet Malta remains in my recollection as an interval of heaven, a short year of glamorous beauty and delight. . . . I cry in my heart: Come back,

magic days! I was sorrowful, anxious, frustrated, lonely—but yet how vividly alive! (*TY*, 290–91)

Unleashed from the stifling demands of her conventional provincial family and from the dreariness of wartime London, where she trained as a VAD in Camberwell, Brittain experienced a peculiar and paradoxical kind of freedom and joy. As her retrospective account makes clear, the war was in almost all respects a great tragedy, an unredeemed and unredeemable episode in European history and the cause of devastating loss for her, and yet it was also a time of undeniable personal excitement and satisfaction, of unprecedented engagement in the collective life of the nation, of independence and heroic exertion. That this could be so—that the cursed war could also be the occasion of release and fulfillment—haunted and shaped her memoir and the war writings of numerous other women and lent a peculiar tension and ambivalence to their novels and recollections.

In some important sense, this paradox became their most salient and distinctive subject, and launched them into a public discussion about the ethics of war from the perspective of a sex that felt it had mainly been kept—sometimes against its will—on the sidelines. "I can't bear the sight of khaki," Rose Macaulay's young heroine, Alix, declares to her mother in *Non-Combatants and Others* (1916), "and I don't know whether it's because the war's so beastly or because I want to be in it. . . . It's both."[2] Revulsion and desire, mourning and envy, sorrow and thrill mingled in women's responses to war. Macaulay's poem "Many Sisters to Many Brothers" (1914–15) manages to convey the conflicting sentiments she feels about her brother's experience at the front. Though every bit a match for her brother's athleticism and, indeed, aggression in childhood ("I was as fit and keen, my fists hit as clean"), she is relegated to the home front, "knitting / A hopeless sock that never gets done," while he sits in the trenches. "Oh," she declaims, "it's you that have the luck, out there in blood and muck: / You were born beneath a kindly star."[3] Macaulay's poem cannot be read as unalloyed irony or unambiguous envy: yes, she feels the injustice of her confinement in light of her implicit physical prowess, and yes, she is, in an obvious sense, far luckier than her lucky brothers.

In *Three Guineas* (1938) Virginia Woolf asks why the "daughters of educated men" flocked to work as nurses, drivers, and factory workers in 1914. In this feminist antiwar treatise, written as England faced the possibility of a second war against Germany, Woolf found especially chilling the idea that these young women goaded young men to fight through sympathy, charm, and the sense that to join the battle was heroic. How, she asks, can we explain this "unconscious influence . . . in favour of war"? Woolf, as she often does, knows the answer to her own question:

> So profound was her unconscious loathing for the *education of the private house* with its cruelty, its poverty, its hypocrisy, its immorality, its inanity that she would undertake any task however menial, exercise any fascination however fatal that enabled her to escape. Thus consciously she desired "our splendid Empire"; unconsciously she desired our splendid war.[4]

Not so unconsciously, perhaps, many young women did desire war, and some were eager to join the fight. Coming of age in a time of suffrage agitation and new opportunities for women in higher education and the professions, they found their trajectories toward emancipation interrupted and, as a result, many transferred their aspirations and feminist passions to the cause of national service.[5] Unlike the American "pioneers" Cather and Orne Jewett, who were devoted to a concept of home and land that was local and regional, these English women imagined patriotism as a national enterprise tied to country and state, as well as to the men of their generation.

Out of the "private house" of their fathers, young women entered—or escaped—into what seemed the most urgent public need of the day. Combining the desire for physical and mental exertion with a heightened sense of duty—"I should welcome the most wearying kinds of bodily toil," Brittain wrote to her fiancé, Roland Leighton—they took on tasks menial and dangerous, as Woolf says, and were willing to fight against their confinement to home and home front in ways that undermined their class identities (*TY*,

140). Nursing, to name but one example, may seem from our vantage point to be a suitably feminine occupation, the extension of private, familial duties, but, as we shall see in the case of Brittain, it required the "daughters of educated men" to transgress the boundaries of proper, bourgeois womanhood over and over again.

Women struggled to avoid the posture of Penelope, weaving, knitting, or darning at home. They rebelled against contributing to the war effort like the sister in Macaulay's poem, or the homebound women in Radclyffe Hall's "Miss Ogilvy Finds Herself" (1926), "knitting socks and mittens and mufflers and Jaeger trench-helmets," or the women of Grasmere who, in Mary Ward's account, awoke at four each morning to make sure that each of fifty soldiers from the town would receive two pairs of socks for Christmas.[6] Young women also eschewed the role of pinup, whose early avatar Edith Wharton mocks in "Writing a War Story" (1919). Wharton's Ivy Spang pours tea in an Anglo-American hospital in Paris but also publishes a short story to inspire the soldiers in a magazine for wounded men, only to discover that the men neglect to read the story in favor of peering at the accompanying photo of her "holding out a refreshing beverage to an invisible sufferer with a gesture halfway between Mélisande lowering her braid over the balcony and Florence Nightingale advancing the lamp."[7]

In their militant efforts to find a life of usefulness and engagement during wartime, women took an unprecedented public role in the national cause. They served as VAD nurses and orderlies, munitions workers, ambulance drivers, and journalists, and as members of the Women Police Volunteers (WPVs) patrolling London, the Women's Army Auxiliary Corps (WAACs), the Women's Royal Air Force (WRAFs), and the Women's Royal Naval Service (WRNS). According to David Mitchell, most of the VADs came from the "cloistral ignorance" of upper-class or middle-class homes, where they might otherwise have waited "until marriage brought release."[8] Sandra Gilbert has observed that women recalled the Great War as the first major historical event that allowed them and, indeed, called on them to use their considerable intellectual and administrative abilities.[9] Gilbert also remarks on the opportunities for mobility—movement and travel—that war work offered.[10] Brittain's excitement about leaving home when she journeyed to Malta was shared by many women who traveled to the Continent as drivers, messengers, and nurses.

How to serve was one question, how to write about the war another. Throughout *A Room of One's Own*, Virginia Woolf weaves a story of women cut off from epic events and thus deprived of weighty subjects for their writing. Could Tolstoy have written *War and Peace* if, like George Eliot, he had lived in seclusion at the "Priory"?[11] Might critics be likelier to acknowledge the value and seriousness of women's fiction if they wrote about the "important" subject of war?[12] Woolf's "very ancient lady" crossing the road at dusk remembers the "streets lit for the battle of Balaclava" at home, but her unheroic, private experience of life will die with her: "Nothing remains of it all. . . . No biography or history has a word to say about it."[13] War as experience and literary subject had been the province of men.

Some women—Woolf and Rebecca West among them—reflected the homebound state and mundane lives of their sex in decidedly oblique representations of wartime. They turned the image of the house itself into a medium for writing about the condition of war and for embodying not just the home front but the nation itself. In *To the Lighthouse* (1927), Woolf uses the Ramsays' deserted summer home to comment indirectly about the war and its losses, both familial and national. In the interlude "Time Passes," sandwiched as it is between the two main movements of the novel, references to the war—to Andrew Ramsay's death and to the war's revival of interest in poetry—are bracketed, literally, as are major events in the characters' lives. Parenthetical deaths, births, and marriages are surrounded by evocations of the seasons, the house, nature, time, and Mrs. McNab's unbracketed efforts to reopen and revive the neglected house. In her bustle and cleaning, all that is "alien to the processes of domestic life," the narrator tells us with no little irony, is kept out.[14] In *Return of the Soldier* (1918), West roots her war story in the shell-shocked soldier's ancestral home, Baldry Court, a place of exquisite English beauty surrounded by "miles of emerald pastureland lying wet and brilliant under a westward line of sleek hills" and, nearer by, "the suave decorum of the lawn and the Lebanon cedar."[15] The soldier's wife and his cousin Jenny, who narrates the story, misread him, mistakenly believing that he holds Baldry Court and his life with them close to his heart as an "amulet" in the trenches, just as they misunderstand his experience of the war and his changeless love for Margaret, the now matronly, déclassé love of his youth.[16] Jenny tries to understand this love with sympathy and has her own vision of the battlefield, all gleaned from the newsreels, but, tied to home and England, even she cannot grasp her cousin's mental state or his indifference to the world for which his class has prepared him. Both Woolf and West seem to suggest the necessarily limited or blinkered nature of the woman's view from home, from England, now both ghostly and imprisoning.

The subject of home occupied the thoughts even of women who resolutely faced outward, toward the front and the war effort. Some of them were adventurers and volunteers who tackled the experience of the front, sometimes in fiction and sometimes in memoirs, journals, or war reporting. For these, home was often most striking for its destruction and transformation under the scourge of warfare. Edith Wharton's articles for *Scribner's Magazine*, posted from France in 1915 as the result of five trips into the war zone during that year, repeatedly describe French towns that have been flattened or deserted. As Hermione Lee shrewdly comments of these forays to the front, Wharton's "passion for cultured tourism was being translated into the ambitious curiosity of that dauntless and idiosyncratic twentieth-century breed, the woman 'special correspondent' at war."[17] "Dead cities," "victim towns," Wharton calls these ghostly places.[18] In Dunkerque a "*bourgeois* house" has had its front torn away, so that "caved-in floors, smashed wardrobes, dangling bedsteads, heaped-up blankets, topsy-turvy chairs and stoves and wash-stands" are exposed.[19] Wharton does not generally focus on people in her war reporting and certainly not on specific individuals but rather on the dwellings, some eviscerated and others bizarrely relocated by soldiers nearer to the trenches. After she travels the French front from "end to end," what sticks in her mind is the "picture of a shelled house where a few men, who sat smoking and playing cards in the sunshine, had orders to hold out to the death."[20] When Wharton came to publish the anthology of poems, stories, and drawings that she hoped would raise money for wartime charities, she called it *The Book of the Homeless* (*Le Livre des Sans-Foyers*) and introduced it, Lee observes, "as if it were a house," with its own foyer, threshold, architecture, and pictures hanging on its walls.[21]

Other writers addressed the problem of the home front "noncombatant," dramatizing in narrative prose both the frustrations of those shut out of battle and the grave doubts about the legitimacy and cost of war harbored by those at home. For women, the question of war often centered on how to pursue their own emancipation by taking a public role while exercising independent judgment and, perhaps, dissenting from the national project of war. Sometimes these impulses were in conflict with each other and, for most, the conundrum of war and peace went unresolved. In time, this ambivalence and divided loyalty became itself a kind of politics, an engagement in public discourse with its own distinctive philosophical force.

Three writers—Rose Macaulay, May Sinclair, and Vera Brittain—entered into the question of war in striking but very different ways. Macaulay (1881–1958), who spent the war years in England as a civil servant, nurse, and propagandist, published *Non-Combatants and Others* in 1916. One of very few novels about the First World War to be published, as well as written and set, during the conflict, it reproduces the unplotted structure of war as it was then lived: open-ended, static, without conclusive denouement or clear moral character.[22] May Sinclair (1863–1946), a generation older than Macaulay, went to Belgium briefly as a member of the Munro Ambulance Corps and produced a record of the experience, *A Journal of Impressions in Belgium* (1915), and a novel, *The Tree of Heaven* (1917), that express both her passion for the war effort and her anxiety about its dangerous pull. Vera Brittain (1893–1970) produced the best known and last published of these works—*Testament of Youth*, a 1933 memoir that looks back on her war experience and the loss of her fiancé and brother in battle. Brittain makes use of her war diaries, with their contemporaneous, youthful, patriotic fervor, but writes from the vantage point of postwar pacifism. Her perspective is double, her glory in the "glamour" and "magic" of war vividly apparent through the scrim of antiwar sentiment. As we will see, all three of these writers express doubts about war as a feeling of disequilibrium related to their status as women.

Though Macaulay's *Non-Combatants* is often placed in the pacifist camp of women's war novels, it is more accurate to see it as an equivocal text and to focus on what Claire Tylee calls its "moral uncertainty."[23] Written in the early years of the war, it juxtaposes a variety of home front reactions and follows a dialectical structure of opinion and debate. Virtually all of the important positions on the war voiced in the novel are women's, not simply because they are the noncombatants, painfully separated from the husbands, sons, brothers, and lovers whose lives are at risk, but because they suffer the anxiety of inaction. However, though Macaulay imagines a gulf between those at home and those who serve abroad, she also draws a parallel between the novel's young, female art student protagonist, the androgynously named Alix Sandomir, and the wounded soldiers who are sidelined by their injuries and therefore adrift, uncertain of their roles. She accomplishes this partly through Alix's physical difference—she is lame, her body stigmatized as the veterans of war are marked—and vexed relationship to her sex. Her bodily limitations mimic the wounds of men like her fellow student Basil Doye, who has lost a finger in the process of defusing a bomb and been sent back to London to convalesce. Like him, she is a reluctant noncombatant and outsider. But, unlike Basil, she is an inveterate and permanent bystander, compelled by circumstance and temperament to watch from a distance: "she looked as from behind a visor, critical, defensive, or amused" (*NC*, 4). The war entices her to depart from the observer's posture, to figure out both what she thinks and how she will act, but her way remains unclear and her stance toward the war unresolved.

As she seeks her own conviction and path, Alix is confronted with two different ways of being a woman during wartime, two competing feminine exempla. Macaulay uses these models of womanhood to structure the novel, which is divided into three parts. The brief section that launches the story is titled "Wood

End," after Alix's temporary home in the countryside, where the subject of war is introduced through a discussion of Belgian refugees and letters from the front. In part 2, titled "Violette," Alix encounters the war posture of conventional femininity when she is sent to live with the Framptons, relatives who live in the home in suburban London that gives this section its name. "Violette," sometimes personified and referred to as if it were an active and sentient woman ("When one had any physical ailment, Violette came out strong."), evokes the conservative feminine sensibility of the household and the England that remains untouched by war (*NC*, 185). Here Alix is exposed to the well-meaning but small-minded example of her aunt Frampton, who favors reading aloud from the local paper. She does so indiscriminately, sliding without change of tone or interest from Belgian refugees, the suicide of a German in Tottenham Court Road, and reports of spies in Harrogate to helpful "Home Hints," instructions for reviving a crushed favorite hat, and a recipe for apple shortcake (*NC*, 50–51). When she intervenes with disapproval in a discussion of woman's role in war, Aunt Frampton insists that Florence Nightingale "kept her place" and identifies the Bible as the source for knowing what that place might be. Arguing against any involvement outside of the home, she cites the case of a woman whose baby fell into the fire and "was burnt to a cinder" when its mother went to a public meeting—"something about foreign politics" (*NC*, 88, 90). For her, domestic obsessions and feminine duties necessarily preclude even psychic engagement with the war.

Aunt Frampton's daughter, Evie, offers a youthful version of her mother's anodyne, blinkered femininity. Healthy, attractive, and insouciant, Evie strikes Alix as her own antithesis—an example of conventionally seductive womanhood as distraction and comforter to wounded men. The reactions of Basil Doye, with whom Alix had had an intensely felt, if unresolved, relationship before the war, bear this out. Confined to England because of his injury, Basil walks down the Strand, sizing up young women and musing on the type that might suit him now. We are reminded of Wharton's Ivy Spang, the aspiring writer whose photo the recuperating soldiers prefer to her fiction: "[Basil] would have liked a healthy, pretty, jolly sort of girl . . . some girl with poise, and tone, and sanity, and no nerves, who never bothered about the war or anything. A placid, indifferent, healthy sort of girl, with all her fingers on and nothing the matter anywhere. He was sick of hurt and damaged bodies and minds" (*NC*, 115). Enter Evie, her "vigorous young bodily life . . . reanimating Basil's own." Alix, "weak-bodied, lame, frail-nerved, with no balance," sits looking at the two of them and assesses Basil's newly focused desire (*NC*, 127). True to her "young buoyancy" and preference for the superficial flirtation, Evie recoils at Basil's intensity. Alix's bodily and psychic wounds make her Basil's counterpart; indeed, they make her too much his equal, but they also disqualify her for the role of consoler and diversion Basil prefers women to play—at least at this moment. Macaulay suggests here that wounded masculinity in the service of war is acceptable, even worthy of celebration, while anomalous femininity is out of place, marked, and relegated to the margins of both war and romance.

Directly opposed to the women of "Violette" is Alix's own mother, Daphne, a free spirit, peace activist, and absent parent who gives her name to the third and final part of *Non-Combatants*. At the beginning of the novel, Daphne has sailed to New York for a peace conference, not content just to work with the Red Cross or Belgian refugees. Her daughter finds her "discomposing"; she finds her daughter indolent (*NC*, 22). Daphne reenters in part 3 as Alix has grown tired of the willful ignorance of war in her aunt's home and frustrated by her own status as a noncombatant. She wants to go to battle and yet she wants to fight against the war. She envies the soldiers and she despises combat. Her mother appears with a solution for her: eurhythmic dancing and militant, indeed bellicose, peace activism.

Macaulay's portrait of Alix's bohemian mother is equivocal, both compelling and satirical. As antidote to Aunt Frampton and cousin Evie, she represents an awareness of life and politics that partly revives her daughter. By this point in the war, Alix has developed something like shell shock, a "case of nervous breakdown" that mimics the "shattered nerves" of soldiers (*NC*, 219). So close is her identification with the combatants that she not only feels jealous of their ability to fight but also shares their psychic suffering. Daphne's mind, however, is energized rather than debilitated by war. She adds her daughter to her list of causes: "You must leave this Pansy, or Violet, or whatever," she orders her daughter, and take up vigorous exercise, health food, and antiwar work, and come to live with her in her flat. At first Alix resists the Society for Promoting Permanent Peace, partly out of the conviction that the idea of a pacifist makes no sense. Everyone, she thinks, is a pacifist at heart and everyone is also, as is Alix herself, ambivalent, capable of both pro-war and antiwar sentiment.

Leaning toward joining the Peace Society by novel's end, Alix is nonetheless left in an ethical and ideological limbo, just as she is left still negotiating her relation to her gender. If she joins with her mother, the free-spirited woman she cannot wholly resemble, she would be compelled to swallow beliefs she might not share. Neither, however, can she reproduce the conventional, blasé femininity of her aunt and cousin. The narrative leaves her with a determination to try her hand at antiwar work and in a state momentarily free of the gnawing sensation of "paradox." Macaulay emphasizes the lack of resolution in Alix's stance toward war and reflects it in the open-ended narrative. This inconclusiveness suits the mood and reality of 1915, a point in time when the war's outcome is unknown and moral certainty elusive, and conveys the in-betweenness of the feelings and even identity of the woman at home whose zeal to participate in the war is matched by her doubt about its efficacy. Part 4 of the narrative is yet to be written, what follows "Violette" and "Daphne" yet to be determined. Alix Sandomir, wounded in mind and marked in body, rejects conventional womanhood and complacent domesticity but stands undecided before outright rejection of the cause of war. What is clear at the end of *Non-Combatants*, however, is that this in-betweenness, this struggle with certainty, has itself become a form of public engagement and political debate.

Like Rose Macaulay, May Sinclair devoted her war fiction to the noncombatants, though her nonfiction signals a longing for the front. As her biographer Suzanne Raitt has remarked, Sinclair seemed uninterested in the politics and causes of the war and instead "explored the psychology of those who were in some way excluded from [it]."[24] Critics, including Raitt, have seen Sinclair as a woman in love with war, even with battle—"war was her romance"—and as an onlooker who savored and identified with masculine aggression.[25] There are signs in both the Belgian journal and *The Tree of Heaven*, however, that she was fully aware of the devastation caused by the war and that her stance toward its "romance" was complicated and, at times, tortured. She saw the Great War, as did others, as a stage in the progress of women's bid for equality and independence and as a symptom of the zeitgeist that required both resistance and submission.

When Rebecca West reviewed Sinclair's *Journal of Impressions in Belgium* in 1915, the year of its publication, she thought it was likely to be "one of the few books of permanent value produced by the war" because of its "extremest timidity and a trembling meticulosity."[26] Samuel Hynes, echoing West's estimation of the journal, praises its "bare, direct, exact, and unmetaphorical" style.[27] Though Sinclair went to Belgium in an undefined role as part of an ambulance corps, she functioned most effectively as a war correspondent, jostling and elbowing her way to a story and telling it, as West and Hynes observe, in a precise, unembellished, and unsentimental way. Her reportage resembles some of Wharton's correspondence, especially in its interest in displacement and homelessness. Her account of four thousand refugees from the countryside in Ghent laid out on straw in the Palais des Fêtes, or of an *infirmier*'s laborious search for socks, trousers, and shirt to fit a badly wounded man focus, without melodrama, on the unheroic, homely details of a country stoically coping with war.[28] The journal is also a tale of exclusion and what Rebecca West calls "humiliations" of Sinclair's desperate and mainly unfulfilled desire to be useful and, indeed, heroic. Deeply frustrated by her inability to join the real mission of the corps, and at one point left behind in a café to take consolation in brioches, she compares herself to a woman going down the Grand Canal in Venice in a gondola, all alone (104). The very purpose of the exercise, whether romantic or medical, is upended by the circumstance of isolation and superfluousness, a state associated with the unmarried woman but given new meaning in the Great War. Sinclair feels superfluous to the war effort, and she represents this through the image of an unattached, unmatched woman. Ultimately, the journal itself becomes her mission, the arresting testimony of a woman willing to take part but relegated to the margins and to navigating the Grand Canal alone.

Glimpses of action make her "foolishly elated." She feels a "quiet exultation" at the firing of her "first near gun of [her] first near battle" (87, 146–47). The "violent noise" that she had imagined would overwhelm her with terror instead provokes a smile and fills her with a peculiar "passionate anticipation" as she awaits the next "boom and shock" (147). But the most exhilarating moment for Sinclair comes at the sight of her first wounded man. Her besotted response to him has unsettled some readers and occasioned the observation that her adoration of combative masculinity was stronger than any empathy or revulsion she might have felt in the face of injury, pain, and death: "He was the most beautiful thing I have ever seen. And I loved him. I do not think it is possible to love, to adore any creature more than I loved and adored that clumsy, ugly Flamard. He was my first wounded man" (169–70). Finally allowed to join the work of the nurses attached to the corps, she relishes the first opportunity to be involved, to be of use. She helps to carry the man's stretcher, assists at the dressing of his wounds, and clothes him. Not in love with him precisely, or with war, she is nonetheless in love with her ability to be a part of the action. She uses the language of romantic and even sexual love ("he was my first") to exaggerate and so convey her elation at having a chance to be absorbed into the compelling, dramatic, and brave effort of saving the injured. Purposefully calling on the image of romance to represent her current state, she accentuates her singleness—alone in the gondola—and the validity of war work as woman's most urgent mission, a mission for Sinclair that equals and perhaps surpasses in importance the calling of heterosexual love.

As the sojourn in Belgium proceeds, Sinclair's exultation at nursing the wounded predictably turns to something else. Caring for a severely injured man near Antwerp, she experiences what she calls "the most terrible night I have ever spent in my life" (216). Alone, she watches him throughout the night and day, sitting by his bedside, trying to move him to make him comfortable, talking to him, reading to him, washing his face and hands over and over, listening to him speak of his mother, supporting his back with her arms beneath him, and desperately listening for his rhythmic breathing. Each of the features she recalls—his hair, his eyelashes, his eyes—is "like a separate wound in [her] memory." "He sums up for me," she writes, "all the heroism and the agony and the waste of war" (222). Her determination to help, and the ecstasy she feels at being allowed to tend the injured, ultimately bring an individual man into focus and the realities of war's devastation to life. In the end, there is no romance.

The Tree of Heaven, published a couple of years after the Belgian journals, follows the Harrison family over two generations and begins with a familiarly jaundiced view of the Boer War. Uncle Morrie, who had gone out to fight in South Africa, disabuses his relations of the idea that war is "all glory and pluck" in words that reverberate throughout this 1917 text:

> It's dirt and funk and stinks and more funk all the time. It's lying out all night on the beastly veldt, and going to sleep and getting frozen, and waking up and finding you've got warm again because your neighbour's inside's been fired on the top of you. . . . You'll find a chap lying on his back all nice and comfy, and when you start to pick him up you can't lift him because his head's glued to the ground. You try a bit, gently, and the flesh gives way like rotten fruit, and the bone like a cup you've broken and stuck together without any seccotine, and you heave up a body with half a head on it. And all the brains are in the other half, the one that's glued down. That's war.[29]

Like the sobering and gruesome conditions of the men Sinclair had so passionately nursed in Belgium, these facts remain with the reader, who tries to thread her way through the history of early twentieth-century Britain this modernist war novel tells. The narrative offers a number of different characters' visions of the Great War. Sinclair's own views are never explicit, so that the novel appears to shift and float between different perspectives. Sinclair, interested in the drift and flow of history and the pull of the zeit-geist, stages a debate about the efficacy of war through the unfixed angle of modernist narrative.

The most interesting and complex participants in the war effort in the novel are two of the Harrison siblings, Dorothy and Michael, each of whom has an ongoing and ambivalent struggle with what Sinclair calls the "vortex." For Michael, who resists going to war longer than any of his male siblings, the vortex—that magnetic force of history and popular opinion that pulls in the young and erases their individuality—is associated with what he thinks of as "the herd." Even as a boy at school, he fears it: "He was afraid of the thoughts, the emotions that seized [the herd], swaying, moving the multitude of undeveloped souls as if they had been one monstrous, dominating soul. . . . He disliked the collective, male odour of the herd, the brushing against him of bodies inflamed with running . . . and the smell of dust and ink" (TH, 86). Michael's unhappiness at school, his detestation of masculinity in the mass, his desire to be alone, and, later, to be a poet, all predispose him to oppose war and to refuse to submit to its call. One by one, his brothers, his sister's lover, and even his fellow bohemians embrace the cause of battle and give in to the romance of violence. But the chill of the "collective soul . . . terrible unanimity . . . the Vortex . . . like the little vortex of school" appalls him, and he continues to resist and to protect his individual will.

Dorothy's vortex comes at first in the shape of the women's movement and the push for suffrage. Jailed in Holloway Prison for her suffrage activities, which she makes clear she pursues for herself and not because of what Michael would call the herd, she is filled with the elation of struggle—"*the* adventure and *the* experience of my life," she calls it—and of the "something bigger, something tremendous" for which she fights (TH, 215, 219; emphasis in original). Staying in the jail cell brings her "a sort of deep-down unexcited happiness" (TH, 219). When she exchanges the solitary state of the cell, however, for the mass experience of a suffrage demonstration, she feels the "old terror of the collective soul"—a terror she shares with her brother—and so goes with a complicated and contradictory set of emotions, both "pride and . . . disdain," to the march (*TH*, 228). It is a hallmark of Sinclair's writing here that Dorothy's ambivalence is neither resolved nor smoothed over and that the novel characterizes the women's movement as both uplifting and oppressive. Indeed, Sinclair's idea of the vortex—the irresistible pull of historical and social forces—seems to be marked by just this doubleness of vision.

Like Macaulay's *Non-Combatants*, *The Tree of Heaven* is divided into three sections. The middle of these, "The Vortex," which covers the year 1914, Dorothy's suffrage activity, and Michael's extended resistance to joining up, gives way to "Victory," the last movement of the novel. Given that Sinclair's book appeared in 1917 and her story ends in 1916, this last title refers not to the ultimate outcome of the Great War but rather to an aspiration or, perhaps, to the victory of the vortex of war over all others. In turns of plot that confirm critics in their conviction that this novel amounts to propaganda for war, Dorothy trades suffrage for war work (organizing for Belgian refugees, driving an ambulance) and Michael, after further resistance, enters the fray.[30] But in a phrase that sheds an ambiguous light on both episodes in history, we learn that the "little vortex of the Woman's Movement was swept without a sound into the immense vortex of the War" (*TH*, 299). By proposing continuity between these two vortices, Sinclair seems to both confer grandeur on the women's movement and to cast an equivocal aura on the war, even as she makes logical and valid Dorothy's progression from one to the next. For Dorothy, war work answers "the shame of her immunity" from risk and suffering and satisfies that desire for "something bigger, something tremendous" first fulfilled in Holloway Prison. The overwhelming craving for action, exertion, and service that marks so much of women's war writing appears in this novel as part of a historical evolution from political feminism to feminist insistence on participation in the national effort.

Michael's conversion comes more slowly than Dorothy's embrace of the war. For her, the war extends a search for woman's meaning in the world. For Michael, acquiescing to the idea of war as a salutary enterprise requires the death of his brother Nicholas and an epiphanic night spent alone in Nicholas's marriage bed in a seventeenth-century house deep in the hill country of Northern England. The house functions as a type of the home-as-symbol-of-England that both Virginia Woolf and Rebecca West deploy in writing obliquely about the war.

Nicholas and Michael had been at odds about going to fight, though close in their friendship and brotherly dispute. A series of letters between them lays out the pros and cons of battle and allows Sinclair to stage her debate about the question of war. Nicholas, who declares, "when you're up first out of the trench and stand alone on the parapet, it's absolute happiness," must be sacrificed in order that his brother may fight. In a moment that falls somewhere between a false note and an example of the narrative's protean point of view, Michael learns of Nicholas's death, awakens the next morning in the old house, and knows he must join the fight: "He would be killed too. And because he was going out, and because he would be killed, he was not feeling Nicky's death so acutely as he should have thought he would have felt it" (*TH*, 381). The indirect discourse of the prose here reinforces the subjectivity of the view that war dulls the pain of loss.

Loss—the absolute dependability of it—undermines the novel's endorsement of war in a muted but persistent way. Every man who goes to war, every male Harrison who signs up and is accepted into the army, is killed, almost immediately. Frank, Dorothy's lover, goes off to war and is killed right away; Michael's bohemian mentor, Lawrence Stephen, is killed; Nicholas dies at the front; then Michael is killed. Not one man lasts in battle for long. The youngest Harrison, John, is conscripted as the novel ends, and there is little doubt that Mrs. Harrison is about to lose her third son. Dorothy, now gripped by a spiritual frenzy of pro-war sentiment, tries to reassure her grieving and bitter mother that her sons have not died in vain, that they have sacrificed their bodies to save the world, and that she had known "something tremendous was going to happen" when she was imprisoned in Holloway (*TH*, 404–5). The novel sets Dorothy's nearly delirious war fervor against her mother's grief, and the reader is left suspended, sensing the daughter's position as an idiosyncratic and unpersuasive point of view and the family's loss as testament to the insanity of the war. In the very last lines of the story, four women dressed in black say good-bye to John as he leaves for the front. Uncle Morrie, the Boer War survivor now a hopeless drunk, sends John off to war with a sodden salute.

If pacifism struggles against the desire to join the war effort in Macaulay's *Non-Combatants*, and war horror challenges May Sinclair's enthusiasm for battle in the Belgian journal and *The Tree of Heaven*, Vera Brittain's internationalist antiwar politics and tragic courtship plot are at odds with the narrative of emancipation under the aegis of war that is *Testament of Youth*. Unaware of the pacifist movement during the war, she began to suspect after returning to civilian life that "my generation had been deceived, its young courage cynically exploited, its idealism betrayed" (*TY*, 470). Even so, she observes in her memoir, she was not "so clearly conscious" of this suspicion at the time of war as she is today. Her conviction that the Great War produced an aversion to warfare and a devotion to the kind of international cooperation that produced the League of Nations in its aftermath came gradually and late and, in all likelihood, postdated the period of her life she covers in *Testament*. As critics have much remarked, however, this conviction caused her to revise her wartime life when she recorded it in the early 1930s and to skew her account toward a critique of Britain's mission in the war. In her forward to the memoir, she characterizes the narrative to follow as the "indictment of a civilization," and this is what she intended it to be, tailoring her war diaries and letters accordingly and inserting a retrospective consciousness of regret (*TY*, 12). The war story she *means* to tell is one of awakening political awareness but, as we shall see, the palpable sense of emancipation she experienced at the time of the war mitigates her antiwar drift and makes the memoir a feminist story instead.

Brittain's rejection of war follows logically from the devastation of loss she experienced and records. Like the women of the fictional Harrison family, she loses the young men she loves best, one by one. Her memoir is launched as an accelerated marriage plot. In the second chapter she meets Roland Leighton, the slightly bohemian and feminist (he was an ardent reader of Olive Schreiner) school friend of her beloved brother Edward, and by chapter 3 she has begun to fall in love with him, he has enlisted, and they have become engaged to marry. By the end of the fifth chapter, Roland has died in France. Their courtship, by letter and infrequent meeting, takes on an urgency and importance that depend on war. "At the beginning of 1915," she writes in a strange locution, "I was more deeply and ardently in love than I have ever been or am ever likely to be, yet at that time Roland and I had hardly been alone together" (*TY*, 121). The night they become engaged, on the evening before he is to depart for France, they sit together for hours on a sofa, afraid to touch each other despite, or perhaps because of, the "electric . . . emotion" they feel (*TY*, 131). It is impossible to separate their courtship—such as it was—from the drama of discovering each other as kindred spirits as war breaks out and knowing almost immediately that they will soon be separated. He is killed, wandering needlessly into No Man's Land as he is about to go on leave to meet her in London and without mentioning to a soul that he would soon see her. "I knew," she observes without elaboration, though perhaps not needing any, "that in his last hour I had been forgotten" (*TY*, 244).

Three years into the war, Brittain suffers a second and then a third major loss: the deaths of Geoffrey Thurlow and Victor Richardson, her brother's and Roland's great friends. After Victor has first been wounded, she dreams of marrying him and sacrificing herself to his care—perhaps this is the way she will write out her marriage plot. But Victor dies shortly after she reaches him in London. Then, in 1918, just before the end of the war, her brother is killed in Italy. Any future that she can imagine for herself has been foreclosed. She becomes, in her mind, the "Superfluous Woman" of her 1920 poem: "*But who will look for my coming? . . . But who will seek me at nightfall? . . . But who will give me my children?*" goes her refrain (*TY*, 535; italics in original). When, in the final pages of her memoir, Brittain does marry, the phantom presence of her brother and first fiancé dominate the ceremony in her account. Her husband, George Catlin, knowingly stands in for Roland, and she carries a bouquet of tall pink roses like the ones Roland had given her ten years before. She asks Winifred Holtby, the companion who will make up the third party in what Brittain calls this "semi-detached marriage," to assume her brother Edward's role in her life as "the element of tender, undistressing permanence" (TY, 658). The marriage plot has turned ghostly, made spectral by the war.

Competing with and ultimately overshadowing these narratives of political transformation and tragic courtship, however, is the story of Brittain's liberation from provincial bourgeois life and stultifying femininity. In this tale the war appears as a chapter in the historical march toward woman's independence and part of the process of individual emancipation begun when Brittain goes off to Somerville College, Oxford. Women's war service is here bracketed by the campaign for suffrage and admission of women to the university in the earliest years of the twentieth century on one side and the successful achievement of the right to vote and granting of Oxford degrees to women in 1918 and 1919 on the other. A strong and self-conscious heir to her rebellious Victorian precursors (she quotes George Eliot and Olive Schreiner throughout the memoir), Brittain brilliantly evokes the priggishness, complacency, and conservatism of her family. Her provincial world was radically circumscribed. Looking back, she realizes that she barely knew of the existence of the Labour Party until she was an adult. Like the parents Ruskin chided in *Sesame and Lilies*, her father was determined that she be raised as "a sensitive plant" and turned into "an entirely ornamental young lady" (TY, 74, 32). He regarded sending her to Oxford as a waste of his money and a distraction from the mission of finding her the proper husband.

Her upbringing deprived her of certain kinds of knowledge, not only of the world, history, and politics but also of the body, sexuality, and even simple domestic duties. The "woolen combinations, black cashmere stockings, 'liberty' bodice, dark stockinette knickers, flannel petticoat and . . . long-sleeved, high-necked, knitted woolen 'spencer'" that covered her adolescent body from toe to neck deprived her of the freedom to move and served as a kind of repressive armor (TY, 34). When she began to train as a nurse, she felt humiliated by her ignorance of basic chores—how to boil an egg, prepare a meal, and launder bedclothes. Her education, begun at Oxford (the "greatest romance of England," she calls it), accelerates with intensity after she leaves Somerville and begins to train as a VAD (*TY*, 63). Most striking, perhaps, is her account of how the war acquainted her with the bodies of men in a way that moved her and made her grateful:

> Throughout my two decades of life, I had never looked upon the nude body of an adult male . . . I had therefore expected, when I first started nursing, to be overcome with nervousness and embarrassment, but to my infinite relief, I was conscious of neither. Towards the men I came to feel an almost adoring gratitude for their simple and natural acceptance of my ministrations. Short of going to bed with them, there was hardly an intimate service that I did not perform for one or another in the course of four years, and I still have reason to be thankful for . . . my early release from the sex-inhibitions that even today . . . beset many of my female contemporaries both married and single. . . . [F]rom the constant handling of their lean, muscular bodies, I came to understand the essential cleanliness, the innate nobility, of sexual love on its physical side. (*TY*, 165–66)

This passage reminds us of all the reasons that nursing was seen as an inappropriate occupation for respectable women, certainly in Florence Nightingale's day but also beyond it. For a young woman like Vera Brittain, ministering to the naked bodies of strange men, like making meals and beds, imbued her with a kind of knowledge and experience that remade or redefined her class identity, as well as her femininity. But it also made her a saner person—less sheltered, inhibited, and afraid. There is, too, an intriguing irony in the contrast between the sexual knowledge she gleaned from nursing and the absolute chasteness of her relationship with Roland. The latter belongs to the narrative of idealized romance and courtship, which constitutes what we might call the fictional plot of *Testament*, while the former fits the story of modern womanhood and emancipation it so powerfully and authentically conveys.

Brittain's escape from provincial life, first to Oxford, then to London to train and work as a VAD nurse, and then to the Continent, is a familiar story with its own fictional models. The young person—usually, though not always, a man—leaves the provinces to shed what Brittain calls "sheltered gentility" and to make his or her way in the world and never look back (*TY*, 213). Like the hero of bildungsroman, she glories in "at last seeing life," and, like the women who flocked to London at the end of the nineteenth century to work with the poor and investigate the slums, she finds it "quite thrilling to be an unprotected female" (ibid.). Her term for the sensation of hard work in the service of the war mission, from "the dressing of a dangerous wound to the scrubbing of a bed mackintosh," is "sacred glamour." Though this phrase is difficult to reconcile with soldiers' suppurating wounds, Brittain's bloody hands, and the daily hour-and-a-half trudge in the dark up Denmark Hill from the nurse's hostel to London General Hospital, Brittain clearly revels in the potent combination of sacrifice, usefulness, independence, and unorthodox middle-class femininity (*TY*, 210).

Called to foreign service and anxious to leave England after Roland's death, Brittain embarks on a period of "glamorous beauty and delight," first at Malta, with its "magic days," and then in France at Etaples, which she found even "more compelling," though "less delirious" than Malta. The idyll of being abroad is marked by effusiveness, especially about the sheer beauty of these settings, and a sense of coming to life again after losing her fiancé. But this coming back to life seems as much the result of the grimmest conditions and most grotesque injuries she encountered during the war as of the stunning Mediterranean light. The grimness begins on the boat that takes her from Mudros to Malta. In another blow to middle-class decorum, the five tin privies on the ship lack partitions between them, and the VADs must trade the fastidiousness to which they are accustomed for this "perturbing . . . publicity" while beset by shipboard-induced intestinal distress (*TY*, 300).

In Malta, after the devastating Battle of the Somme, she sees "men without faces, without eyes, without limbs, men almost disemboweled, men with hideous truncated stumps of bodies" (*TY*, 339). Once in Etaples, her growing competence lands her an assignment in the German ward, where she both fears for her own bodily safety and experiences "a regular baptism of blood and pus" (*TY*,

375). The steady stream of hemorrhaging and gangrenous bodies brought in from the front, the 3:30 a.m. hour of waking, and the dozens of men to be washed each day in icy water oppress and yet revive her. The mixture of "magic" and gloom animates and sustains her, so much so that when her parents call her home because her mother is ill and they cannot manage without her, she is filled with rage and despair. After the intensity and urgency of wartime, she is reduced to the status of dutiful daughter and "maid-of-all-work," and she feels "marooned in a kind of death-in-life" (TY, 429–30). Without irony, Brittain writes that she can "look back more readily . . . upon the War's tragedies . . . than upon those miserable weeks that followed my return from France" (TY, 429). Stultification in comfort was more painful than constant exertion and exhaustion under devastating conditions and in the face of continuous loss. We think here of Woolf's conviction that the "education of the private house, with its cruelty, its poverty, its hypocrisy, its immorality, [and] its inanity" drove young women to take refuge in the "menial" tasks of war.

In 1920, after the war was over and Vera Brittain had returned to Oxford to finish her degree, she, like Rose Macaulay's Alix, suffered a breakdown. "No one," she writes in *Testament*, "realized how near I had drifted to the borderland of craziness" (TY, 496). Worst of all for her during those hallucinatory days was looking in the mirror, where she saw her own reflection as something utterly transformed and terrifying. She detected a shadow on her face: Was she developing a beard or "turning into a witch" (TY, 497)? Who was she? Had she become monstrous in some way, unsexed, her face made masculine and her single state made permanent? She could tell no one what she saw in the glass and, at the time, had no understanding of her psychological state. The reasons for such distress are not hard to fathom. Not only had she lost her brother, fiancé, and closest male friends in the war, not only had she experienced enough stress and devastation to qualify her for shell shock, not only did she seem to have become a "superfluous woman" (or a witch), but she had returned to a world where, according to the title of the chapter that describes her breakdown, "Survivors [were] Not Wanted." Like Macaulay's Alix and like May Sinclair in Belgium, Brittain was a woman out of place, at sea as both a woman and a citizen.

She felt out of step with the younger men and women she encountered at Oxford who could, with the benefit of hindsight, blithely criticize those who had made and gone to war. Not only were her womanhood and her very being superannuated, but so too were her convictions, or at least her allegiances. She writes with muted bitterness:

> Patriots, especially of the female variety, were as much discredited in 1919 as in 1914 they had been honoured . . . No doubt the post-war generation was wise in its assumption that patriotism had "nothing to it," and we pre-war lot were just poor boobs for letting ourselves be kidded [elsewhere she says "hoodwinked"] into thinking that it had. The smashing-up of one's youth seemed rather a heavy price to pay for making the mistake, but fools always did come in for a worse punishment than knaves; we knew that now. (*TY*, 490)

What is striking here is that her own critique of Britain's war mission—her "indictment of a civilisation"—does not displace or supersede the loyalty she feels to the experience and fervor of her generation or her pride in having severed the bonds of conventional femininity through the crucible of war. She does not renounce her patriotism, even as she recognizes it as problematic and misguided. Brittain ultimately finds the politics of internationalism and feminism as solutions to the feeling of being an anachronism, superfluous and unmoored from her time, but the memoir is finally most compelling as a "testament" of the power of war to remake womanhood.

Virginia Woolf read *Testament of Youth* in 1933, the year of its publication, when she was working on *The Pargiters* and beginning to meditate on the material that would later become *The Years* (1937) and then *Three Guineas* (1938). She wrote in her diary that she didn't find Brittain's mind sympathetic but could not deny the power and originality of her memoir. "But her story," Woolf concedes, "told in detail, without reserve, of the war, & *how she lost lover & brother, & dabbled her hands in entrails, & was forever seeing the dead, & eating scraps, & sitting five on one WC*, runs rapidly, vividly across my eyes."[31] Woolf recognized something new here, and she zeroed in on what it was: a woman born at the end of Victoria's age, raised in bourgeois propriety and constraint, and able to experience and write freely, without the self-imposed, inhibiting admonitions of the "angel in the house," about the horrors and degradations of wartime. "I give her credit," Woolf concludes, "for having lit up a long passage for me at least." With echoes of her evocation in *A Room of One's Own* of the new woman writer "Mary Carmichael," who "will light a torch in that vast chamber where nobody has been," Woolf signals that she finds a radical power in Brittain's memoir. Unsettled by the frankness and "urgency" of the book, Woolf notes that her hand shakes and her writing grows indecipherable as she writes about *Testament* in her diary.

It seems likely that Woolf was unsettled by, among other things, the comingling of feminist aspiration and patriotism that she saw in *Testament of Youth*. For Brittain's generation, the latter could be embedded in the former, part of a history of progress and emancipation. For Woolf, of course, especially as she articulated her views in *Three Guineas*, these two impulses were utterly at odds. Indeed, feminism and the Great War constituted all the argument she needed against warfare in general and the war she feared now faced Europe in particular. If we understand *Three Guineas* as a book about the Great War, it can be seen as a culmination of the antagonism toward war that began to emerge in the writing of women like Macaulay, Sinclair, and Brittain. Woolf distilled this antipathy and virtually stripped it of the countervailing sentiments that drew women to the war effort. The ambivalence and divided sensibility that emerge in many women's World War I writing seem absent from Woolf's more clearheaded condemnation of war. And yet even in *Three Guineas*, a hint of contradiction breaks in. Addressing those who would enlist her help in a war against fascism, Woolf argues that "feminists" of the last century had been fighting for the same things that animate her interlocutors today: "They were fighting the tyranny of the patriarchal state as you are fighting the tyranny of the Fascist state."[32] Though their interests are different, their enemy is the same. "You are feeling in your own persons," she writes, "what your mothers felt when they were shut out, when they were shut up, because they were women. Now you are being shut out, you are being shut up, because you are Jews, because you are democrats, because of race, because of religion."[33] Feminist resistance to patriarchal order during the Great War, abhorrence of the hypocrisy of what Woolf called "the education of the private house," compelled women to escape into involvement in a national enterprise that in later days many could call patriarchal—or worse. In Woolf's case, feminism and disgust at the "cruelty, . . . poverty, . . . hypocrisy, . . . immorality, . . . inanity" of the private house fuels her critique of war. But it also brings her to a deep sympathy for—not to say identification with—those who passionately promote it. Even in Woolf's refusal to endorse war, we hear a muffled call to arms.

PART II: THE SECOND WORLD WAR

Woolf never recanted her belief that war originated in the discreditable "desire for aggression, the desire to dominate and enslave," but her pacifism was qualified, then rendered effectively moot by a world war that blurred and eventually erased the dividing line between home front and battlefield, between civilians and combatants.[34] The decisive battles of the Second World War were no longer confined to sodden trenches across the Channel but were fought everywhere and by everyone. "The fronts are everywhere," Churchill emphasized in a speech delivered to the House of Commons on April 20, 1940, a crisis point in the Battle of Britain: "The trenches are dug in the towns and streets. Every village is fortified. Every road is barred. The front line runs through the factories. The workmen are soldiers with different weapons but the same courage."[35] Churchill's homage to home front workmen as soldiers—the terms are generic rather than gendered—served as a public notice that women were no longer relegated, as Rose Macaulay complained, to the sidelines of battle. They were in the thick of things.

But being in the thick of things also made it harder to take in what was actually happening. Looking back on the stories written in wartime London, Elizabeth Bowen emphasized "the *desiccation* [her italics], by war, of our day-to-day lives": "The outsize World War news was stupefying; headlines and broadcasts came down and down on us in hammerlike chops, with great impact, but, oddly, little reverberation. The simple way to put it was: 'One cannot take things in.'"[36] Soldiers in a war whose necessity none disputed, women and men writers alike struggled to find new ways to take things in, to record and in recording help combat the desiccation, the moral stupor that war wrought on life every day. Where women writers differed from men and from each other was in the manner they fought and the strategies they devised to salvage or create "indestructible landmarks in a destructible world."[37]

That Woolf's choice of weapons changed from pacifist critique to moral defense of the wartime effort was perhaps inevitable once the fighting was on home ground and the aim less to defend the "splendid Empire" than to protect English freedoms against totalitarian aggressors. For Woolf the front line ran through the environs of her country home, Monk's House, where she was subjected to the terror of night bombings across the Sussex countryside. But the war's devastation was brought home to her most agonizingly during her periodic visits to a London "cramped and creased" by incessant aerial bombardments. The woeful spectacle churned up emotions she hardly knew how to account for: "Odd how often I think with what is love I suppose of the City: of the walk to the Tower: that is my England: I mean, if a bomb destroyed one of those little alleys with the brass bound curtains and the river smell and the old woman reading I should feel—well, what the patriots feel."[38]

This unexpected burst of patriotic feeling must have been difficult for Woolf to acknowledge, if only to herself. In *Three Guineas* she had proclaimed her freedom from all nationalist attachment, declaring that as a woman she had no country, that her country was the whole wide world,[39] but the din and destruction of the relentless bombings prompts her to lay claim, with as much tenacity as tenderness, to "my England." Like Cather, Woolf cherishes her country not in the august form of a nation-state, but in the more neighborly guise of a patria. Her England is not symbolized by Windsor, Whitehall, Westminster, or Churchill's war rooms but is conjured by the neighborhoods formed by little alleys with brass-bound curtains and permeated by the smell of the Thames. The tutelary figure for her England is an old woman reading, silently engaged in those civilized pursuits that the war threatens with irrelevance, if not outright extinction.

In light of these feelings, she can no longer dismiss political oratory, as she emphatically did in *Three Guineas*, as "claptrap."[40] In "Thoughts of Peace in an Air Raid," she even resorts to the nationalist rhetoric she had spent her life impugning and embraces the consensus view that "the fight going on up in the sky is a fight by the English to protect freedom, by the Germans to destroy freedom." She concedes that the battle against patriarchy and the war against fascism have become one fight that is being waged on overlapping rather than parallel fronts. She acknowledges that the battle is hers as much as anyone's; the question is not whether but how to contribute to the war effort. Her answer was totally in keeping with her conviction that war was wrong but that this one must be fought. She would exercise the option, which for her amounted to an absolute duty, "to think peace into existence."[41] Dismissing any objection that "all the idea makers who are in a position to make ideas effective are men," she takes heart in the thought that "there are other tables besides officer tables and conference tables." The writing table for one. There she could mount a defense against Nazi aggression while continuing her lifelong battle against the "unconscious Hitlerism" that opportunistically lurked at the heart of patriarchy.[42]

Yet even as she intensifies her "mental fight" against fascism in all its forms, Woolf battles her own dispiriting sense of impending catastrophe as rumors of invasion gained momentum and credibility. In the diary entry for May 15, 1940, she is plagued by the latest government appeal "for home defense—against parachutists," which she juxtaposes to the conversation she has had earlier that morning with her husband Leonard about what they would do "if Hitler land [sic]": "Jews beaten up. What point in waiting? Better shut the garage doors." This tense and wearisome day, one of many to come, culminates in an idea that, by clarifying her place and role among the fighting forces, heightens her commitment to moral as well as armed resistance: "the army is the body. I am the brain. Thinking is my fighting."[43] The incipient defeatism that threatened her fighting spirit earlier in the day is, at least for the moment, subdued by this morally fortifying image that conjoins and equates mental fight with physical combat.

The realization that war not only changed what but *how* one thought also haunts Elizabeth Bowen's wartime fiction, where it acquires the unanswerable authority of "an awful illumination."[44] The phrase is used—twice—by Justin Cavey, a dour but unmistakably prescient character in "Summer Night," a meandering Chekhovian story set in a rural "outpost" of neutral Ireland. Bowen depicts Cavey as a city man whose "impersonal, patient look of a thinker" establishes him as the reflective center of a story set in a country that, although a nonbelligerent, is nonetheless caught in the surge of the "black tide coming in" (CS, 599). Cavey, mindful of the approaching surge, is neither patient nor impersonal in sounding the alarm:

> I say, this war's an awful illumination; it's destroyed our dark; we have to see where we are. Immobilized, God help us, and each so far apart that we can't even try to signal each other. And our currency's worthless—our "ideas," so on, so on. We've got to mint a new one. We've got to break through to the new form—it needs genius. We're precipitated, this moment, between genius and death. I tell you, we must have genius to live at all. (CS, 590)

Cavey's cri de coeur epitomizes the plight of women writers who, precipitated between genius and death, wrote in the glare of an awful illumination that their patria, with its sustaining ideas of home and homeland, community and tradition, was hurtling toward a point of no return beyond which extinction was all but certain.

The plight was general, but individual responses reflected who you were, where you spent, and what you did in the war. Bowen, for example, served as a "native informant" for Churchill during the war, reporting on the popular mood in neutral but strategically vital Ireland, while Olivia Manning held a more official position as press attaché to the American Embassy in Cairo and later served as press assistant to Jerusalem's Public Information Office. Martha Gellhorn unhesitatingly joined the ranks of foreign correspondents who "had been reporting the rise of Fascism, its horrors and its sure menace, for years." History, sadly and horrifically, vindicated the prescience of this "Federation of Cassandras." As Gellhorn reminded her readers, the "doom they had long prophesized arrived on time, bit by bit, as scheduled." Confirming their status as Cassandras, their warnings went unheeded: "For all the good our articles did, they might have been written in invisible ink, printed on leaves, and loosed to the wind."[45]

The "good" of fiction during wartime is even more dubious, if good is defined and measured by the number of horrors averted, actual lives saved. And yet fiction continued to be written with an urgency and inventiveness that should make us reconsider and expand our notion of wartime heroics. Woolf and Bowen are instructive figures in this respect. Their war was fought on a home front so battered by the "violent destruction of solid things" that, as Bowen recalled, "we all lived in a state of lucid abnormality."[46] In a world in which abnormality is the norm, the mind reaches out for some glimmer—never a flash—of the peace to come. (In war any flash portends annihilation before it announces insight.) Woolf, who believed that peace could be achieved and preserved by acts of the mind as well as of armed bodies, wrote in the distant but active hope that it might be possible "to live differently—differently," the vague but urgent imperative that reverberates throughout the closing pages of *The Years*.[47] Bowen, too, devotes much of her wartime fiction to prophetic exhortation, dramatizing the pressing need for "new forms of thinking and feeling," even as she remarks how impoverished the world feels as the old forms begin to disappear, sometimes violently, under the stress and assault of war.

Gellhorn and Olivia Manning, both of whom spent the war near and sometimes actually in combat zones, were more immediately preoccupied with testifying to what war was and did rather than how the world might return to the normalcy of what Gertrude Stein called "the ordinary business of daily living."[48] Their novels unblinkingly record life on the battlefields overseas where death was imminent and everywhere: the three novels composing Manning's *Levant Trilogy* track the uncertain fortunes of British colonials stranded in the Middle East during the historic military campaigns in North Africa; Gellhorn's *A Stricken Field* recounts the "appalling days" following the German annexation of the Sudetenland in 1938 when the Nazis began systematically to persecute Jews, round up and torture dissidents, and turn native Czechs into exiles in their own country, precipitating a refugee crisis that was to be repeated in other countries that came under German occupation; her *Point of No Return*, set at the end rather than the beginning of the war, follows an American battalion enlisted in the Ardennes Counteroffensive, the so-called Battle of the Bulge. The novel describes the battles they fought, the women they romanced, and the awful illumination that awaited them at the end of an ordinary street in Dachau.

However different Woolf's war was from Gellhorn's, Bowen's from Manning's, they were sisters in one respect: all found it difficult, at times impossible, to "think back through [their] mothers,"[49] as Woolf ventured that women writers invariably did, for models and precedents. The daughters of literary women who wrote of the Great War might have inherited their mothers' genius for living, but they were dispossessed of the "dark" in which their immediate predecessors confidently expressed their genius in daring amalgams of adventure and critique, in stories of self-development that unfolded amid the slaughter and shell shock of trench warfare. There are few, if any, self-secure protagonists to be found in women's fiction of the Second World War, which take as their central theme the shock, disorientation, and desperation of characters whose everyday reality has been reduced to a heap of "scraps, orts and fragments."[50] This is how Woolf characterized the rubble that clutters *Between the Acts*, her last and most explicit "war" novel, in which shattered psyches and crumbling traditions acquire the alarming reality of an accomplished and perhaps irremediable fact. Both the fact and Woolf's title register Cavey's temporal sense of the war as an in-between time in which things are prone to disintegrate in a blinding flash, never to regain their rightful form or place in the world.

Under such harrowing conditions, the reality of who and, as Cavey adds, "where we are," becomes less and less discernible. As the mind becomes more and more accustomed and attuned to war's phantasmagoria, any vision of where we are and are violently heading is likely to be seen less like an awful illumination than the projection of a distraught and disordered brain. The delusions of the shell-shocked are as much a staple of "homeland" as "battlefield" fictions. They, too, dramatize how war's "lucid abnormality" can distort perception and unsettle the mind.

Bowen, who detected "a rising tide of hallucination" in her collected wartime stories, contended that all such "[i]mpulsive movements of fantasy are by-products of the non-impulsive major routine of war."[51] This hallucinatory tide crests in "The Demon Lover," the title piece in the collection. As the story opens, Mrs. Drover, whom the narrator dismisses, with just a whiff of contempt, as "the prosaic woman," returns to her London flat to retrieve some personal items. She is briskly going about her errand, hardly registering the "unfamiliar queerness" of the "once familiar street" that war has depopulated and left forlorn until "a shaft of reflected daylight"—the activating agent and medium of her awful illumination—directs her attention to a letter lying in wait for her, like a buried bomb waiting to explode. The very sight of the letter stops Mrs. Drover dead in her tracks and sends the story catapulting into another dimension where all the rules of time and space are eerily abolished.

The letter is addressed to her. It advises that she is to expect the writer "at the hour arranged." What gives the letter *its* unfamiliar queerness is that the tone and the signature identify the sender as her former fiancé, presumed killed in the First World War, and that the hour arranged, which was set twenty-five years earlier, has obviously long since come and gone. Intensifying the queerness, and giving it a nasty edge, is her memory of their final parting, in which "without very much kindness, and painfully" he pressed her hand on the breast buttons of his uniform, leaving an imprint of his domineering will. This imprint, we are told, "was, principally what she was to carry away." She can recall nothing about his face except that he seemed to have "spectral glitters in the place of eyes," a foreshadowing of the inhuman and possibly malevolent designs he had and still may have on her. Now he seems to have returned from some dark netherworld to fulfill those designs, designs whose shape and purpose were manifest in his disquieting, because peremptory, assurance that he would come back *for* (not *to*) her "sooner or later" (CS, 663).

In this assurance, which is barely distinguishable from a threat, Bowen gives a macabre and malicious twist to two scenarios that were a staple of women's fiction written in and about the Great War—the sentimental leave-takings of newly recruited soldiers going off to war and their troubled homecomings as veterans shell-shocked, unmanned, or disillusioned by the horrors of battle. Given that Kathleen (her first name is only revealed when she recalls the nightmarish courtship plot in which she found herself conscripted) feels that "no other way of having given herself could have made her feel so apart, lost and foresworn" (CS, 664), it is easy, perhaps too easy, to conclude that the return of this soldier represents a return of the repressed. The title conspires in this impression, putting us on the alert that sooner or later the demon lover will make his/its way back into the life and heart of this prosaic woman. Unlike the soldier in Rebecca West's emotionally delicate novel, Kathleen's ex-lover seems insusceptible to rehabilitation or even appeasement, so intent is he on keeping an appointment and a promise made in a world that has long ceased to exist.

It was in that vanished world that Kathleen was pressured into making an "unnatural promise" intended to "drive down between her and the rest of all human kind" (CS, 663–64). In her demon lover's "drive" to divide her from the rest of mankind, we hear a weak echo but strong pun ("drove her") on her current married name, as if putting a linguistic seal on his too implacable campaign to make her his exclusive possession. The linguistic slippage from drive to driver (it is as a driver that the demon lover returns to keep his appointment) further splinters the perspectives of the story as it shuttles back and forth between past and present, the First and the Second World War, the scrupulous realism of its narrative manner and the implied supernaturalism of its central event. The feeling of "unnatural queerness" that initiates the story becomes so pronounced that it eventually becomes impossible to decide whether Kathleen is a heroine haunted by an erotically possessive and possibly vengeful ghost or a woman the war has slowly but irreversibly driven mad by a guilt too subtle or too shameful even to name. The story ends with her screaming and pounding hysterically on the glass pane separating her from the taxi driver who is "accelerating without mercy . . . down the hinterland of deserted streets" (CS, 666). Is she pounding to be released from the demon lover and the ghost story he has made of her otherwise prosaic existence or is the glass she so furiously pummels actually a mirror in which she sees, like some glittering hallucination, the distorted reflection of her own panic-stricken, guilt-ridden face?[52]

Bowen claimed that the hallucinations common in wartime, even those as extreme as Mrs. Drover's (if, that is, hers *is* a hallucination), were a counterresponse to the lucid abnormality of wartime life, an "unconscious, instinctive saving resort," perhaps the *last* resort for a mind besieged by the strain of life "mechanized by the controls of wartime, and emotionally torn and impoverished by change." Under such constraints and impoverishments, Bowen insists, "life had to complete itself in *some* way."[53] In investigating this claim, it is advisable to trust the tale over the teller. Despite Bowen's disclaimer, it is difficult not to see mental peril in the undeniably uncanny ordeal visited upon the prosaic and timid Mrs. Drover, a woman unambiguously marked by her tendency to give assent rather than to offer resistance, a weak character trait at any time, but one more troubling, even dangerous, during wartime, when standing fast is one of the incontestable moral imperatives of the day.

Even when fantasy is active in translating the mind to a place of greater, if not ultimate, safety, as it does in "Mysterious Kôr," the new purchase on reality is fraught with peril, jeopardizing as it does any attachment to the human. That, in fact, is Kôr's major attraction for Pepita, a young woman who cannot imagine how anyone can "think about people if they've got any heart" (CS, 730). Her mind therefore instinctively and gratefully turns to Kôr, the "completely forsaken city," in response to the challenge of being alive. At no time does Kôr seem more within reach than when

London is so drenched with moonlight that it "looked like the moon's capital—shallow, cratered, extinct" (*CS*, 739). The very thought of Kôr, a capital city without a history, soothes Pepita's war-beleaguered consciousness, not because it is a place where one might live differently but because it idealizes the notion of extinction. Kôr, among whose whitened ruins there "is not a crack . . . anywhere for a weed to grow in," offers the mind, distraught and disoriented by war, a serene emblem of a civilization that has survived some unchronicled catastrophe intact. Fantasy here does not so much complete life as replace reality. So much is hinted when Pepita defends the immaterial but real existence of Kôr by claiming that "[t]his war shows we've by no means come to the end. If you can blow whole places out of existence, you can blow whole places into it" (*CS*, 730). The war also showed how quickly whole places could be blown out of one time into another. "You never escape the war in London," Woolf notes during a visit to London in 1941: "Very few buses. Tubes closed. No children. No loitering. Everyone humped with a gas mask. Strain and grimness. At night it's so verdurous & gloomy that one expects a badger or a fox to prowl along the pavement. A reversion to the middle ages with all the space & the silence of the country."[54] It is easy to understand how visions of Kôr, the mysterious city, might materialize amid the strain and grimness, the space and silence of a London in which people equipped with gas masks scurry to safety, leaving empty pavements where country creatures, badgers and foxes, prowl unchallenged.

The reversion to a more primitive and surreal mode of life was even more pronounced in the war zones of Italy and France. One of the most detailed and intimate accounts of civilian life under these conditions is given by Iris Origo in *War in Val D'Orcia*, the remarkably vivid, yet emotionally temperate diary she kept in the perilous years of 1943–44, when Tuscany, where she spent most of the war, was virtually under Nazi occupation. Origo, who was of Anglo-Irish descent, spent most of her childhood and young womanhood in Italy (she was a friend of Bernard Berenson, with whom her mother had an affair). She left for a brief time to live in England, then returned to Italy and married the (illegitimate) son of an Italian countess, upon which she moved in and renovated a country estate in Tuscany where she was to spend the rest of her life. There she practiced and refined her skills as a historian and biographer of romantic talents, personalities, and historical epochs. She was the biographer of the Italian poet Leopardi, wrote a short life of Allegra, Lord Byron's daughter, and recounted the affair between Byron and Countess Guccioli (*The Last Attachment*). Her most famous historical work remains her life of Francesco di Marco Datini, the so-called thirteenth-century Merchant of Prato, but her most affecting work may be *A Need to Testify*, which offers intimate and admiring portraits of four dedicated antifascists who were remarkable figures in their own right: the writer Ignazio Silone, the politician Gaetano Salvemini, the American actress and incomparable monologist, Ruth Draper, and Lauro De Bosis, the Italian aviator-poet who died disseminating antifascist leaflets over Rome from his low-flying airplane.

Origo's historical subjects were illustrious and romantically larger than life. In yet another example of how war changed how women thought and wrote, Origo writes of her own experience of war in Val D'Orcia in a plain, unemphatic style that conveys the "lucid abnormality" of a time when even the most commonplace actions and emotions seemed at once routine and surreal. The blending of historic and homely details is accomplished unobtrusively by Origo's deft use of the diary form, which answers to her wish to record how everyday life went on, yet was no longer ordinary under fascist rule and German occupation. She imperturbably reports on the major events of the war that are fast encroaching—the Allied invasion of Sicily and the mainland, the bombing campaigns against nearby Turin and Genoa, troop movements in and out of Tuscany, and the threat of civil war as the Germans retreat and the Americans advance, energizing the partisan opposition. She takes particular notice of how daily life was reverting to a medieval pattern: "as the outside world is more and more cut off, we must learn, not only to produce our own food and spin and weave our own wool—but to provide teaching for the children, nursing for the sick, and shelter for the passerby-by."[55] Cut off from modern life and its conveniences, but also immersed in the deadliest of modern conflicts, Origo and her family fended off fascist officials and Nazi officers while aiding the partisans, harboring refugee Italian children, and providing cover and shelter for escaping British airmen and prisoners of war. If discovered, she faced summary execution.

Amid such dangers, Origo experiences her own awful illumination, one that occurs on August 15 during a birthday celebration for her daughter, Benedetta:

> In the middle of Blind Man's Buff a military lorry drives up and two German officer[s] come clanking down the garden path. They belong to the division, encamped beneath Radicofani, which crossed the Brenner on July 28. . . . As they sit, very correct and polite—drinking their glasses of wine and proposing a formal toast—I feel that they are the most highly specialized human beings that I ever encountered: the "fighting man."[56]

Origo kept her diary as a private citizen intent on recording her own local experience of war, but it is the historian in her that notes the transformations the war has made in the general fabric of life and in the character of men. Certainly, it was the historian Origo who rather dispassionately observed that these young soldiers, who fight with an "absolutely single-minded, self-denying devotion, with no half-shades of humour, self-criticism, or doubt" represent an alarming specialization in modern manhood—the "fighting man." The fighting man, born of the male genius for war, is more sinister in his ability to mimic the polite forms and join in the celebrations that belong to the everyday life of peace.

Against this uncanny image of the fighting man who toasts his (captive) host before resuming the hunt for Jews and partisans to deport or execute outright, the figure of the fighting woman, the defender rather than the taker of life, stands in stark, if often oblique, opposition. Whether at home or near the battlefield (in Origo's case home was on the battlefield), the fighting woman is perhaps most formidable when thinking peace into existence. Writing half a century after "Thoughts of Peace in an Air Raid," Gellhorn, who shared very little with Virginia Woolf in the way of temperament, upbringing, and life experience, echoed the credo of the fighting woman in her own unvarnished idiom: "I believe that memory and imagination, not nuclear weapons, are the great deterrents."[57]

For Gellhorn, the peculiar creative power, at once summoned and challenged by the devastating realities of war, a power we have been calling, after Bowen, the "genius for living," inheres in memory and imagination. These are the faculties that restore continuity and intelligible form to the ordinary human world, which war disrupts and obliterates. Bowen, as fearless as she is precise in devising new forms to capture the magnitude of the psychological damage the war inflicted upon civilian populations, retrospectively understood her wartime stories as a series of "disjected snapshots—snapshots taken from close up, too close up, in the middle of the mêlée of the battle." Seen from so close up, the war unfolds and is experienced as a series of moments too disconnected and dispersed to cohere into a single and unified narrative. In such circumstances, Bowen relates, "[y]ou cannot render, you can only embrace—if it means embracing to the suffocation point."[58] There is something unnerving in the thought of an embrace, however artful, that, like that of the demon lover, suffocates rather than enfolds and protects.

This pervasive sense of emotional disarray, of a stifling helplessness before an overwhelming and incomprehensible reality, characterizes the work of women writers, struggling as it were for their artistic breath. The struggle is evidenced by the halting or disjunctive syntax, by excursions into fantasy or outright hallucination, by the imaginative withdrawal into an inhuman, if not posthuman, world, like Kôr, that is outside time, or that, like the world contemplated by the depersonalized narrator of *Between the Acts*, contains no life, no death, and no danger, but no happiness or kindness either, nothing but "the still, distilled essence of emptiness, silence" (*BA*, 37). And yet, the forms these writers invented, at times literally, in the middle of the mêlée of the battle, *did* hold together, locking reality in a firm and determined embrace. In Gellhorn's *A Stricken Field*, this embrace takes the form of an unvoiced lament by Mary Douglas, an American war correspondent based, with not a jot of self-approbation, on Gellhorn herself. (One of the dissidents she is trying to help escape the Nazis acknowledges that Mary is "a good woman," admires her "fine legs," but thinks "she is not politically developed."[59]) Mary has been dispatched to Czechoslovakia by her American editor "to get the rounded picture . . . the complete bird's eye view of tragedy and defeat," to avoid "propaganda," and to report "the inside story" as it is disclosed to her through interviews with "big executives, politicians good for quotable sentences; some high army men; and perhaps even some literary celebrities" (*SF*, 82). Mary prides herself in her professionalism but still cannot help regretting that "in a world hurrying between large disasters," there is no time to report the other "inside story," the story of those without much money or power, and certainly without fame; the story of refugees running out of food and hope; the story of children without a home and about to lose whatever future they might have had; the story in which the suffering, cruelty, and pity of war is told over and over again to an unheeding world. Writing for an audience who is either not listening or has disappeared completely is a recurrent plaint in the literature of war. Gellhorn herself bitterly denounced Chamberlain, whom she reviled for being "deeply committed to having Franco win" in Spain: "You only hear what pays."[60] Her exasperation is reflected in Mary, heartsick at what she witnesses yet cannot report as "news." "If I knew how," she determines, "I would write a lament."

But Mary does know how, as attested by the lament she immediately composes without hope of its ever being heard:

> I heard the children sing once in Spain, in Barcelona, that cold and blowing March when the bombers came over faster than wind, so that it would all happen in three unending minutes, but if you saw them they were hanging in the sky not moving, slow and easy, taking their time, you'd think, not worried about anything. But usually the planes were higher than you could see or hear and suddenly the streets beneath them fountained up, in a deep round echoing underground all-over-the-sky roaring that seemed never to finish, and the windows bent inward and the furniture shook on the floor and in the

stillness afterwards you would hear one voice, wild and thin and alone, crying out sharply, and then silence. (*SF*, 82–83)[61]

A Stricken Field is dedicated to Gellhorn's then husband, Ernest Hemingway. It can be read as her homage to the writer who made the "specific problem of construction, imagination and sentences" (*SF*, 311) *the* problem for the writer. The lament Gellhorn composes in *A Stricken Field* is one solution to that problem, one that discharges her debt to Hemingway while minting a stylistic currency all her own. Hemingway's skill in accumulating details, hard little pellets of sensation, into a stream of words that gathers momentum, clarity, and force until the "one true thing" is finally and permanently stated, is echoed but also transfigured in Gellhorn's virtuoso recording of the voice of children singing exultantly despite the cold and the roar of bombs, whose loud denotations set up a "deep round echoing . . . that seemed never to finish" but that eventually dwindles to the sound of a voice "wild and thin and alone, crying out sharply" before it is silenced and absorbed into the void of a deathly quiet.

Lamentation is a form, especially in its biblical iterations, that speaks to and on behalf of the forsaken. The forsaken, those dispossessed of their lives, their loves, and at times their reason, also dominate the emotional foreground of Bowen's wartime stories. Her "Sunday Afternoon," like "Summer Night," for which it serves as a pendant (the desultory and dwindling light of day yielding to the saturated blackness of night), conjures up a pastoral peacefulness that the story itself disturbs and, ultimately, ironizes, going so far as to intimate that in the "new catastrophic outward order of life" wrought by the war, the very "idea of summer has been relinquished." Henry, the brooding intelligence of "Sunday Afternoon," is a man who, like Justin Cavey, is suspended between the provincial society still clinging to all the "country sweetness" of its traditions and the bitter realities of the war-torn present. He, however, goes even further than Cavey in proclaiming that the demise of the old "view of life may be just as well." Miranda, the young girl to whom he delivers this historical verdict, dismisses his lugubriousness: "The trouble with you is, you're half old" (*CS*, 622).

Miranda is not wrong, but she is not right in the way she thinks she is. Like her namesake in Shakespeare's *The Tempest*, the world is new to her. To be caught between two orders of time, as Henry and Justin are, is to be half-old, but not, as we shall see, without hope of beginning anew.

For Bowen, prophecy is inextricably linked to elegy, a form congenial to the mixed feelings of the half-old since it honors steadfast, if often ambivalent, attachments to dead or dying ways of thinking and feeling. But the half-old are still half-young, and so Henry and Cavey, for all their cheerless rhetoric, take up the burden of thinking the unthinkable—how to live differently in a postwar world that most likely will have no place and less need for the old ways of life, the old self. This uneasy but potent twinning of unquiet elegy with uncertain prophecy also underlies the rhythm of Woolf's *Between the Acts*, a novel that takes place, like Joyce's *Ulysses*, in one day, but whose narrative, also like, if less grandiloquently than, *Ulysses*, encompasses the past and future of the country, the race, and, indeed, the planet, now convulsed by war. This history is told primarily, again as in Joyce, through pastiche and parody. In *Between the Acts*, Woolf embraces—to the point of suffocation—the mock-heroic, a daring stance to take up when the nation's survival was by no means assured. Woolf was not alone, however, in looking to the comic arsenal for her weapons of choice in the (mental) battle of Britain. The provincial world seriocomically evoked in *Between the Acts* is akin to the quaint, lovingly satirized country villages that were enduring mainstays of the wartime fiction of popular comic novelists like Angela Thirkell, whose *Cheerfulness Breaks In* (1940) buoyed home front audiences with its evocation of an insular Trollopian world besieged by war shortages and an influx of children relocated from the perilous streets of London; or like E. M. Delafield, whose "diaries" of a West Country provincial lady, a national treasure in the gallery of British humor characters, gave her devoted readers a daily dose of the "ordinary English citizen's reactions to war" in *The Provincial Lady in Wartime*, reactions that oscillate between "a patriotic desire to obey all regulations" mandating blackouts and gas masks and "private inner convictions" that such regulations are a bother and a nuisance (a motif that will reverberate in more sober registers in serious wartime fiction of the period);[62] or like Stella Gibbons, author of the incomparably droll *Cold Comfort Farm*, in her wryly amusing novels of wartime love and lovemaking, *The Bachelor* and *The Matchmaker*.

The studied and intractable provincialism of these works infuses without commandeering Woolf's *Between the Acts*, a novel set in a village close enough to London to hear war planes overhead, yet far enough away to proceed with the yearly pageant meant to raise money for the local church. As conceived, produced, and directed by Miss La Trobe, or Old Bossy, as she is sometimes resentfully called behind her back, the pageant reaches beyond traditional village fare ("Gammar Gurton's Needle" was the production the preceding year) and attempts an ambitious, if ramshackle, history whose protagonist is England herself, from her birth as an isle "Sprung from the sea . . . Cut off from France and Germany" (*BA*, 77) through her multiple incarnations in Chaucerian, Elizabethan, Restoration, and Victorian times up to and including the present moment, a June day in 1939. Though the pageant is synoptic in scope, the action unfolds in a desultory and disjunctive manner reminiscent of Bowen's "series of disjected snapshots." English history is played out in the war-strained mind of the playwright and her audience as a loose assortment of "orts, scraps and fragments" rather than as a majestic sequence of cultural touchstones. Adding to this sense of disjunctiveness, the performance is constantly being interrupted both by planned gaps in the timeline and in the spoken text, and by unplanned disturbances (like war planes flying overhead). Interspersed between the more extended scenes of the pageant are fragments culled from nursery rhymes, lyric poetry, and dramatic verse that La Trobe, in a manner recalling T. S. Eliot in *The Waste Land*, shores against past and impending ruin. Still, cheerfulness breaks in with the deft comic turns on British dramatic conventions, particularly as they were elaborated in playlets, like "Where there's a Will there's a Way," evocative of the verbal glories of Shakespearean and Restoration comedy.

The audience in attendance, delighted as they are to recognize their neighbors acting various roles in the national saga of Home and Empire playing out before them, are mostly bewildered by the "game" La Trobe seems to be playing with venerable traditions. Nothing befuddles them more than the form and subject of the final act: "Present Time: Ourselves." No wonder they are unsettled, for La Trobe's last theatrical effect does more than bring the pageant up-to-date. She modernizes it by rendering present time with all the aggressive iconoclasm of the avant-garde. Present time is not represented by a person or a tableau but as the medium in which La Trobe immerses her audience, giving them no choice but to experience, in unmediated "real time," the minutes ticking remorselessly away. Presently (the pun is active in La Trobe's dramaturgy), the audience's consciousness of themselves in the present moment becomes the very stuff—as well as the entire point—of the play.

This coup de théâtre is achieved when the stage is given over to mirror bearers who, "malicious; observant; expectant; expository" (*BA*, 186), turn their glass toward the audience, showing them an unflattering and deeply disquieting image of themselves. The demeanor of the mirror bearers is indicative of the unstable mix of emotions that infuse the pageant and, indeed, a great deal of wartime writing, especially by women. The word "malicious," first in the sequence, calls special attention to itself. Few if any would dispute that artists, especially those so observant and expository in showing the form and pressure of the "present time," are perhaps bound to be read as malicious, their works deemed an insult to national character and ideals, especially when the country is at war and when maintaining civilian morale is of the utmost importance. The telltale mirrors the artist holds up to the very body and form of the time may even be seen as seditious, giving fuel, if not solace, to the enemy. But the war, rather than softening Woolf's pronounced gift for caricature, brought out a more astringent tone to her satire. The opening sequence of *Between the Acts* begins with a discussion of a cesspool and closes with a wife's revengeful fantasy prompted by the adulterous emotion circling around but excluding her: "In the car going home to the red villa in the cornfields, she would destroy it, as a thrush pecks the wings off a butterfly" (*BA*, 6). From such sullying details we take our initial sounding of the form and pressure of the very age in which the novel is written.

As if to recover, or at least disarm, this satiric malignity, the novel ends with the suggestion, fundamentally comic in form and feeling, that the estranged couple, Isa and Giles, will reconcile, and out of their reconciliation a new life might be born. They retain their recognizable character traits—she is the discontented house-wife poet who has so far failed to find the right emotion or the right rhyme to join the outer life of strife with the inner life where love struggles to survive; he is the restless hero manqué whose yearning for action is finally relieved when, between the acts of the pageant, he smashes a snake "choked with a toad in its mouth," a ghastly symbol "of birth the wrong way round—a monstrous inversion" (BA, 99). This incident is the most important thing that actually *happens* between the acts, since it alone relieves the grow-ing need to do something other than wait for bombs to fall. Giles, associated throughout the day with the stage figure of "valiant Rhoderick," the English fighting man *"Armed against fate / Bold and blatant"* (italics in original), is for once the man of the hour, even if it leaves him rather ingloriously with blood on his shoes.

The poet, whose art is painfully described as abortive, and the warrior, who, albeit symbolically, strikes out at the monstrous in-versions that proliferate during wartime, are brought together in the fertile mind of Miss La Trobe at day's end. Feeling dejected and nursing a consolatory beer, Old Bossy is "sitting arms akimbo with her glass before her" when her "floating visions" crystallize into a "high ground at midnight" against which are silhouetted "two scarcely perceptible figures." A few pages later, the place and role of the two perceptible figures are assumed by Isa and Giles, who are translated in the final sentences of the novel back to a "night before roads were made, or houses" onto "some high place among rocks" (BA, 219).

When the curtain rises on what may be the final or only one more act in the pageant of human history, we might rightly won-der whether the tableau that seems to materialize a vision that came to Miss La Trobe as she sat, dejected and solitary, nursing her beer, might represent one more hallucination. The measured, sure cadences of the final lines—"Then the curtain rose. They spoke"—suggest otherwise. No trace of hysteria or of compensatory fantasy disturbs the declarative mood of those concluding words. Contributing to this impression that vision and its fulfillment, drama and prophecy, are now indistinguishable is the narrator's brisk assurance that before Isa and Giles sleep, "they must fight; and after they had fought, they would embrace" and from that embrace "another life might be born." The mood may be conditional, but it seems fairly certain that their first words will be fighting words.

Bowen claimed that she wrote stories of wartime, not war stories. But there were women novelists, Gellhorn preeminent among them, whose fiction ignored this distinction. They often wrote novels in which war stories—its battles, its atrocities—alternated with stories of wartime recounting the travails of soldiers and civilians looking for, or trying to hold on to, love, hope, or the sheer luck that meant the difference between life and death. The three novels that formed Olivia Manning's *Levant Trilogy—The Danger Tree*, *The Battle Lost*, and *The Sum of Things*—constitute perhaps the most ambitious and sustained attempt by a woman to write stories of wartime that were also war stories.[63] The trilogy follows the fortunes of its central couple, Harriet and Guy Pringle, whose work for the British Council takes them first to Romania, then to Greece (recounted in the so-called *Balkan Trilogy*), and, when war breaks out, to the British enclaves in Egypt. Though the Pringles occupy the epicenter of the trilogy, the more involving stories revolve around those British who experience the war, as the public-spirited but emotionally distant Guy cannot, as a human disaster. If Harriet is Manning's own testament of a youth spent and wasted in war, Guy is her satire on a man whose "easy certainty" about the rightness of his actions and judgments comes from "having found that people usually did what he wanted them to do."[64]

You don't have to have the faintest idea of who Olivia Manning was or how she spent the war to grasp that Harriet is a thinly disguised version of herself. The novel is a roman à clef that can be unlocked by any determined picklock curious to discover the real-life originals of those characters who Manning depicts as having spent the war in promiscuous dalliances, adulterous liaisons, and unacknowledged homosexual longings, and, when these escapist tactics failed, killed themselves. Less sensational but more upsetting is Gellhorn's *A Stricken Field*, a novel that is a transparent firsthand account of Gellhorn's own experience as a war correspondent. The dramatic confrontation between dozens of Czech refugees and one very young Nazi soldier patrolling a recently established and completely arbitrary border is almost a verbatim transcription of an incident Gellhorn personally observed. The autobiographical dimension looms large in these works, endowing them with the emotional appeal of fictions sprung directly from history, from lived rather than imagined experience.

This is emphatically not the case with *Point of No Return*. Gellhorn, who followed the British Eighth Army in the Italian campaign, chose to write her most personal war novel about an American infantry battalion engaged on a front she had only observed for a week and even then surreptitiously, having been forbidden by the US Public Relations Office in London to report in combat zones. (Under wartime rules, a magazine was allowed only one correspondent in the war zones, and Gellhorn ranked second in hers.) Despite knowing little of the routines and collective character of the American platoon, she chose a genre very much in the American grain and one usually reserved for men who had sustained contact with a fighting unit. In her afterword she owns that she invented it all—"the men in the battalion, their daily life, their combat."[65]

The men who fight and love in this novel, then, are thoroughly imagined, independent creations rather than thinly disguised portraits of actual people. This is particularly true of the novel's protagonist, Jacob Levy, who emerged, Gellhorn tells us, fully formed in her imagination as "a good, simple, unthinking young man." From the minute she conceived him, she found him to be "so constant and so real that for an uneasy while he invaded my sleep and I thought I was dreaming his dreams not mine" (*PNR*, 328). The dreams were nightmares, the only form in which the realities of war could be rendered by a consciousness forced to witness atrocity after atrocity. Invented as it was, *Point of No Return* aimed at a historical truth that factual reporting could not render, much less embrace.

If *Point of No Return* indicates a threshold where journalism crosses over into fiction, it also marks the gender divide that Gellhorn crossed in writing the war novel she wanted—that she *needed*—to write. Not only the war but men look different on the far side of that divide. Imagined rather than directly observed, the fighting man who appeared to Origo as the most highly specialized human being she had ever encountered begins to reveal a more varied character and appearance. The opening pages of *Point of No Return* introduce us to fighting men coming from different regions of the United States and representing different ethnic, religious, and cultural traditions—a microcosm, in other words, of the America that went to war in 1941. Gellhorn is deft in individualizing these representative types through the telltale idioms, prejudices, and manners that distinguish the urban pugnacity of Sergeant Postalozzi, born and raised in Detroit (*PNR*, 19) from the easy sociability of PFC Bret Hammer, whose "expression of joyful and intimate obedience" (*PNR*, 2) in answering to his commanding officer betrays the amiable cunning of a "sensible person" who knows how to keep out of trouble or prevent it from developing.

In such quickly but sharply etched profiles, Gellhorn elaborates a complex typology of manhood enlisted in, but also transformed by, war. The most idiosyncratic and at the same time the most literary character belongs to Lieutenant Gaylord, an avid reader of pulp fiction with its "dope peddlers, gamblers, blackmail, murder: frightened platinum blondes, draped with rubies, escorted everywhere by ominous hard-faced men" (*PNR*, 32). The lurid adventures of these paperback puppets are typical of the escapist fare that offered many soldiers relief from the long stretches of boredom between battles. Pulp also offers Gaylord a model of manhood to emulate in "that infallible man, the private detective, with his mocking smile and cold wit, his chivalry, his magic appeal to women, all women, his Charvet ties, and the client's grateful gift of twenty grand that closed the case" (ibid.). Gaylord—his name is a clue to the baronial ebullience of his nature—knows that in war there are no infallible men and certainly no twenty grand awaiting soldiers on their return home. But the desperate idiom of violent action and the skewed, but genuine, chivalry that gives moral luster to that American knight-errant, the private detective, answers to the wish for outsized heroics that is denied expression in ordinary life. War finally grants that wish by providing Gaylord with the opportunity to lead a daredevil attack that costs him his life but saves the day.

These men, vivid as they are, are but satellites who orbit around their commander, Lieutenant Colonel Smithers, and his newly assigned driver, Jacob Levy. Gellhorn makes Smithers a lower-caste Southerner, a type Postalozzi derides as "anti-union slave-driving KuKluxers, at heart," although he finds Smithers himself "allright" (*PNR*, 19). Raised in a culture in which caste and race are social absolutes, Smithers smarts at the thought of belonging to a "family that went to the wrong church and didn't keep servants" (*PNR*, 8). War helps Smithers surmount ingrained prejudices and discover common interests among men whose politics and background are utterly foreign and antagonistic to each other. But Gellhorn is also alert to the limits to war's leveling and democratic alchemy. At the close of the novel, Smithers confesses that he knew Levy was a Jew but that in working with him he "forgot all about it." It is the form that his forgetting takes that exposes the anti-Semitism that is as entrenched, if not as murderous, in him as it is in the Nazis: "I don't know how many times I said to my officers that Levy was a real white man" (*PNR*, 297). Smithers's masculine and national ideal is the "real white man," a standard that obliterates even as it pretends to assimilate the Jew, the Italian, the Eastern European, all those displaced and dispossessed people for whom America promised a life of freedom but also equal dignity.

Much of the ambiguity and eventual poignancy attaching to Smithers's moral character stem from his attempts to fulfill his official role and duty as "Lieutenant Colonel John Dawson Smithers, commanding the Second Battalion, 277th Infantry, Twentieth Division, U.S. Army" (*PNR*, 24). The leader is and must appear to his men as "the certain man" whose rank and whose orders are beyond dispute. Such certainty seems to confer immunity, since Smithers enters and leaves the war—and the novel—without a scratch. Levy, who has been wounded twice, hopes Smithers's luck will rub off on him. But if he is not a lucky man, he is "a good steady man" (PNR, 29), an invaluable character to have around when nerves become frayed by days of endless waiting.

Levy's goodness and steadiness, like the colonel's certainty, will be sorely tested by the war. The first bastion of moral certitude to be battered by doubt is the idea of home. At first, the bastion seems impregnable. Home is at once the goal and the polestar for soldiers wandering from front to front, contending with bone-chilling cold, the rancid smell of fear, the stupefying boredom between battles, and the constant threat of sudden death. It is their one absolute, the value that unites them across the chasms of class or ethnicity, the differences in speech and manners that separate a man from the North from a denizen of the South, the Midwesterner from the Easterner. Wherever they come from, Levy feels sure, "This was what everyone wanted: a fine home of your own, settling down, knowing today what you would be doing tomorrow" (PNR, 124–25). War not only increases the desire for a fine home; it incites a renewed appreciation of home as an existential and moral ideal. As befits an ideal, a fine home confers on those who find and inhabit it "a sense of possession and permanence, and this belonging somewhere" (PNR, 149).

This homage to traditional ideas of home and homeland may seem unexpected coming from a woman who lived as if her home and her country were actually the whole wide world. Gellhorn may be the most restless, as she is the most battle-weary of those heroines we have called the peripatetics, always on the move and on the lookout for new territories for the mind and spirit to explore. Perhaps only a woman writer of her itinerant temperament could appreciate what home might mean to men who have passed the point where homecoming is no longer emotionally, even if it is physically, possible. Levy, who goes to war hoping only to return home alive, soon begins to feel that St. Louis, his hometown, is so far away that he can't believe it actually exists, at least for him. "Maybe it was there, as he remembered," Levy reflects with hardly a flicker of interest, "but it had nothing to do with his life" (PNR, 145). War proves the beginning of his own personal diaspora, one that takes him so far from home that he loses all desire and hope for return. The promised land that beckons him is not the home and people he left behind but a historical mirage located in some yet-to-be discovered or created place, a "dream of a new place and unknown life."

This dream, vivid and credible enough to resist the criticism of common sense, vanishes when Levy enters Dachau. It is on this grim threshold that autobiography and fiction finally align. Dachau is Levy's point of no return, just as it had been Gellhorn's, with the important difference that Levy doesn't realize that he has passed it. He thus attempts to put distance between himself and the sight and smell of a historical hell that mocks the very idea of a common humanity and an individual destiny. But the reality of Dachau permeates him, is absorbed into his flesh, and is seared into his brain: "The smell went with him, he thought he could taste it. He felt it sticky and oozing and thick, on his hands, his clothes, his hair. He would have been warned of what he was walking into, had he not thought the smell went with him" (*PNR*, 287). Earlier in the novel, Gaylord had sardonically taken note that "people had different smells the way they have different eyes," smell being as indelible an imprint of individuality as the particular color of one's eyes. Overwhelmed by his own smell, Gaylord wonders "how many smells did that make in the world?" (*PNR*, 31). The smells that make up a world, however foul, are nonetheless living smells. Gellhorn asks us to savor the democratic stink. The stink of death in Dachau has, in contrast, no distinct odor; individuality is not detectable and traceable within it. Yet its smell sickens and appalls, saturated as it is by the acrid scent of ashes, which are all that remain, except for a few gold teeth, of countless bodies who perished within its ovens.

Seeing what he has seen, and learning what he has learned in the camp, Levy finds it difficult to reenter the living city of Dachau and resume the work of bringing peace back into existence. The smell has disordered his brain, which becomes even more inflamed on returning to a world where "everyone looked healthy and occupied and cheerful." He sees a group of Germans laughing and takes directed aim at them:

> The people in the freight cars must have screamed a long time before they died. When the wind was right, the ashes from the chimney must have blown down this way. Not a mile away,

not even a mile. They knew, they didn't care, they *laughed*. Hate exploded in his brain. He felt himself sliding, slipping. It was hard to breathe. He held his fist on the horn and pressed his foot until the accelerator touched the floor. At sixty miles an hour Jacob Levy drove his jeep on to the laughing Germans. (*PNR*, 292; emphasis in original)

If after Auschwitz poetry is impossible, after Dachau, so is laughter, at least to Levy, for whom laughter in the face of so much death—death one can smell, death one can hear, death that one inhales—constitutes the supreme human offense, itself punishable by death. Levy will survive his mad and futile attack on death and those who laugh in the face of it. He even seems to regain something like a genius for living in the last pages of the novel, as he lies recuperating from injuries that go deeper than the flesh and reach his inmost heart. What restores his sanity and his will to live, as Woolf says in *Three Guineas*, "differently—differently," is the memory of his home and homeland, "the wonderful country of woods and mountains" of his patria. The last words of the novel assure us that Levy "found his hope again" (*PNR*, 325). But the hope of return is not the same as the reality of doing so. The title of the novel may have not just the first but the final word in deciding whether returning to a life of peace is, for Levy, an actual possibility.

Did Gellhorn write of a hope of return she did not share? In her 1959 introduction to *The Face of War*, a collection of fifty years of writing about war—in Spain, Finland, the various other theaters of the Second World War, Java, Vietnam, the Middle East during the Six Day War, and Latin America—Gellhorn reflects on her life as a modern Cassandra: "[W]ar was our condition and our history, the place we had to live in."[66] Gellhorn is speaking here of her time as a war correspondent in the 1930s, but it is clear from the reports from other battlegrounds that she has never outlived that condition or that history. She no longer regards war as a time to be lived through and, hopefully, survived. War has become a permanent habitation, a place we must all learn to live in. Nothing in contemporary history suggests she was wrong to think so.

But neither does anything in contemporary history suggest that she was wrong to persist in the hope that things might be different. At the conclusion of *The Face of War*, her hope takes the form of an admonition that we "always remember that we are not the servants of the state":

> As the British Attorney General said in his final speech at the Nuremberg Trial, "The State and the law are made for man that through them he may achieve a fuller life, a higher purpose and a greater dignity." The state has fallen down on its job; instead of a fuller life, that state has led man to a haunted life.
>
> There had to be a better way to run the world and we better see that we get it.[67]

It was the aim of a political vanguard of women writing between and after the two world wars to find a better way to run the world. Although they were not part of Gellhorn's nomadic federation of Cassandras, they did assume the mantle of beleaguered prophecy in agitating for political reforms that would protect and advance everyone's right to a fuller life, a higher purpose, and a greater dignity. Their writings, in which their vision of freedom and peace contended with their satires on the failures to achieve either, articulated the depth of their commitment to egalitarian ideals, ideals the realization of which in large part depended on women taking a greater part in democratic rule, in having, as Gellhorn hoped they would, a greater say in running the world.

CHAPTER 5

Politics

"IN DEMOCRACIES, EVERYONE HAS A SHARE IN EVERYTHING." The "everyone" envisioned by Aristotle as having a share in democracy extended only to the ranks of free men. Women in Athenian democracy were not accorded the rights, nor did they share in the obligations, of citizenship, whose main task, according to Aristotle, "is the preservation of the partnership that is their system of government."[1] Modern women hardly fared better, though not for lack of cogent argument and determined efforts. Neither the revolutionary outbursts that regularly convulsed nineteenth-century Europe nor the de facto egalitarianism that often prevailed among the frontier settlements resulted in women's participation in civic or national governance. It took a world war to dismantle the tenacious opposition to women's suffrage, which was extended to American women in 1919 with the passage of the Nineteenth Amendment and to Irish women with the establishment of the Irish Free State in 1922. British women over thirty were granted the vote in 1918, but did not vote in a national election until 1944.

Yet even when legally secured, the right to vote did not itself settle the issue of what or how women "shared" in the governance and preservation of democracy. The franchise offered, but could not guarantee, women the two freedoms that Aristotle identified as the primary political goods of democratic governments: "1) being ruled and ruling in turn, since everyone is equal according to number, not merit, and 2) to be able to live as one pleases."[2] Gender inevitably complicates and often forestalls the vigorous exercise of these political rights, since as little as a hundred years ago women were "ruled" with little hope, and even less experience, of ruling in turn. For modern women, female governance was a tradition more to be imagined than reclaimed.

Nonetheless, that the ruled might rule in turn and that everyone should be free to live as they pleased were principles abstract and universal enough to survive whatever restrictions were first (and still) attached to them. Such was Margaret Fuller's conviction in arguing for the political good and moral benefits of women's participation in democratic rule. In *Woman in the Nineteenth Century* Fuller examines the history of democratic ideals from the Greeks to the moderns and concludes that "[i]f principles could be established, particulars would adjust themselves aright."[3] In the fervor of her democratic hopes, Fuller surely ranks as one of the "Over Mothers"—the name Charlotte Gilman gave to the female guardians who rule in her feminist utopia, *Herland*—to succeeding generations of women writers like Tess Slesinger, Josephine Herbst, Mary McCarthy, Grace Paley, and Joan Didion, who seized the historic opportunities afforded by the franchise and an expanded voice in public life to monitor and defend democratic principles at the very time when America's political as well as economic institutions were under siege. Their fiction was the testing ground for Fuller's optimistic proposition that to establish just principles was to find ways to live by them.

For the particulars and principles of her own vision of the democratic partnership, Fuller looked not to Athens but to Sparta, whose women she commended "for being as much Spartans as the men." Spartan women impressed Fuller as models and harbingers of a civic parity we have yet to achieve: "The 'citoyen, citoyenne' of France," she proposed, "was here actualized" (54). (It certainly wasn't actualized in France, as Fuller well knew, and wouldn't be for some hundred years after Fuller wrote, when women were granted suffrage by the interim French Provisional Government in 1944.) Turning to her own times, Fuller imagined a revolutionary vanguard of ardent women she called the Exaltadas. She knew the name, taken from a Spanish political party, might invite derision but maintained that the "world would not sneer always, for from them would issue a virtue by which it would, at last, be exalted, too" (155). The virtue of the Exaltadas was potent and contagious enough, Fuller believed, to lay the moral groundwork for the social transformations to come. "I have in my eye a youth and a maiden," she wrote, "whom I look to as the nucleus of such a class":

> They are both in early youth; both as yet uncontaminated, both aspiring, without rashness; both thoughtful; both capable of deep affection; both of strong nature and sweet feelings; both capable of large mental development. To them I look, as, perhaps, the harbingers and leaders of a new era, for never yet have I known minds so truly virginal, without narrowness or ignorance. (ibid.)

Fuller, a friend of Emerson's, was arguably a more ardent transcendentalist in prophesying a "new age of Man" whose most notable feature would be a greater role for women in national life. The Exaltadas she envisioned would constitute not only a new political class but a new order of sovereign beings impelled as much by feeling as by ideology and endowed with an innocence that Fuller takes care to distinguish from "narrowness and ignorance."

Fuller is poised here on the brink of myth, and part of her originality as a political prophet lies in her audacity in crossing that threshold. Although she contrasted her own imagination to the Greeks, "who saw everything in forms, which we are trying to ascertain as law, and classify as cause" (105), her own power as a polemicist owes as much to her visionary descriptions of an emancipated society as to her closely reasoned arguments for giving women equal opportunity and adequate scope for self-development. She was eager to discover and ready to devise emblematic figures to body forth the laws she ascertained as first causes. Thus, to illustrate the fundamental principle that "Union is only possible to those who are units"—a principle that applies to political as much as marital unions—she invokes an Indian legend of a woman who dreamed she was betrothed to the Sun and "built her [sic] a wigwam apart, filled it with emblems of her alliance, and means of an independent life" (101).

Yet even in her exultant moods, Fuller recognized that the "calm equality" she attributed to the women of Sparta in "sharing the ideal life of their nation" would be harder to secure and maintain for modern women, whose lives "must be outwardly a well-intentioned, cheerful dissimulation of her real life" (159). This continual effort to dissimulate a cheerfulness one does not feel was the secret cause of the "crisis" in the life of women (121). A century later, Betty Friedan would see the same silent crisis transmogrified into the more sinister, because unacknowledged, "problem with no name" that afflicted generations of women in private but wholesale subjection to the Feminine Mystique. Fuller, convinced that history would yield to the ardent efforts of Exaltadas like herself, could not foresee, much less imagine, how this rival ideology of feminine subservience would insinuate and entrench itself into the consumerist culture of the postwar era, a time when freedom of choice for women often reduced itself to the confines of a shopping list. She had hoped that her Exaltadas would usher in a new egalitarian, democratic culture that would promote and protect "the perfect of each being in its kind—apple as apple, Woman as Woman." With the dawn of that new era, women might aspire and indeed expect to live a life that would "be a beautiful, powerful, in a word a complete life in its kind" (177).

For Fuller, as for Friedan more than a century later, the rights of women fundamentally entailed a right to life on one's own terms, a life dedicated as much to self-fulfillment as to the care of another person (husband, child) or to meeting the demands of an ideological but very real entity (the family, the nation, the race). This certainly qualifies as among the most generous, as it may be the most unrealizable construction put upon the democratic freedom to live as one pleases, in accordance with one's own nature. The problem for democracies has always been the problem of reconciling the rights of the individual with the will of the majority, the personal with the collective good. For women, this is the problem behind the problem with no name. It is a problem that seldom admits of happy solutions, since women traditionally have been socialized to put the general good above their personal inclinations and desires.

At no time did the problem seem more intractable than in the thirties, when democratic societies were being tested by economic and social disorder from within and threatened by totalitarian aggressors without. The foremost women writers of political fiction in the twentieth century—Tess Slesinger, Josephine Herbst in her Trexler family saga, Mary McCarthy, and Joan Didion—were not as sanguine as Fuller about the future of democratic ideals. They questioned how or even whether to preserve democratic institutions increasingly discredited by crippling unemployment, unconscionable disparities in income and opportunity, and alarming concentrations of power in the hands of the well-provided and self-interested few. All but Didion embraced communist or socialist platforms for radical reform with varying degrees of enthusiasm and firmness: Herbst never wavered in her dogged loyalty to Stalinism; Slesinger lampooned but never abandoned the progressive politics of an urban intellectual vanguard whose small numbers betrayed their large ambitions to right the wrongs that seemed to multiply daily around them; McCarthy's initially accidental, then increasingly vehement and informed, allegiance to Trotskyism and anti-Stalinist politics was tempered by an intractably skeptical intelligence quick to detect and call out casuistry and outright hypocrisy wherever they showed themselves—in the marketplace of ideas and in public debates but also within the quieter forum of her own conscience. Didion insists that her beliefs "are a logical product of a childhood largely spent among conservative California Republicans (this before the meaning of 'conservative' changed) in a postwar boom economy."[4] In accord with this upbringing, she was an ardent supporter of Barry Goldwater in the 1964 presidential election. After the Republicans "jettisoned an authentic conservative (Goldwater) and were rushing to embrace Ronald Reagan," she became the first member of her family to register as a Democrat, only to make the "novel discovery" that the shift in party affiliation "did not involve taking a markedly different view on any issue" (ibid.). Out of this realization would issue her excoriating dissections of the American political establishment.

Like their male counterparts, these "committed" women writers who came of age under the shadow of totalitarianism were faced with the urgent task of devising literary forms that would not just indict but reimagine the existing social forms of a democracy that had lost, it seemed, the instinct and habit of sharing. Indeed, they probed the viability of the very concept of sharing at a moment when there seemed less and less to go around. These writers didn't dispute the moral value of communitarian principles, but unlike most of their male counterparts, they refused to suppress or even subordinate their consciousness of the gender inequities that riddled even the most egalitarian political creeds. They dissented from radical solutions that demanded women relinquish their hopes for a personal life, an abiding and fulfilling love, a child as well as a job. In the political fictions of Slesinger, McCarthy, and Didion, we encounter radical heroines increasingly divided between their own impulses to give what was asked of them and to keep something for themselves, to live, that is, as they pleased and, like Fuller's woman betrothed to the Sun, be ultimately answerable to no one but themselves.

Another image—that of a working woman with a pencil in her hair—offers a modern counterpart to Fuller's ideal of a free and utterly self-reliant woman. The image appears in Slesinger's *The Unpossessed*, a work Lionel Trilling proclaimed the first "novel of the thirties" to deal with the American radical intellectual class "in an effort of realism."[5] That effort of realism was bound to falter when it came up against, as it invariably did, Slesinger's satiric intelligence. We can see that intelligence at work deconstructing the ideologically bright image of a modern woman very much "at home" at her job, her implement close at hand, lodged in a nest of hair that displays while pleasantly disarranging the tokens of traditional femininity. Slesinger, who was unfailingly alert to the ways the radical intellectual vanguard professed one thing and secretly felt another, brings out depths of feeling, most of them sour, in delineating an emerging social type rapidly becoming familiar in offices where money and policies were being made.

As etched with a bitter knowingness by the novel's central female protagonist, Margaret (Meg) Flinders, a lightly veiled portrait of Slesinger herself, the girl with a pencil in her hair becomes a kind of affrighted and frightening gargoyle, drained of whatever personal charm she might originally have possessed.

> [W]e are sterile; we are too horribly girlish for our age, too mannish (with our cigarettes, our jobs, our drying lips) for our

sex. . . . Was this what my mother meant for me, sending me off to college, a book of Ibsen under my eager arm? O Economic-Independence Votes-for-Women Sex-Equality! you've relieved us of our screens and our embroidery hoops, our babies and our vertigo; and given us—a cigarette; a pencil in our hair.[6]

Although this diatribe is spoken by "Margaret Flinders to Margaret Banner-that-was," it is not ultimately clear who this "silent scream" is directed *against*—the feminist Over Mothers who fought for their daughters' rights and freedoms or herself for believing that sex equality in the marketplace and at the polls would leave her free to live her life in her own way. Meg's unvoiced rage, composed of equal parts chagrin and resentment, distorts her normally cheery countenance, giving her the look of a "cheated Madonna" (*U*, 94). The New Woman here confronts her aggrieved progenitor and doppelgänger, the dethroned Madonna or deposed Over Mother who has no place or role in the brave new world of comrades. The tradition of exalted Motherhood hangs like a pall over the world of *The Unpossessed*, intensifying the fetid atmosphere that pervades the hothouse world of radical reformers the novel depicts. Beneath all the talk and active, if largely futile, efforts to initiate sweeping political reform runs an unvoiced, disquieting question about the role of women in the postrevolutionary world: Who will have the babies? This question inevitably provokes another: Does putting this concern at the heart of her narrative make *The Unpossessed* a satire or an example of a higher feminine realism?

To frame the question this way is to absolve Slesinger from any latter-day charges that she was a reactionary Total Woman avant le lettre, the ungrateful and resentful child of feminist Over Mothers who had sent her into the world equipped with Ibsen and all the other standard baggage of doctrinaire feminism but otherwise unprepared for the realities that would confront her. On the contrary. No one was more prepared to assume the mantle of a twentieth-century Exaltada or to fulfill the bright social hopes held out to young women of her generation. Raised by a freethinking, enterprising mother who trained as a lay analyst with Karen

Horney and Erich Fromm and helped found the New School for Social Research, educated in the progressive enclaves of the Ethical Culture School and Swarthmore College, Slesinger was very much at home in the radical milieu of New York Jewish intellectuals. She began her career as a writer for the *Menorah* journal, a radical Jewish magazine whose editor, contributors, and politics are lightly disguised, some might say caricatured, in *The Unpossessed*. Even when she moved to Hollywood, she remained politically active until her death in 1945 at the age of thirty-nine. Although she never joined the Communist Party, she was a signatory to the letter denouncing the Dewey Commission's investigation into the Moscow trials, supported the Scottsboro Boys, the Abraham Lincoln Brigade in the Spanish Civil War, and the Hollywood Anti-Nazi League, a communist front organization that until the Stalin-Hitler Pact was closely allied with the Screen Writers Guild. A member of the executive board of the Motion Picture Guild, which promoted "the production of liberal and progressive films,"[7] Slesinger fought against the studio moguls who, through intimidation and company edicts forbidding fraternization, tried to block "white-collar" industry workers from unionizing. Her testimony in the 1937 hearings, held by the newly established National Labor Relations Board, helped secure the guild their rights to collective bargaining, which in 1941 resulted in the first industry-wide contract for writers.

A woman of such broad, bicoastal, and yet blinkered experience of democratic politics may have clung to certain political tenets, but never for a moment did she write as if the utopia promised to women upon achieving sex equality, economic independence, and moral freedom—a kind of Herland with men—was anywhere on the horizon. This understanding of how gender complicates the politics of vision is more apparent in her novel. Her penchant for satire was muted in her screenplays, as evidenced by her reverent adaptations of Pearl Buck's *The Good Earth*, a kind of peasant epic of a rural Chinese family in prerevolutionary China, and Betty Smith's *A Tree Grows in Brooklyn*, a proletarian female bildungsroman set in pre–World War I Brooklyn (the tree that grows there is native to China and Taiwan, an apt symbol for emigrant efforts to establish roots in new cultural soil). These works, which celebrated the resilience and unvanquished optimism of the dispossessed of the world, resonated with democratic audiences struggling to keep their families, homes, values, and lives more or less intact. It was only in some of her more routine assignments that Slesinger indulged her sardonic wit, most notably in an intriguingly busy comedy, *Are Husbands Necessary?*, which centers, as *The Unpossessed* does, on a couple who are deciding whether or not to have a child. The film ends with the announcement, the novel with the termination, of the wife's pregnancy.

The Unpossessed, which Slesinger dedicates to "her contemporaries," began as a barely fictionalized short story about the abortion Slesinger had. The abortion marked the end of her marriage and, as a consequence, her affiliation with the Menorah circle, where her ex-husband, Henry Solow, served as assistant editor and whose other members included such future luminaries as Lionel Trilling, Diana Trilling, Clifton Fadiman, and, on the periphery, Sidney Hook and Max Eastman. In expanding a private sketch of a marriage into a group portrait of New York Jewish intellectuals, Slesinger foregrounded the precariousness not just of modern marriage but of any form of democratic partnership at a time when sharing—food, employment, power—was neither easy nor especially common. The novel's title suggests that her contemporaries experienced life under these conditions as a catastrophic series of deprivations. The word "unpossessed" itself verges on faulty diction, indicative, perhaps, of the felt need for new idioms to voice the widespread depredations of the times. Trilling sees it as a conscious echo of Dostoevsky's *The Possessed* (Slesinger would not have known its later, more faithful translation as *The Devils*), and contends that Slesinger wanted to recuperate the positive sense of "being possessed" as entailing "an accession of vital energy in the service of some great personal vital intention."[8] If this is so, the meaning is only recuperated through its negation, for it is hard to see any such positive and active intention at work in a political group "whose common factors . . . are negatives, rebuttals, refutations" (*U*, 85).

The intellectuals bound together in common cause against existing social arrangements and, as it turns out, floundering amid the miserable state of their personal lives, are Meg and her husband Miles, a puritanical soul who cannot believe in salvation except through pain, a legacy of the brutal floggings he endured as a child; Jeffrey, a successful, sexually adventurous novelist, and his placid wife, Norah, who winks at his infidelities; Elizabeth, the novel's most au courant version of the New Woman who tracks the latest artistic or social trend to its epicenter in Paris before returning to New York in hopes of entering a relationship with Bruno, the charismatic, eloquent, and noxiously self-hating leader of this motley band of radical reformers busily working, or pretending to work, toward a revolution few of them actually believe possible. Bruno rallies but also derides his Marxist flock adrift in troubles, many of their own making, by reminding them of their status as "bastards, foundlings, phonys, the unpossessed and unpossessing of the world, the real minority" (*U*, 327). The title word "unpossessed" figures so prominently and strategically in this catalog of "outcasts, miscasts and professional expatriates" that we might take Bruno's view to be Slesinger's own, were it not the rhetorical hiccup of that wiseacre word "phonys," which makes one wonder if this is a self-appraisal of an honest man confessing his inauthenticity or of a congenitally phony one pretending to be honest. This is one example of how Slesinger's effort of realism runs afoul of her satiric skill in dissecting the contemporary situation in all its morally ambiguous particulars.

Even the group's "vital intention" to start a little magazine is caricatured as a petulant rather than principled expression of their political will. "Why Can't We Have a Magazine?" is the title of the chapter that introduces the project that promises to unite the unpossessed in a common purpose. The magazine is envisioned as the child of their collective labors, a cherished possession that belongs to all of them. Reviewing the novel, Elizabeth Hardwick was less generous but more accurate in describing the magazine as an "instrument of arcane propaganda and personal identity for the band of pinkos."[9] Whether considered an instrument of timely political intervention or a vehicle for arcane propaganda, the magazine provides the otherwise floundering band of pinkos a concrete objective. It is precisely in this guise that Meg silently contests it, countering the question posed at the head of the chapter with another within it: "*Norah, why don't we have children?*," a question italicized to ensure that we attend to it. Even though Meg doesn't have the courage to utter it aloud, that question, "battling its way through her pounding temples," is clear and direct enough to "[clear] the air of confusion and wrong" (*U*, 93).

The confusion and wrong are private, but they are rooted in the public disorder of the times. The economic harm inflicted by a disintegrating economy and ineffective, when not corrupt, political institutions is not limited to the unemployment line but extends to personal relationships that are blighted, like that of Meg and Miles, or that are unconsummated, like Elizabeth and Bruno's. These unhappy marital and sexual pairings deepen the novel's sense of what it means to be unpossessed of mutually beneficial personal relationships. The word "possession" first appears in the novel in connection with Jeffrey's hands after his bungled sexual embrace of Meg while their respective spouses chatter amiably on the other side of a closed kitchen door. Once the "shameful" groping has reached its quick and unsatisfying end, Jeffrey's hands are "back in his possession again"; he then proceeds to rub "them one against the other as though he washed them and forgave them." Neither Jeffrey nor Meg can escape the shame incurred by their sexual fakery, which leaves them "both embarrassed like a pair of tired actors wishing the curtain would fall on a play they knew was rotten" (*U*, 69). The title interprets this exhaustion as a deprivation, a fatal depletion of the will to futurity. The play is rotten, but even if the curtain falls on it, there is no promise or even evidence that it will rise again on a new act with a better scenario.

The poignant symbol of this deprivation is the empty womb. The choice between a magazine and baby does not require a Solomon to adjudicate, not because the "right" choice is morally self-evident, but because it is not. For Slesinger's contemporaries, for whom these choices were becoming increasingly common, the choice will be decided differently according to which gods one serves—the new god of economics or the ancestral God who enjoined humankind to increase and multiply. Even though Meg submits to her husband's god, she harbors heretical thoughts: "Giving up a baby for economic freedom which meant that two of them would work in offices instead of one of them only, giving up a baby for intellectual freedom which meant that they smoked their cigarettes and looked out of the windows of a taxi onto street and people and stores and hated them all" (*U*, 345). In her unvoiced dissent, Meg is protesting against an economic independence and intellectual freedom that will leave her childless while filling her with social hatred. She is also demanding a more equitable share in the democratic partnership, one that would honor women's sense of what freedom, indeed, what life is *for*. The right to bear children is one way to define that freedom, as the most cursory history of the ongoing political battle over women's reproductive rights reminds us.

Without the prospect of children, the traditional relation between women and home comes under profound pressure for revision. By turns questioned, ideologically refurbished, desecrated, but never fully abandoned, Home is the "X" in the new social equation being worked out in the distressed democracies of the thirties and forties. *The Unpossessed* assigns new values to the idea of home according to its location—in this novel one can find, or at least feel, at home in an office or a coffee shop—but more often according to its emotional decor. The home of the wealthy Middletons, precursors to the Radical Chic socialites of the sixties, is turned into a public circus offering lavish entertainment to publicize the plight of the starving poor. By contrast, Meg's home is the scene of intimate emotional devastation. The novel begins with Meg returning home with provisions to nourish and comfort her husband, wounded in his ongoing battle with the world. It ends with her returning home from the Maternity Hospital with a basket of fruit, rather than a baby, in her arms.

These searing depictions of home mark a historic turn—indeed a radical deviation—in the dialectic of home and world that propelled women forward while keeping them anchored in certain life-sustaining values, customs, and relationships. That dialectic seemed in danger of coming to an abrupt halt on the threshold of a revolutionary transformation in social relations in which comrade would supplant husband and an identification with a "larger and deeper fraternity" (*U*, 7) supersede traditional allegiances to the nuclear family. Poor Elizabeth, who has purchased a ticket on what she calls the Fast Express, hurtling toward a world where all traditional values are either inverted or eliminated, takes little pride and even less comfort in her up-to-dateness: "Home is where you hang your hat and drop your skirt, my dear by the time I'm thirty I'll be at home anywhere in this cock-eyed world, I speak the universal language, the twentieth century snappy dead language, of no-love loving, of lust without love, I belong anywhere and nowhere (self-pity is the lowest form of wit), a gal without a country—a ship without a port" (*U*, 129). The peripatetics who traveled to unknown countries or into the outlands of the American frontier aimed to create a new home for themselves. Their daughters are wanderers who are at home anywhere and nowhere, spiritual vagabonds with no prospect of setting down roots.

If Meg, not the au courant Elizabeth, is the one who can still hope for a home and a country—a *patria*—of her own, it is because, as her husband realizes, she has "the intelligence only of a homing bird." That "only" is meant to be disparaging, but it is the judgment of a man who "implacably" puts a sign in block letters above his desk "announcing him 'Not at Home' to life" (*U*, 351). Meg's intelligence proves much more capacious and exalted than her husband allows or will admit, as attested in her vision of conjugal partnership, which is delineated with all the rhetorical grandeur of an epic simile:

> As when a thousand people gather in a square, an enigma called "mob" is born, so two people cannot live together without giving birth to a third entity, at once a part of themselves and greater than the whole. This entity, so Margaret thought, was a thing to be reckoned with, wooed, its presence constituting the aura in which lovers must live. They are never alone. This thing that is born of their being together is a censor, a chaperon, made of their separate consciousnesses meeting, not quite merging, wavering in a pattern they never can see, which nevertheless (dancing on the bathroom walls, the ceiling over their bed at night) dominates their life together. Ignored, it stretches forth an icy hand and claws their joy to death. Wooed, it hovers like a blessing on their heads. (*U*, 178–79)

In making such solemn pronouncements, Meg sounds less like a girl with a pencil in her hair than a high priestess declaiming the terms of salvation. She thereby may take her place among the modern Exaltadas, prophesying the terms of a more hallowed sexual, but also decidedly political, dispensation in which the Whole is greater than its parts. Meg's vision of people united by a love that is at once part of and greater than themselves possesses for her the reality of a natural law to which societies, like individuals, must submit if they are to prosper. Without this shared and exalted love, the greater and patterned whole of which they form a part and which they in turn create becomes accursed. The simile suggests that the curse may take the form of a mob, the specter that haunts democratic rule.

Bruno, Meg's intellectual counterpart but temperamental antitype, offers a different vision of the relation between the one and the many. If Meg sees herself as the girl with the pencil in her hair and an empty lap where a child should be cradled, Bruno sees and presents himself as an "all-purpose one-man three-ring self-kidding self-perpetuating exhibitionist circus divided, like all of Gaul into partes tres. One part sour grapes, one part wish-fulfillment, nine parts subconscious" (U, 75). Observing the unmerry band of pinkos who surround and empower him, Bruno

> saw them, each in his separate groove, traversing parallels in an endless treadmill; a chorus composed entirely of temperamental first violins. Their energies combined would make terrific force, a powerful and vital symphony; but they seemed each to prefer being first violin in a small puddle to throwing in his lot with the common orchestra. So the strength of each, turned inward on himself, bored like a cancer in the tortured brain; his music, bursting and swelling, remained milling and unexpressed in his own private head. (U, 85)

The magazine represents Bruno's attempt to externalize this symphony, a symbol, steeped in nostalgia, of his youthful faith in the notion of a "heroic whole" (U, 163).

Such a conception would give continuity as well as nobility to the vibrant, diversified social formations of democratic culture.

Of German Jewish descent, Bruno may subconsciously be deriving his symbol for a vital collective intention from Walter Ruttmann's *Berlin: Symphony of a Great City* or from other city symphony films like Paul Strand's *Manhatta* (also *New York the Magnificent*), an early prototype of the form, or Dziga Vertov's *Man with a Movie Camera* and Alberto Cavalcanti's *Rien que les heures*, all of which offered dynamic images of the city as a field of energy, innovation, industry, and play that belonged to everyone and that everyone belonged to in turn. These were avant-gardist works whose innovative cinematic techniques—dissolves, superimpositions, double exposure, and nonnaturalistic editing—gave modern city-dwellers a new visual understanding of the whole of which they formed a vital part. But even in a "realist" Hollywood film like Gregory La Cava's *Symphony of Six Million* (1932), the story of a young doctor who rises above and abandons his lower-class community to minister to hypochondriacal Park Avenue matrons, the people are the source and symbol of all genuine personal and social happiness.

The richly polyphonic form of the symphony film and what we might call the symphony novel, of which *The Unpossessed*, along with John Dos Passos's multivoiced, multigeneric *U.S.A.* are the richest examples, are models of how a democratic society might become better attuned to the contending but also converging voices, needs, enterprises, and energies active within it. In the novel, Jeffrey recalls that the philosopher George Santayana "reduced everything to a common denominator, to different numbers of atoms floating democratically—all of equal importance—in the general life stream" (*U*, 145). Democracy so envisioned reduces everyone to atomistic integers, each of equal standing but none of special significance or importance. This is what Aristotle meant when he observed that democracy treats everyone equally according to number (the democratic unit) rather than merit. Bruno's conception of the society as a symphony is not only anti-atomistic, but anti-narcissistic, enlisting the separate orchestral instruments that, left to their own devices and impulses, would turn inward. In extolling the symphony's "concerted rhythm" (*U*, 262) as a model of a transfiguring social harmony, Slesinger is pledging her allegiance to the tradition of Fuller's idealistic Exaltadas rather than Santayana's pragmatists.

This vision of the heroic whole, undercut but never ridiculed by Slesinger's satire, triumphs in the longest chapter in the novel, "The Party," a fund-raising event for Hunger Marchers, where guests and donors can feast on food ostentatiously arrayed on a "Brobdingnagian refectory table" that creaks under the weight of "six whole Virginia hams, two sliced turkeys, six plates of devilled eggs, sturgeon and salmon, a tray designed in canapés, of caviar, cheese, and anchovies, bowls of olives . . . and so on" (U, 246). To those who give and attend it, the party is a carnivalesque entertainment in which classes and races, Jews and Gentiles, who normally keep to themselves, mingle democratically, albeit without any particular understanding or liking of each other. As a doctor who has come to contribute his money and his opinions observes, the party is society "psychoanalyzed, all the cross sections exposed as in a tree" (U, 252).

And as in psychoanalysis, all depends on the talk. In this respect, "The Party" is a marvel of diagnostic orchestration. Narration yields to an onrush of talk, spoken confidences, and asides uttered by a succession of voices, some of them nameless, many of them minor, each with their own contribution to make. People come and go, drifting in and out of conversations, pausing only to listen to Bruno's toast to the hostess and the assembled party-goers, in which he mockingly extols them as sponsors of "sublimation, constipation, procrastination, masturbation, prevarication, adumbration, equivocation, prestidigitation, moral turpitude, split personalities and rape; pornography, salacity, apostasy, hypocrisy, erotica, neurotica—in plain words, fellow-victims, anything that's phony or a fake" (U, 326).

This is witty, but as Bruno knows all too well, "nasty wit . . . is the opiate of the intellectual," just as, according to Elizabeth, self-pity is the lowest form of wit. Slesinger recognizes the need for a profound counterirritant to her own acrid satire, which can have a narcotic effect in numbing us to the appeal of genuine emotion or the possibility of actual change. She locates this antidote in the consciousness of Elizabeth, a portrait, perhaps, of Slesinger herself as a young and too easily disillusioned young woman. In the midst of the party, Elizabeth comes to the sudden realization that her drawing "which started each time large and fine," was ultimately defiled because "she never let go until she had spoiled it, apparently without volition, by some comic touch." The party may be society psychoanalyzed, but Elizabeth is the artistic psyche psychoanalyzed. This is how Elizabeth ultimately understands her own proclivity to court failure, to live without hope of love or home, and to disguise the feeling of unpossession that inevitably attends misdirected or inappropriate laughter:

> Success perhaps was insupportable; somewhere along the line she must, she felt, have missed out badly and forever after would take no substitutes. And so she ran away or laughed accidentally at the wrong moments or stopped her ears with a roar when some truth battered for entrance; and so she would go on until she had laid the ghost of what she missed, or found the magic number; or else she would come face to face one day with the main issue, in some narrow passage, where she could not turn aside or make a joke. (*U*, 310–11)

Political fiction at its best leads us to reassess the very terms of our social pacts. It conducts us through the corridors of satire or those of melodrama, which inevitably intersect and conjoin in that narrow passage where we come face-to-face with what Slesinger unflinchingly identifies as "the main issue." Satire was, for Slesinger, the hardest and truest effort at realism, since only satire could expose the main issue without any of the euphemisms, alibis, and casuistry designed to hide political "truth" from public view. But she also understood that once she had stripped the main issue of all the platitudes and pieties that obscured it, she could no longer turn aside or make a joke. The truth battering for entrance *would* be admitted. The women who wrote in her wake and within her tradition often found themselves facing the same predicament.

No writer opened the door more widely to unattractive, distressing truth than Mary McCarthy, a writer who seemed to relish the unseemliness of reality and of her own indiscreet pursuit of it. Was any social satirist as merciless to herself as she was to her targeted subjects in *The Company She Keeps* and *A Charmed Life*, the first of which shows her heroine and alter ego scrambling on the floor of a Pullman compartment to retrieve her stockings—and her dignity—after a night of fumbling sex with a man she doesn't find the least bit attractive or, in the latter, drunkenly succumbing to the advances of an imperious ex-husband (based in part, the least flattering and most alarming part, of Edmund Wilson) and becoming pregnant by him just at the moment when she hoped to salvage her current marriage to a more reliably loving man?

It was McCarthy who first naturalized the Exaltada as a modern woman whose increased freedoms of association, movement, and sexual activity marked a new stage in the enfranchisement of women and her greater and more vocal involvement in public life. As with all leaps forward, there was bound to be some backsliding and scrambling for a foothold along the way, not to mention the unforeseen difficulties in finding and, once found, in standing one's ground. So it is with *The Company She Keeps*, which chronicles the uneven but unstoppable development of a young woman testing her values, her judgment, and her own talent for astute, hence generally unwelcome, social and political observation, as she ventures from suburbia to the commercial and social hubs of New York, from the conjugal bed to the psychiatrist's couch, and from bourgeois respectability to an unorthodox socialism devoted to "literature and the Fourth International."[10]

The vagaries of mood and fortune that define the modern Exaltada are given stability and dignity in an image of self-secure womanhood that the novel's heroine clings to like a lodestar. This image appears almost epiphanically amid a "torrent of explicitness" that courses through the most famous, and certainly the most scandalous, story McCarthy wrote, "The Man in the Brooks Brothers Shirt." Meg Sargent, the protagonist of the story, finds herself pretentiously quoting poetry to her compartment mate on a train heading east. She finds the man's porcine looks and social background faintly repugnant, yet through a kind of reflected narcissism, he attracts her as a "connoisseur of women" who "from his divine position at the center of things where choice is unlimited" has "chosen *her*" (*CSK*, 87; emphasis in original). In the banter that tests the sources and limits of this attraction, she reveals, against her better judgment, that her favorite line of poetry is spoken by Chaucer's Criseyde: "I am myn owene woman, wel at ese" (*CSK*, 81).

Criseyde's assertion is made not as a boast but as a statement of fact. She is a woman who simply (simply!) knows her own worth. Fuller's Exaltada or the disheveled girl with a pencil in her hair may have lost their original luster over time, but, like Shakespeare's Cleopatra, Chaucer's Criseyde resists the depredations of age and custom. The self-possession Fuller extolled in her Exaltada is an aspect of Criseyde's character that requires no extraordinary moral exertion to achieve; and in her moments of distraction the girl with the pencil in her hair may be dreaming that she might one day feel as "wel at ese" as her sister some five hundred years before. In her moral poise, Chaucer's Criseyde hovers over *The Company She Keeps* as an ego ideal, the goal of Meg's quest for self-sovereignty.

The man in the Brooks Brothers shirt—so branded, apparently, because he is *not* his "owene man"—looks at Meg in "bald admiration," and once he understands the full import of the Middle English, exclaims: "Golly, you are, at that!" (*CSK*, 81). That "Golly" should alert us that what he admires is probably a figment of his sex-addled imagination, one of those overestimations of the coveted object typical of infatuation, especially midlife infatuation, that obscures judgment almost in exact proportion as it recharges libido. For Meg is hardly "at ese" with herself and with the "absurd, ugly love story" in which she has allowed herself to become enmeshed. Not only enmeshed but weirdly spellbound, as if fascinated by the spectacle she is making of herself. She is chagrined but also pleasantly astonished to feel herself overwhelmed by a "sense of guilt, of social responsibility, of primitive awe . . . watching and listening, waiting to be ground to bits" (*CSK*, 91). However inevitable—and masochistically gratifying—she might find the spectacle of her own moral dismemberment, such moments of self-dramatization hardly comport with the notion of a woman "wel at ese."

McCarthy, who at times seems almost vindictive in calculating the moral and psychological distance that separates her heroine from Criseyde's self-possession, shows an unaccustomed tenderness toward her heroine's plight in the foreword to the novel, where she notes that Meg is "fumbling in her spiritual pocketbook for a missing object, for the ordinary, indispensable self that has somehow got mislaid" (*CSK*, 14). The ordinary, indispensable self is still mislaid in *A Charmed Life*, a novel that literally revolves around the painting, meaning, and possession of a portrait of the female protagonist, the most self-sabotaging and doomed of McCarthy's fictional alter egos. Martha, the subject of this contested portrait, may see herself as an absolutist who aspires to "be a paragon uniting all the virtues," but her portrait, in which her face is "refracted all over the canvas," creates the impression that "her personality-nucleus was blown apart into its component solids."[11] McCarthy seems to exult in the sheer force and virtuosity of her own analytic cubism—what she terms "explosive cubism," as if to underscore that her cubism will have only a disintegrative, not a reintegrative or synthetic phase.

Were such fierce assaults on her own personality-nucleus heroic in their candor? Or were they misguided salvos against everything she disliked about herself and condemned in others, as Randall Jarrell suggested when, in *Pictures from an Institution*, he caricatured her as a novelist of superior intelligence but inferior humanity who "had not yet arrived even at that elementary forbearance upon which human society is based"?[12] McCarthy was aware and seemed to worry about this trait in herself, especially when it took the form of a "compulsive didacticism" so vigilant that "no cliché, no ineffectual joke could pass the rigidity of her censorship" (*CSK*, 14). But she did not let that worry deter her from stating truths in danger of being defaced by cliché or deflected by defensive and ultimately lame jokes. The central truth she needed to confront was that of her own moral character; she was relentless in exploring whether she was a paragon or a wanton parody of free democratic womanhood, a question she hoped to decide in "The Man in the Brooks Brothers Shirt," a story Saul Bellow dismissed as bullshit, but which Norman Mailer admired, so awed was he by McCarthy's willingness, as he put it, to let herself be found out.[13]

Found out, but only in segments or one facet at a time; she never outs herself all at once. Meg's moral and political education, for instance, does not follow the well-laid tracks of the classic bildungsroman but is fitful and anecdotal. Her self-development is tracked across a series of discrete, loosely continuous stories, each of which isolates her relationships, most of them brief, with men who nudge her forward toward an enlarged and increasingly forbearing knowledge of herself and of the world. Among the most notable of these tutelary and invariably monitory figures are: Mr. Sheer, whose name abets him in deceiving his clients about the value and provenance of the artistic wares he cheerfully hawks in his "Rogue's Gallery" (in which he is the prime exhibit); the man in the Brooks Brothers shirt to whom she drunkenly, but not unwillingly, submits, partly because she discerns behind the regulation dress and bromides of his trade a survival of the "omnivorous" businessmen of the "Golden Age of American imperialism" who had been "great readers, eaters, travellers, collectors . . . small-town men newly admitted into world-citizenship, faintly uneasy but feeling their oats" (*CSK*, 75); her editor at a left-wing journal, Jim Barnett, a socially and economically well-situated Yale man "who came to socialism freely, from the happy center of things" and who recognizes and reverences in himself an "intelligent mediocrity" that makes him the perfect incarnation of "the Average Thinking Man to whom in the end all appeals are addressed" (*CSK*, 127). She gleans from these workmates and bedmates a knowledge of how business works, how public opinion is formed, and how power operates, a knowledge that makes her more credible—and affecting—as a modern woman newly admitted to the polling booth and to world citizenship.

Meg's erratic but ongoing education, which prompts her to recalibrate her moral view of herself and of the world, the wrongs of which she hopes to amend, is reflected in the different grammatical positions she occupies vis-à-vis the narrator: "the intimate she and the affectionate diminutive you, the thin, abstract autobiographical I." McCarthy says, "If the reader is moved to ask: 'Can all this be the same person?' why, that is the question both the heroine and the author are up against. For the search is not conclusive: there is no deciding which of these personalities is the 'real' one: the home address of the self, like that of the soul, is not to be found in a book" (*CSK*, 7). One might reasonably ask where the home address of the self and the soul is to be found, if not in the book where their existence is posited. It is a question that will continue to plague women novelists, especially those who, as one century ends and another begins, will chronicle the inconclusive searches of a new generation of heroines in political and existential transit—those we have given the name of multinationals, since their quest for a "home address of the self" takes them beyond their native lands. These heroines, like Meg, also find that they have somehow mislaid the essential self somewhere in the passage from the old world to the new, from traditional to modern societies, from natives at home in their patria to uneasy, often displaced citizens of the world. Yet even if the self has no permanent home address for Meg and her multinational descendants, traces of its "real" existence can be located and recovered by tracing its passage from the place and ranks of the unpossessed to the place, yet to be discovered, where they can feel "wel at ese."

To find a home address where Meg might be "wel at ese" would require not just a change of place but a change of heart. It would require, that is, something on the order of a conversion. Whatever democratic hopes McCarthy's fiction entertains are pinned on the prospects for spiritual rather than political transformation. When McCarthy entered the public realm of vigorous political commentary, protest, and debate, she brought with her the intellectual ballast of a classical education and schooling in Catholic dogma that she, like Joyce's Stephen Dedalus, rejected but whose moral coherence she could respect. These traditions intermingle in one of Meg's more intriguing demonstrations of compulsive didacticism. Her tutee is also her analyst, to whom she is more prone to relate her political convictions than her emotional troubles. They are not easy to keep apart, however. In one particularly instructive moment, Meg rather grandly confides her theory that the class war between capital and labor is best understood as a clash between the Elect (the Protestant, philanthropic Philistine) and the Reprobate (the villainous aristocrat or criminal proletarian, both Catholics).

Meg professes personally to know all about the Elect, having married one. She offers him up as a perfect specimen of the "Protestant pragmatist" whose unqualified syllogisms—"If I say this, it is true. If I do this, it is justified" (*CSK*, 208)—are the assertions of a man certain that he is and will remain in a state of grace. His is the "religion of the Pharisee." She, on the other hand, is the lapsed Catholic who still identifies with Catholicism as "the religion of the proletariat and of what is left of the feudal aristocracy." "Our principles" she explains,

> are democratic; we believe that original sin is given to all and that grace is offered with it. The poor man is democratic out of necessity, the nobleman is democratic out of freedom. Have you ever noticed . . . that the unconscious hypocrite is a pure middle-class type? Your aristocrat may be a villain, and your beggar may be a criminal, but neither is self-deluded, puffed up with philanthropism and vanity like a Rockefeller or an Andrew Carnegie. And the French, who are the most middle-class people in the world, have produced a satirical literature that is absolutely obsessed with this vice. (*CSK*, 208–9)

Meg justifiably takes a somewhat jokey pride in her "beautiful psychology," which demonstrates her intellectual grasp of the representative types, political allegiances, and moral proclivities of classes occupying every position along the democratic spectrum— the aristocrat, the industrial tycoon, the financier, the corporate businessman, the bourgeois merchant, the hardworking or criminal proletarian—all of whom understand and exercise their democratic freedoms in different, often diametrically opposed ways that are not easily, perhaps never can be, reconciled. The problem is that however beautiful her psychology may be, it does not account for or satisfy her "thirsty spirit" (*CSK*, 222)—thirsty and still distressingly without a "single self" to call and claim as her own. Meg may never be "wel at ese," yet acting out of that moral scrupulousness, which is possibly her most active virtue, she holds herself accountable as her "owne woman," distinct and self-responsible: "There are other girls in the world," she declares, "but there is only the single self" (*CSK*, 207).

She hopes to recover this self, mislaid en route to what she thought was a meaningful place and role in the world, on the analyst's couch. Despite having "lost the life-giving illusion, the sense of the clean slate, the I-will-start-all-over-again-and-this-time-it-is-going-to-be-different" (CSK, 203–4), she has not lost her hope in the efficacy of conversion, a turning away from the darkness of her own soul and of her times. As the title of the novel's concluding chapter, "Ghostly Father, I Confess," indicates, errant Meg, who has spent most of her life searching not just for enlightenment but for absolution, treats the analyst's couch as a secular confessional. Both the religious and Freudian science of self-examination require voluntary acts of confession, an out-pouring of shameful deeds, thoughts, dreams, and desires that, by their very telling, can lead to a vision of Truth that can set the spirit free.

Such is the theory, both in theological and psychiatric doctrines of soulcraft. The theory is tested in Meg's most scandalous con-fession, which is saved for last. That it involves a thing dreamed rather than a thing done does not diminish its shamefulness. The dream, as dreams are wont to do, at once symbolizes and displaces her deepest and deeply contradictory wish to be and yet to change herself. In the dream she is matriculating from Eggshell College. (McCarthy has Nabokovian fun ridiculing the garishly obvious symbolism of this womb fantasy, which Meg insists was "custom-made" to please her therapist.) She finds herself in an "outing cabin," where she meets and then begins to flirt with a young man "of dun color, awkward, heavy-featured, without charm, a little like the pictures of Nazi prisoners that the Soviet censor passes" (CSK, 221). She unaccountably—this is a dream, where the un-accountable is precisely what counts—endows him with Byronic qualities, kisses him, then realizes that he is hardly the romantic rebel that in her aroused state she thought or hoped he might be. Still, when he kisses her a second time, she keeps her eyes closed, since, she admits, she "wanted him anyway." Meg remembers this dream in every detail—how could anyone forget it!—and is ap-palled at herself for dreaming it: "Oh my God . . . how could I, how could I?" (CSK, 222).

There are many girls in the world who, were they to have such a dream, would undoubtedly react the same way. What singles out Meg is her refusal to disown the dream: "It belonged to her," she admits. It doesn't matter whether the dream represents a wish fulfillment, in which blind Eros has its way, or whether it dramatizes Meg's justified anxiety about graduating to some unspeakable depravity of spirit. Whatever its import, the dream is her dream, and for Meg to be her own woman, to own, that is, herself, she must accept this morally hideous aspect of herself. The only mitigating detail appears at the end of her dream, in which "her eyes are closed, but the inner eye had remained alert": "She could still distinguish the Nazi prisoner from the English milord, even in the darkness of need" (*CSK*, 222). Meg's relief in still being able to distinguish a Nazi from an English milord may strike us as one of those tasteless jokes she censures so vigorously in her waking life or, what is worse, as a sign of how little, really, she morally expects or asks of herself. Such responses would not only be appropriate but almost inevitable had Meg disowned the dream and the darkness of need it symbolized and exposed. But she doesn't disavow her dream and the darkness of her need; she acknowledges both the dream and the need as her own. In claiming them she is also claiming possession of the spiritual capacity to look Truth in the face without flinching.

This capacity is what qualifies, if it does not yet establish, Meg as a modern Exaltada, a democratic seer whose "inner eye" can tell the difference between the ordinary and the standardized self, the democratic from the authoritarian character. Being modern, and being as transgressive as Mary McCarthy by her own account was—in her late-in-life *Intellectual Memoirs*, which are devoted primarily to her sexual adventures, she admits to sleeping with three different men within twenty-four hours—Meg is neither as innocent nor as morally impeccable as Fuller's woman who betrothed herself to the sun. Yet she does consider her calling a sacred one, answerable to, but also protected by, some transcendent presence or force: "Oh my God," she inwardly prays, "do not let them take this away from me. If the flesh must be blind, let the spirit see." To this supplication she appends a final vocal appeal:

"Preserve me in disunity. *O di . . . reddite me hoc pro pietate mea*" (Oh gods, render me this in return for my devotion) (*CSK*, 222–23).

The gods to whom Meg appeals are not to be found in any orthodox pantheon and, indeed, the last thing we learn about Meg is that she does not believe in God. Thus, we must presume that this prayer, uttered as far as we can tell without a trace of her customary and very caustic irony, is addressed to her own enlightened spirit. Typically, Meg does not pray to be made whole but to persist in her disunity. The prayer implies that she henceforth plans to devote herself to adjudicating the rival, often irreconcilable claims of bodily need and spiritual yearning, discouraging fact and robust hope. She does not foresee and certainly does not want an "integrated" life, which she presumably can only attain by surrendering "her sense of truth . . . and wonderful scruples" (*CSK*, 205). It is an article of her democratic faith that if she can hold on to these possessions, she might one day become her "owne woman," ready to take, but also ready to contribute, her share in everything.

What seems a personal striving to live within the light of truth is thus revealed to be essential to preserving what we may rather grandly call the democratic way of life. If we believe in the moral grandeur of democratic ideals, and lament the failure of democratic practices and institutions to fulfill them, it is partly due to the efforts of the Exaltadas, who were committed to articulating the elevated standards to which they held themselves, their government, and their times accountable.

By the middle of the twentieth century, the voice of the Exaltada might have changed its pitch, but it was still strong and compelling enough to be heard above the din of fractious Cold War politics and the clamorous birth pangs of emerging third world nations. One of the most stubbornly idiosyncratic and idiomatic of these voices belonged to Grace Paley's Faith (short for Faithful) Darwin, a midcentury woman "asweat with dreams" who when she feels especially "in the swim of things" considers "crawling Channels and Hellesponts and even taking a master's degree in education in order to exult at last in a profession and get out of the horseshit trades of this lofty land."[14] Exaltadas, apparently, can come from anywhere, even from the beachfronts of Coney Island, where Faith was born and whose brash colloquialisms enhance her authority as a seer of the playground, where, as a single Jewish mother, she spends a good deal of time. Her first name confirms her optimistic character but also her perplexity as "an American . . . raised up like everyone else to the true assumption of happiness" (*GP*, 148). Her last name, Darwin, is a New World name assumed by an immigrant Old World Jewish family who, despite the Holocaust and the "new little waves of anti-Semitism" that "lap the quiet beaches of their accomplishment" (ibid.), are buoyed by evolutionary hopes for "a sensible, socialist, Zionist world of the future" (*GP*, 177).

Though the title of the volume where many of her experiences are related augur *Enormous Changes at the Last Minute*, both her own history and her capacity for human observation have taught Faith that great changes, whether in the self or in governments, are never as final or as lasting as one had hoped. But they can happen, and when they do, they are survivable. This is the insight that comes to her as she contemplates her "place in democratic time," perched on "the twelve-foot-high, strong, long arm of a sycamore" (*GP*, 176). Looking down on the playground where her children play and the inhabitants of her patria saunter by, this urban Exaltada makes her own inimitable pronouncements:

> I don't think that civilization can do more than educate a person's senses. If it is truth and honor you want to refine, I think the Jews have some insight. Make no images, imitate no God. After all, in his field, the graphic arts, He is preeminent. Then let that One who made the tan deserts and the blue Van Allen belt and the green mountains of New England be in charge of Beauty, which he obviously understands, and let man, who was full of forgiveness at Jerusalem, and full of survival at Troy, let man be in charge of Good. (*GP*, 185)

A good Jewish woman, Faith does not presume to imitate God, only his rhetoric, when she enjoins her democratic flock: "Let man be in charge of Good." This is the first principle of her politics, by which the particulars of truth and honor, those monitors of power, might be refined or, as Fuller would say, might adjust themselves aright.

Such changes would be enormous, since they could hardly be slight, concerning as they do truth and honor. But even Faith, who casts her lot with the "revisionist Communist and revisionist Trotskyite and revisionist Zionist registered Democrats" (*GP*, 225), doesn't count on such enormous changes occurring soon, much less at the last minute. In *Later the Same Day*, a title that humorously deflates the apocalyptic expectations raised by *Enormous Changes at the Last Minute*, Faith, as if revisiting her morning and midday efforts to retell and remake the world, recalls pamphleteering against the Vietnam War and distributing pamphlets demanding that the "U.S. Honor the Geneva Agreements." These literally bold-faced protests, however laudable, are of doubtful efficacy, as Faith is reminded when her partner voices his skepticism that "the U.S. would ever honor the Geneva Agreements": "Well, then," Faith remarks in a sad parenthesis, "sadness, Southeast Asian sadness, U.S. sadness, all-nation sadness" (*GP*, 378). In the full flurry of her principled and mostly ineffectual activism, Faith has never been more sensible: she sees that there is no point, really, in arguing a point that only events will settle. At the same time she has never been more loyal to her principles of truth and honor. Her "Well, then," accepts but also warns against the sadness of broken promises and betrayed ideals, a sadness that she sees spreading like a plague from region to region, nation to nation, until it blights the globe. It may be objected that this is an emotional rather than a geopolitical argument against American interventionism, but Faith, were argument her mode, which it is not, would dismiss that distinction as a false and morally indefensible divorce of policy from its human consequences. She does not so much argue as foresee the consequences of a violation of the Geneva Agreements—a local disaster that cannot be contained but metastasizes into a palpable scourge that reaches every corner of the world.

Faith's political creed is literally proclaimed from her prophetic aerie in a tree. Her father, who likes stories to be short, simple, and redolent of truth, feels his daughter's tales fail to measure up to his notion of what stories are and what they are supposed to communicate. "I do not object to facts," he tells her, "but to people sitting in trees talking senselessly, voices from who knows where"

(*GP*, 233). Well, then, here is a more earthbound perspective on the disturbances, little and great, that rattle and unsettle the world:

> [A]s the granddaughter of a geologist I learned early to antici- pate the absolute mutability of hills and waterfalls and even islands. When a hill slumps into the ocean I see the order in it. When a 5.2 on the Richter scale wrenches the writing table in my own room in my own house in my own particular Wel- beck Street I keep on typing. A hill is a transitional accom- modation to stress, and ego may be a similar accommodation. A waterfall is a self-correcting maladjustment of stream to structure, and so, for all I know, is technique.[15]

This passage appears in a novel by Joan Didion called *Democ- racy*. The title alone is worthy of remark, so unperturbed is the implied promise that the fiction to follow will parse this abstract word in all its worrisome particulars. Didion seems to renew, if not fulfill, the promise in giving us, hardly two pages into the novel, this geological metaphor as a way of understanding the stressful and committed nature of her writing, which she pursues no mat- ter what seismic upheavals are occurring around her. It alerts us to the prospect that this novel, like all her political novels about democracy gone awry—*A Book of Common Prayer* and *The Last Thing He Wanted*—is a construct built on ground that is beginning to buckle. It gives us a scientific model for the historical collapse of democracy, while reminding us that the collapse of a system, how- ever cataclysmic, represents but a "transitional accommodation to stress." Who knows what future accommodations the government of the people, by the people, and for the people may devise to ensure its own continuance amid the changing landscapes of the geopolitical world? If Didion can keep on typing when a tremor registering 5.2 on the Richter scale wrenches her writing table, then might not democratic institutions serenely carry on with the business of governance even when wrenched by crises at home or abroad? This is a doubtful outcome, but it cannot be ruled out.

Not everyone might appreciate or even credit this analogy. In reviewing the novel, Mary McCarthy confessed to a rare moment of stupefaction as to what Didion could possibly have meant by her title (the first of many irritable queries she puts to the book). "I found it hard to make out," she complained,

> what connection there can be between Joan Didion's "Democracy," opening with a memory of the pink dawns of early atomic weapons tests in the Pacific, and Henry Adams's "Democracy," which deals with the dirty politics of the second Grant Administration. And, leaving aside Henry Adams, I do not quite see how democracy comes into the Didion tale except for the fact that two Democratic politicians (both Vietnam-war opponents) and a C.I.A. man play large roles in it. For Adams, "democracy" had become a coarse travesty of the ideal of popular rule, indissociable from the gravy train and the grease spots on the Congressman's vest. For Miss Didion, too, the term is rich in irony, though corruption by now is so universal that it can no longer be identified with a party or tendency or grand ideal betrayed.[16]

Given her own penchant for ironizing the general terms that define and indeed distinguish democracy as a political system, we might be surprised at McCarthy's inability—or unwillingness—to see a similar dissecting, skeptical intelligence at work in Didion's entangled tale of democratic politics in an atomic age. Perhaps McCarthy was nonplussed because Didion's irony, unlike her own, is not a vehicle for compulsive didacticism.

Not that Didion doesn't have her own "teachable" moments. One that makes the sharpest impression occurs when Didion, who appears in the novel in propria persona, relates her experience of teaching a class at Berkeley in the spring of 1975—a key period in the Vietnam War. Once a week, Didion tells us, she met with a dozen or so students "to discuss the idea of democracy in the work of certain post-industrial writers." That discussion took the form of "pointing out similarities in style, and presumably in ideas of democracy (the hypothesis being that the way a writer constructed a sentence reflected the way that writer thought)" (D, 71).

This proposition bears examination, since the claim, as McCarthy objected, is by no means self-evident. The "certain post-industrial writers" Didion selects to advance her hypothesis—Hemingway,

Orwell, Norman Mailer, and Henry Adams (who wrote about himself in the third person in *The Education of Henry Adams*)— suggest that an unflinching directness, a militant dismissal of cant, and a capacity for self-distancing are the hallmarks of a democratic style. None of these qualities are necessarily the unique possession of male writers, a fact whose import is by no means easy to determine, given that it is a question never discussed, not part of the syllabus, we might say, in this novel's course of instruction.

Didion prefers to concentrate attention on her putatively gender-neutral training in reportage, which taught her to "distrust other people's versions," "triangulate the coverage" to "handicap for bias," and, most of all, "consider what filter is on the lens. So to speak" (*D*, 124). Gender, of course, is a lens that magnifies and distorts like any other filter of perception, but Didion triangulates her coverage to reduce any distortions attributable to her sex. This becomes an interesting ploy, especially given that we learn that her first job was as a features writer for *Vogue*, a woman's magazine whose interest in politics and political actors is primarily sartorial, and that her initial intention was to write "a study in provincial manners, in the acute tyrannies of class and privilege by which people assert themselves against the tropics" (*D*, 22). Such a study would have placed her in the direct line of the Victorian realists, especially George Eliot, whose *Middlemarch*, one of the most worldly novels ever written, was subtitled "A Study of Provincial Life."

The outlines of Didion's original study is still there, as is the primary focus on women as the primary custodians, interpreters, enforcers, and, ultimately, victims of the stultifying sexual and social codes of colonial island life. But these gendered dimensions of *Democracy* are themselves filtered through the putatively wider and corrective lens whose use she learned from male authors. This lens magnifies particulars in order to reveal the emptiness, if not the villainous deceptiveness, of stock phrases and abstract words. As the literary daughter of Hemingway and Orwell (to whom we should add her most cherished paterfamilias, Joseph Conrad), Didion learned to make her own singular accommodations to the stress and the language of public life. Reading dispatches from

Saigon, she finds in "those falling capitals a graphic instance of the black hole effect," of accelerated collapse. She initially accepts the image of "falling" capitals until she speaks to antiwar students, who use the term "being liberated." The next time she speaks to them about the disintegrating situation, she modifies "falling" to "closing down" (D, 73).

Her accommodations to stress (caused by the half-truths, sentimental nostrums, routine misrepresentations, and outright lies disseminated in the public sphere where no one takes responsibility for particulars) never come, as Slesinger's, McCarthy's, and even Grace Paley's do, in torrents of prophetic denunciation and satiric invective. What she defines as "the self-correcting maladjustment" of narrative stream to narrative structure lacks the force, the fluency, and the sheer flamboyance of their outpourings. The "flow" of her narrative and of her sentences is not even continuous. *Democracy* meanders back and forth in time and across space from the chic political enclaves of the East to the colonial verandas of Hawaiian colonials (where murders as well as afternoon cocktails take place), from army posts and air bases in Saigon to refugee settlement camps in Kuala Lumpur. Facts are recorded and scenes evoked in halting or truncated phrases that often seem to stumble over their own knowing but impotent irony. Didion's famously laconic sentences, in which her accommodations to stress are calibrated with lapidary precision, are not meant to encourage debate or create a safe haven for dissent. Her writing reflects a notion of democracy that is ruminative rather than deliberative.

Didion does not, for example, "debate" the political necessity or moral wisdom of the American pullout from Southeast Asia. Rather, she concerns herself with particulars, noting, for example, that the

> colors of the landing lights for the helicopters of the roof of the America embassy in Saigon were red, white, and blue. The code names of the American evacuation of Cambodia and Vietnam respectively were EAGLE PULL and FREQUENT WIND. The amount of cash burned in the courtyard of the DAO in Saigon before the last helicopter left was three-and-a-half million

dollars American and eighty-five million piasters. The code
name for this operation was MONEY BURN. (D, 73–74)

We hear echoes of Hemingway in her concentration on the details
that evoke the "atmosphere" of mad flight, of Orwell in her appalled recollection of the code names that mask clandestine "op-
erations" of questionable legality and doubtful efficacy. But here
we also see the "self-correcting maladjustment" of her style to the
stream of half-formed or concealed thoughts, perceptions, and re-
ported—if not confirmed—facts in which we might ascertain the
reality of events, or at least the most plausible, disinterested version of them.

Didion, both as a novelist and essayist, has never shown the
slightest proclivity for "the final cause, the unambiguous answer"
that she saw frenetically at work in the fiction of Doris Lessing.[17]
Didion is a doubter, though less as a matter of fashion than of
temperament. Because she entertains no exalted notion of her own
power to see and in seeing transform the blighted world before
her, Didion is the most bereft of the modern Exaltadas. In the most
wrenching of the essays comprising *The White Album*, in which
she chronicles a social revolution that never took place, Didion
writes of the time she retreated to Honolulu. It is hard to decide
whether she is being honest or belligerent when she announces
that she wants her readers "to know, as you read me, precisely
who I am and where I am and what is on my mind." You are getting, she explains, "a woman who for some time now has felt radically separated from most of the ideas that seem to interest other
people. You are getting a woman who somewhere along the line
misplaced whatever slight faith she ever had in the social contract,
in the meliorative principle, in the whole grand pattern of human
endeavor."[18] Meg Sergeant had mislaid her ordinary, indispensable
self; Didion has misplaced something equally precious but harder
to locate and recover—her faith in the social contract, in the meliorative principle, in the whole grand pattern of human endeavor,
in sum, in the first principles of the Exaltadas' creed.

This period in her life marks an intensification of that sense of
spiritual anomie and dispossession that troubles all of Didion's

work, fiction and nonfiction alike. But even in the extremity of her distress, she, like McCarthy, refuses to barter her sense of reality for a more consolatory vision of better times to come. Not that she isn't aware of that option or of the way to avail herself of it. In her brief but trenchant appraisal of Doris Lessing, she is at once fascinated and appalled by the spectacle of a writer "undergoing a profound and continuing cultural trauma, a woman of determinedly utopian and distinctly teleological bent assaulted at every turn by fresh evidence that the world is not exactly improving as promised."[19] Didion was determined not to ignore the evidence, even while remaining sympathetic to those traumatized by the failure of their revolutionary hopes. She concludes by conceding that "the impulse to final solutions has been not only Mrs. Lessing's dilemma but the guiding delusion of her time."

Loss of faith in the social contract remains the abiding dilemma for the Exaltadas contemplating the fate of the democratic way of life as the "American" century drew to a close. In a 1962 interview with the *Paris Review*, McCarthy maintained that she still believed in the political creed of her youth, "a kind of libertarian socialism, and a decentralized socialism." This libertarian strain is crucial to understanding her democratic politics. It signals and reaffirms her allegiance to the idea that the ordinary, indispensable self is the legitimate political actor in a democracy. But, she continues,

I don't think that the problem of social equality has ever been solved. As soon as it looks as if it were going to be solved, or even as if it were going to be confronted—say, as at the end of the eighteenth century—there's a mass move to a new continent which defers this solution. After '48, after the failure of the '48 revolutions in Europe, hope for an egalitarian Europe really died, and the forty-eighters, many of them, went to California in the Gold Rush as forty-niners. My great-grandfather, from central Europe, was one of them. The Gold Rush, the Frontier was a substitute sort of equality. Think of Chaplin's film . . . And yet once the concept of equality had entered the world, life becomes intolerable without it; yet life continues without its being realized. So it may be that there will be another displacement, another migration. The problem, the solution, or the confrontation, will again be postponed.[20]

But there comes a time when the problem, the solution, and the confrontation can no longer be postponed, a time when the limits of the known world contract and those migrating from one part to another realize that soon there will be no new place to run to, that displacement has become not a moral option but a permanent condition of the striving self. As the desire for equality and a meaningful freedom disseminates across once-impermeable borders, the world itself becomes the home address of the self and soul.

And yet one cannot call the world a home. The dimensions are too large and unaccommodating, the soul misses its patria, its neighborhood. This is the plight and dilemma confronting the multinationals, the unpossessed of the age of the global migration of people and capital. The multinationals of our own time don't have names like Margaret or Faith or even Inez. They have names like Sai and Ka, yet they, too, might be considered the legitimate heirs of the Exaltadas, that special class of women born of democratic aspiration who envisioned crawling Channels and Hellesponts to reach that brave new world where the single self might finally feel "wel at ese."

CHAPTER 6

❧

Multinationals

PART I: THE POLITICS OF HOME

For Mirah Deronda, née Lapidoth, who sails with her new husband to find an unknown but much-desired homeland at the end of George Eliot's *Daniel Deronda*, a journey of adventure, dislocation, and homecoming is about to begin. In a continuing narrative that we readers can only follow in our imaginations, Mirah will struggle to create a home for herself and her family in the Levant, a part of the world remote from England in ways geographical, social, spiritual, and linguistic. More than a hundred years after the publication of *Daniel Deronda*, at the turn of the twentieth century into the twenty-first, a cluster of fictions by women writers not only follow their migrating protagonists to unknown lands across vast seas but also find ways to represent old home and new simultaneously, in a single narrative. Novelists like Anita Desai, Nadine Gordimer, Jhumpa Lahiri, Monica Ali, Edwidge Danticat, and Kiran Desai take on the subjects of twentieth- and twenty-first-century emigration and relocation, mobility and deracination, through the juxtaposition of two disparate cultures. We call these writers the multinationals, not only because their narratives occupy more than one part of the globe at a time but because their own frames of reference and life experiences have produced in them multiple national and cultural affiliations. Some are immigrants, some children of immigrants, others have lived in a polyglot world from childhood, and some inhabit a mixed community of refugees, émigrés, and displaced peoples.

Migration in their fictions most often moves in the direction of the more prosperous, developed country—the metaphorical West—and away from poverty, chaotic and sometimes brutal politics, and insistently patriarchal religions, but not always, as we shall see. It is usually a matter of "pulling up anchor and going somewhere else," as the narrator of Gordimer's 2001 novel *The Pickup* puts it, "either perforce or because of the constrictions of poverty or politics, or by choice of ambition and belief." But migration is also, this narrator continues, the result of an "inexpressible yearning that cannot be explained by ambition, privilege, or even fear of others."[1] These novels and stories explicitly or implicitly pose the inevitable and deceptively simple questions: Where is life better? Where are people—and especially women—freer? Where is the location of home, in its most meaningful and deepest sense? And where, in Gordimer's phrase, is "the exact location of a person," in Mary McCarthy's words, "the home address of the self"? These writers deploy the technique of juxtaposition to create a natural ground for comparison, a means of posing and trying to answer these vexing questions. Some of their narratives are geographically divided, split down the middle in location; some emphasize memory as a means of bringing two places and two cultures into rhetorical proximity; some rely on letters as the conduit for a culture not directly seen; and some are palimpsests, with the faint outlines of a previous life appearing below the bolder strokes of the present. "I think of writing as transparent," Anita Desai has said, "so that one can see many layers underneath, made up of different languages and all the different literatures that have gone to make up your mind and your own world."[2] Unlike the US pioneer and immigrant fiction of the late nineteenth and early twentieth century—of Cather and Orne Jewett, of Antin, Abraham Cahan, Anzia Yezierska, and Henry Roth—which tends to remain fixed geographically (if not always linguistically) in the new land, this body of work straddles two cultures and two geographies, never quite settling in one place.

When Mirah and Daniel Deronda set sail for the Levant at the end of Eliot's novel, the text leaves them on the brink of adventure, a risky voyage that uproots them from the safety of the national home they have heretofore known but promises them a return to what Eliot elsewhere calls the "parental hearth" of their people.[3] Similarly, as we have seen in chapter 1, Anne Elliot embarks on a life of possible distress and impending war at the conclusion of Austen's *Persuasion*, as she consents to reside on board her husband's man-of-war, living with him in full companionship, intimacy, and unity of purpose. Lucy Snowe, leaving England impulsively and inexplicably for Labassecour near the start of Charlotte Brontë's *Villette*, propels herself into a strange land, where she will live independently and yet without a home of her own. These heroines are left suspended somewhere between exile and the exhilarating promise of a wholly new kind of existence, a new world. Our protagonists in these "multinational" texts have arrived, however, and struggle to put down roots in a strange land. Heroines in a new form of immigrant story, they prompt us to ask if mobility always means emancipation and if those parts of the world that pride themselves on promoting the freedom of women always fulfill their promise. In ways that are often provocative and sometimes even perverse, these works challenge many of the assumptions of British and American women's writing in preceding centuries.

The migrating protagonists of Anita Desai, Nadine Gordimer, and Jhumpa Lahiri all travel great distances, but we most often meet them after they have arrived at their destinations, settled in unambiguously domestic settings. For them travel means, paradoxically, the need to reconstitute a domestic existence, albeit in an alien and sometimes mystifying context, and an ultimate inability to cross the threshold and venture into public life—a kind of paralysis or confinement to a constricted space. They achieve a form of mobility—that much-prized and hard-won achievement of nineteenth-century heroines—that also produces radical dislocation and isolation. All three of these writers are drawn to exploring the most constraining and stultifying of environments: the suburbs, that emblem of female entrapment identified for another, non-journeying Western generation as the locus of the "feminine mystique." Here they find the most available and vivid setting for the purposes of cultural juxtaposition and for representing the antithesis of life in those countries where struggle and material deprivation prevail. They also distinguish the home, and especially the suburban home, from cohesive or comforting family life. Though domestic space is the destination and setting for their migrating heroines, the traditional occupants of home are pulled apart by the centrifugal forces of modern life.

But, as even this brief account suggests, comparisons between home and abroad are not a simple matter, and questions about where life is better and where one belongs are hard to answer—and that is precisely the point. Through a close focus on the domestic and conjugal lives of women—the household, the family, marriage, sexuality, and the female body—these writers meditate on the relative value of differing cultural systems and gender ideologies. Through the narrow sphere of home, in its most literal sense, they broach the broadly political. At times they speculate on a third sphere, a realm in which the division of West and East, industrialized and developing, colonizer and formerly colonized, prosperous and deprived, can be transcended. This third sphere, or term, can take the form of art, or love, or the imagination: those places where cultural difference might be banished. In the end, however, these narratives imagine relocation as an existential affair, the necessary quest of individuals—rather than national, ethnic, or migrant groups—to find a place or a mode of belonging and, in Gordimer's words, to "discover and take possession of oneself" (*TP*, 47).

In an essay called "Various Lives," published in 2003, Anita Desai compares her rich and varied cultural background to an umbrella with many panels and spokes. Born in India to a German mother and Bengali father, her childhood combined the languages, architectures, literature, games, foods, religions, holidays, music, and even flora of a variety of nations and ethnic strains:

> In my home in Old Delhi, a rambling old bungalow weighed down with bougainvilleas of the kind the British left behind all across their empire in Asia, we listened to my mother sing us German lullabies and play Schubert on her piano . . . while

my siblings and I spoke Hindi to each other and our neigh-
bours, a Hindi that actually was mixed with Urdu to form—
conveniently, usably—the hybrid Hindustani spoken in north
India. . . . At Queen Mary's High School for Girls we sang
hymns . . . and we played rounders and badminton in the
playgrounds. . . . We played hide-and-seek amongst the tombs
of emperors and empresses of the Moghul Empire [and] came
home and read for the hundredth time our treasured copies of the works of Dickens, the Brontë sisters, Wordsworth
and Milton, or old copies of comic books like Superman and
Beano that we had bought with our pocket money in the ar-
cades of Connaught Circus. Or we listened to my mother tell
us one of Grimm's fairy tales or of Christmastime or Easter
in Germany, or heard my father talk of his childhood among
the rivers and rice fields of Bengal, so far to the east and in the
past as to be quite mythical.

After this long and vivid evocation of the "pied, patchwork structure" of her life, Desai wonders if the object she held over her
head, the protective parasol "fashioned by our motley ancestors,"
was absurd, impracticable. "Was it schizophrenic?" she asks, likely
astonished by the degree of cultural mixture in her own experience
as she records it on the page.[4] For Desai, this question about her
life became a question about her writing. How could she marshal
and then distill these various and sometimes conflicting influences
in fictional narrative?

After publishing eight volumes of fiction about Indian subjects
in English but wishing still to make use of the most important
linguistic and national strands of her being, she sought a way to
combine German and Indian stories. The difficulty was at least
twofold: as a woman of around fifty, she found that German was
"buried, hidden, locked up" within her, perhaps wholly inaccessible, and beyond that, she had never lived in Germany, even if
she could quote Goethe and recite the German nursery rhymes
her mother had taught her. The answer came unexpectedly, in
the form of a character: "Finally I found him: Baumgartner," she
writes. "His name dropped out of a tree and struck me on the

head as I walked in Lodi gardens in Delhi on a dusty summer evening, and I went home and started writing a book about a German émigré who escapes from the Holocaust to India."[5] In *Baumgartner's Bombay* (1988), Desai brings the polyglot world of India's most populous city into contact with the Berlin of her protagonist's childhood through the aging Baumgartner's recollections and reveries. Passages in German—mostly songs, nursery rhymes, and memories of his mother—are sprinkled, untranslated, throughout the text. Two cultures coexist on the page, a formal innovation and personal solution for Desai. But her protagonist had to be a man, she told an interviewer, because she wanted "to walk out into the wider world and bring in history and experience and events," and the traditional roles of Indian women would mean confining their stories to family and home.[6]

Desai identifies *Baumgartner's Bombay* as "the beginning of my move away from India." Living on different continents during regular stints of teaching in Britain, and especially in the United States, piqued her desire to "mesh [these experiences] together, and make a pattern of them."[7] But the formal means of accomplishing this remained elusive, and she wondered if she could still write about India while living in the United States and, once she found she could, if she could say anything cogent about this new setting and alien culture, a place where her literary experience of English couldn't help her and where she felt "on the outside . . . looking in."[8] Almost as a leap of faith and apparently without a clear plan, she completed the first part—the Indian part—of *Fasting, Feasting* (1999) and then "contrived a way" to push on with an American section because the material was so "vivid" to her at that moment. Unsure of whether there would be a link between the two parts of the book, she "realised eventually that these two novellas were mirror images of each other—not exact images, but as if the mirror were distorted."[9] She also discovered how she might combine the insistently domestic existence of an Indian woman with the story of a young man who had "walked out into the wider world."

Fasting, Feasting is a brother-sister story, a rewriting of those nineteenth-century English narratives, like George Eliot's *The Mill on the Floss*, that capture the asymmetrical upbringings of boys and girls in a culture that places a painfully high premium on masculinity. The narrative prepares us for this asymmetry very early on, when Uma, the daughter, witnesses her parents' jubilation at the birth of her much younger brother, Arun, even though this late child has arrived as an unplanned addition to the family. Uma and her beautiful sister Aruna (who escapes parental pressure by marrying promptly and getting away) watch "awe-struck" as their father screams with joy and leaps over chairs "like a boy playing leap-frog, his arms flung up in the air and his hair flying."[10] Their mother struts with pride as the bearer of a son, her "chin lifted a little into the air," and attains a new level of importance, perhaps Papa's equal now, because of her "achievement" (*FF*, 31). Uma is abruptly removed from the convent school she attends and groomed to become the boy's nurse. School ceases to be a part of her life and, by contrast, "education" is the word that will "sum up [her brother's] childhood" (*FF*, 118).

Desai, like many other multinational writers of this period, includes a gallery of what Mary Wollstonecraft called the "wrongs of woman." Uma is drawn to these eccentric, persecuted, and outcast women, both exhilarated by their daring and horrified by their fates. A distant relative, Mira-masi, travels the country pursuing fulfillment "like an obsessed tourist of the spirit" (*FF*, 38). Uma's cousin Anamika wins a scholarship to Oxford but is prevented from taking it by her parents, who consign her to a hateful husband and a mother-in-law who beats her. Anamika's life ends in self-immolation or, more likely, a fiery death at the hands of her in-laws. Uma herself, deprived of an education and, later, a chance to escape her parents' home to live alone and to have a career, is subjected repeatedly to the humiliations of the marriage market, the traffic in women. In her demeaning experience, betrothal is an occasion for female enslavement, corrupt dealings, trickery, ruin, and shame.

Desai's narrative is divided geographically, the first two thirds devoted to the sister's story in India, the final third to the brother's sojourn in America. Sent to school in Boston in order to further his education and improve his chances for material success, Arun is the male protagonist able to venture forth into the "wider world" while his sister is almost literally tied to home. But Arun also calls to mind, as we shall see, Cather's desire for male protagonists because they were more in need of fresh air. The bifurcated and symmetrical title—*Fasting, Feasting*—teases us into expecting a story of deprivation in India and plenty in the United States, asceticism in the first culture and indulgence in the second, suffering and want for the sister and abundance and opportunity for the brother. However, Desai's narrative confounds this expectation and challenges the neatness of these distinctions on a number of levels. Indeed, the American section of the novel, in which we encounter Arun's horror at American family life, sends us back to the Indian story of his sister and to clues regarding his own character and likely fate, which we might otherwise have overlooked.

When forced to leave his university dormitory during the summer months, Arun finds himself living, much to his dismay, in the suburban home of an American family, the Pattons. The anonymity and "total absence of relations, of demands, needs, requests, ties, responsibilities, commitments" of dormitory life had felt glorious to him. There, he had "no past, no family and no country" (*FF*, 172). But at the Pattons' he feels repulsion and nausea, disgust at both their modes of consumption and their vexed family relations. As a vegetarian (from the putative land of "fasting"), he is sickened by the sight of a piece of meat "bleeding in a stream across Mr. Patton's plate," by the Patton son's constant "prowling . . . in search of victuals" like a raccoon, and by the "false religion" of a summer night's barbecue (*FF*, 167, 189). This "feasting" is inseparable, however, from the "fasting" of Melanie Patton, the family's bulimic daughter. The Pattons' food derangement extends from the gluttony of the carnivorous men in the family and the compulsive overshopping of Mrs. Patton to the daughter's gorging and disgorging. Desai attends to the relationship between food and tradition on the one hand and food and modernity on the other.

Though this American family appears grotesque to Arun, he is ultimately able to recognize its resemblance to his own. He sees in Melanie's face the familiar "enraged sister," unable to directly express her "outrage against neglect . . . misunderstanding . . . [and]

inattention" (*FF*, 214). Not only does she reproduce Uma's distur-
bance of mind, but she also reflects back at him what he himself
feels: nausea, disgust, a phobic reaction to food, the sensation that
his throat muscles contract when he sees the quantity of groceries
Mrs. Patton has bought at the Foodmart. And beyond this, he realizes that he has been pulled back into the psychological maelstrom
of family life, the "sugar-sticky web of family conflict" (*FF*, 195),
the oppressive hovering of the mother, and the suffocating pressure
of expectations: "No, no he had not escaped. He had travelled and
he had stumbled into what was like a plastic representation of
what he had known at home; not the real thing—which was plain,
unbeautiful, misshapen, fraught and compromised—but the unreal thing—clean, bright, gleaming, without taste, savour or nour-
ishment" (*FF*, 185). Here, then, is the distorted mirror image of
India in American life that Desai discovered only in the writing of
her own story. Contrasting veneers hide the common woes of the
psyche that lie beneath.

By the end of Arun's stay at the Pattons', we come to see not
only that family life allows no one—not even the favored male
child—to escape its pressures but also that Arun himself suffers
from certain deformations of the soul and mind. His reaction to
the gluttony and self-starvation in the Patton home strikes the
reader as extreme though perhaps understandable. His disgust
at another kind of flesh—the near nakedness of Mrs. Patton—
complicates and makes more disturbing the boy's general squeamishness. The sight of Mrs. Patton sunbathing, her overexposed
and reddening body stretched out like a slab of meat on the grill,
unsettles him, fills him with "turbulent feelings" and "distress"
(*FF*, 213–15). Her lined flesh "seems to be frying in the sun because she has spread quantities of oil over it . . . and it gleams
brown and shiny" (*FF*, 213). "She might have been on display in
the Foodmart," Arun thinks to himself, "a special order for the
summer, gleaming with invitation" (ibid.). Aroused and repelled
all at once, he retreats, shuns her, averts his eyes in fear. The narrative, which reproduces the boy's perspective in this part of the
novel, conflates the bloody, raw meat of the barbecue with the
mother's body, as well as with the daughter's body lying in its own

vomit. The appetites, disturbances, and failures of the flesh—and especially female flesh—disgust and terrify him.

The son sent out into the world cowers in the face of its exposed bodily truths. Rather than meeting new experiences and alien ways of life with interest, he retreats from them. It is only at the end of Desai's narrative that we fully understand which sibling is the more radically stunted child. As a small boy, we recall, Arun had sequestered himself in his room, withdrawing to the "outermost limits" of the household. His food fetishes, mirrored in Melanie's, begin at an early age. Maternal imposition and parental anxiety around the subject of his eating take their toll. Surrounded by happy eaters who love even to talk about food, the abstemious Arun is a natural vegetarian whose teeth clench when his mother brings him a boiled egg. He bites his sister's finger, drawing blood, as she feeds him cod-liver oil. The implied association between the female body and food begins here, as does Arun's confused antipathy to both.

Joyless, Arun walks with "the gait of a broken old man" (*FF*, 119). Years of academic toil and enforced study deaden him to most pleasures (save his beloved comic books), and he occupies the "deep well of greyness that was his existence" (*FF*, 122). It is Uma, the oppressed, unmarried sister, the drudge of her family denied education and independence, who is capable of experiencing true joy, even ecstasy. She evinces a childlike delight in food even into middle age and delights in the sensation of a forbidden ritual bath, which produces in Uma the "thrill of license," "a kind of exultation" (*FF*, 110–11). Uma hungrily reads the poems of Ella Wheeler Wilcox and aspires to transcendent spiritual experience. When her mother discovers and angrily disparages Wilcox's aptly titled *Poems of Pleasure* in her daughter's room, Uma "screams at [her parents] silently," emitting the singular words of the poems: "Rosebuds. Wild waltz. Passionately" (*FF*, 137).

In *Fasting, Feasting* Desai dissects the sexual politics of Indian culture and does so exclusively through contrasting portraits of domestic life. Even the brother's entry into the wide world is conveyed within the claustrophobic environment of home and family. This brother-sister story is told with full and sustained consciousness of gender inequity, and with a ruthlessness that surpasses

Desai's nineteenth-century predecessors. Desai goes beyond this, too, to an exploration of cultural difference in the sphere of gender and, even more strikingly, to the revelation of family paradoxes that no system of female oppression can fully control. Just as the United States, with its suburban plenitude and openness to individual expression, mirrors the pinched and repressed circumstances of Indian life in surprising ways, so too does the sister's capacity for pleasure in the face of its constant denial defy our sense of the expected. The feasting culture fasts and starves itself, the fasting culture makes room for the appetites. The well-fed brother fasts, while the sister, starved of love and freedom, feasts on the pleasures and passions that abide.

Like Anita Desai, Nadine Gordimer claimed both a strong national affiliation and a multinational identity. Born in South Africa to two European immigrants, she described herself as "an African writer in the English language."[11] She drew on French, Russian, Commonwealth, American, and, above all, English literary influences, with a special early fondness for the New Zealander Katherine Mansfield—"also living at the end of the world"—and a large debt to the "British liberal writers" of Bloomsbury. Forster's *A Passage to India*, with its evocation of both the promise and the impossibility of understanding between occupier and occupied, spoke to her in a way she didn't quite understand at first: "it referred to a foreign country in the way that my own country was a foreign country."[12] Her maternal grandmother worked as a feather comber at Buckingham Palace, and Gordimer herself remembers celebrating George IV's ascension to the throne as a child, collecting branches from her garden to decorate the house and feeling tremendous patriotic pride.[13] Her Jewish father came to South Africa as a largely uneducated teenager from Lithuania, fleeing czarist rule on his own. Part of a left-wing émigré world and firmly identified with other African writers, Gordimer wrote from the position of both the colonizer and the colonized, and it is precisely this mix and clash of identities that inform *The Pickup* and its predecessor, *July's People* (1981).

Both of these novels, published some twenty years apart, one dystopian, the other set in partly invented places, imagine a woman from a comfortable background in an industrialized society who is transplanted to a developing, non-Christian land (what used to be called a "third world" country). In the case of *July's People*, this distinction is complicated by the fact that both locales are in the same country, South Africa. Maureen Smales, the novel's female protagonist, has taken refuge with her family in her servant July's village during a period of revolutionary upheaval that has made life in the cities and suburbs, where her family resides, impossible. Gordimer sets her story in the village but manages to achieve the effect of juxtaposition and contrast through her characters' memories of lives past. In *The Pickup* Julie Summers marries Abdu, a man from an unnamed Muslim country who has been working as a gas station attendant in hers (a developed African country like South Africa, though never identified as such), and emigrates to her husband's home after his work papers have expired. The novel juxtaposes two cultures by dividing the narrative in a manner similar to Desai's *Fasting, Feasting*. Both of Gordimer's novels underscore the hypocrisy and unwarranted complacency of modern societies by transplanting their heroines and placing an economically advanced, socially enlightened way of life alongside what "Westerners" might consider a benighted culture. In the end, however, as with Desai, Gordimer's protagonists cannot depend on predictable and absolute distinctions between cultures or on reflexive liberal responses to them.

Gordimer's use of female protagonists to tell these particular stories might suggest that she sees in this juxtaposition of cultures an opportunity to explore and critique ideologies of gender. This is true, but only in a counterintuitive, not to say contentious, way. Julie Summers, after all, eventually chooses to remain alone, without her husband, in his Muslim country, where she will have to wear the *hijab* when she leaves the house and where women who commit adultery can be stoned. Her father, expressing shock that she would voluntarily migrate to such a place, challenges her: "You, you to whom independence, freedom, mean so much, eh, there women are treated like slaves" (*TP*, 98). But Gordimer employs a familiar critique of progressive Western societies by suggesting that sexual politics in Julie's own country leave something to be desired. Her father, the well-meaning but blinkered enlightened man, understands only part of the story. Her uncle back home, a gynecologist and a decent man, is falsely and very publicly accused of sexual harassment by a disturbed patient, as if to suggest that liberal gender politics have gone too far or at least have their own potential for perversity. Gordimer has repeatedly claimed that in her culture, race outstrips gender as the salient human and political distinction: the "basis of color cuts right through the sisterhood or brotherhood of sex," she has said, and further, "Women's Liberation is, I think, a farce in South Africa . . . a black woman has got things to worry about much more serious than these piffling issues."[14] A circumscribed and culturally specific political realm, in which gender played only a limited role, interested Gordimer. Her focus on women and on ideologies of gender in these texts, then, seems linked in her writing to a desire to probe the most private, the most domestic spaces of life—the conjugal and sexual—and to see them as grounds for understanding both the social ties and the deepest aspirations of individuals.

In *July's People* the words "master bedroom" signify the comfortable, bourgeois life the Smales enjoyed before the revolution and become a metaphor for the comfortable but inadequate assumptions and postures that went with that life. The revolution, Maureen muses, means "an explosion of roles . . . the blowing up of the Union Buildings and the burning of master bedrooms."[15] The word "master" begins as a loaded term, suggesting hierarchies of race, sex, and station, and these varying kinds of differential power come to be associated through the word "bedroom" with the conjugal tie. Over the course of the narrative, the term comes to signify an entire political and economic system (who can afford to have a bedroom with an en suite bath?) and the social customs, one of which is marriage, that underpin it. If you want to attack and destroy a power structure, burn master bedrooms, both literal and symbolic. In time we come to see that without a particular social structure, and perhaps even an edifice to provide context for the marriage bond, it quickly dissolves.

The disintegration of Maureen and her husband Bam's conjugal life reflects its dependence on both the creature comforts and the structure of gender roles in their suburban home. In July's village Maureen places wadded rags between her legs when she menstruates and goes to the river with the rest of the women to wash them out for reuse. When she and Bam make love for the first time after their flight from home, Bam awakens "in a moment of hallucinatory horror" at the sight of blood on his penis (*JP*, 80). Before he realizes the blood is his wife's, he thinks it must belong to a wild boar he had helped to slaughter the night before. His implication in the rituals of hunting, and his now very intermittent sexual contact with his wife, seem fused in his psyche as signs of his weakening grip on his former, socialized self.

The relationship between husband and wife has been stripped of its social, affective character but also of what the text refers to as "the deviousness natural to suburban life" (*JP*, 89). The old Bam becomes for Maureen "someone recollected," and her own physicality is utterly transformed, her body defeminized (*JP*, 93). Her breasts are now shallow, her neck weathered and reddened, her wardrobe a thin cotton T-shirt. "The baring of breasts," we read, "was not an intimacy but a castration of his sexuality and hers; she stood like a man stripped in a factory shower or a woman in the ablution block of an institution" (*JP*, 90). To Bam, Maureen now looks like her father, a shift boss on a mine. Without the master bedroom and all that it stands for, the roles of husband and wife, legible gender difference, and even sexual relations, cannot be sustained. Maureen ceases to look after her children; they learn to fend for themselves. As the novel ends, Maureen runs for a helicopter on her own, "trusting herself . . . like a solitary animal at the season when animals neither seek a mate nor take care of young, existing only for their love of survival" (*JP*, 160). By focusing on the most intimate parts of Maureen's private life, Gordimer exposes the tenuousness of what is widely understood as civilized and moral behavior, the product of what Maureen had once believed was a "humane creed" (*JP*, 64).

For her epigraph to *July's People*, Gordimer uses a quotation from Antonio Gramsci's *Prison Notebooks* that invokes a new social order struggling to be born out of the old. Her novel, she implies, takes place in what Gramsci calls the "interregnum," the chaotic middle period between what is dying and what is new and as yet unimaginable. A third way may emerge, then, out of the dialectical process of repression and revolution she imagines in the novel. In the epigraph to *The Pickup*, from a poem by the South African writer William Plomer, this third way is imagined in terms not of time but of space. The poem is repeated in its entirety later in the novel. "Let us go to *another country* / Not yours or mine," it begins, "And start again" (*TP*, 88; emphasis added).

Neither one lover's country nor the other's—neither Julie Summer's Westernized African land nor the nameless Muslim country of Abdu—but a third place, a hypothetical home, will be the couple's refuge or promised land. At first the "other country" where they meet isn't a place but a state of being: "The capacity returned to him, for this foreigner made him whole. That night he made love to her with . . . reciprocal tenderness . . . the kind of love-making that is another country [he thinks, echoing Plomer's poem], a country of its own, not yours or mine" (*TP*, 96). Abdu is made whole through trust, tenderness, the possibility of mutual feeling, and the ability to transcend self. For the privileged, willful Julie, this other country comes, temporarily, in the form of acquiescence, first to the idea of emigrating to Abdu's country and then to the idea that they will leave his land in search of opportunity in the West. "There is something beguiling about submission," the narrator muses, perhaps reproducing Julie's own thoughts, "for one who has believed she has never submitted. Something temptingly dangerous, too. The Suburbs; The Table; *a third alternative*" (*TP*, 239; emphasis added). Rejecting both her parents' comfortable home in the suburbs and "the table," the regular bohemian gathering at the L.A. Club in town, Julie seeks her own third term by following her husband. For each one, then, the other promises a means to transcendence, to completion. "She was the country," we read, "to which he had emigrated" (*TP*, 193).

Emigration is at the core of this novel, and yet the novel finally undermines conventional liberal assumptions about emigration. So, too, does it challenge the idea that "reciprocal tenderness" can be redemptive in some enduring way. Ultimately, Julie's delight in submitting will be undermined by her ambivalence about leaving Abdu's country, where she has come to feel at home, and her conviction that, in going to America (the "harshest country in the world"), he will be exploited (*TP*, 230). At the last moment she decides to stay in Abdu's home surrounded by his female relatives, "at peace, at her place in the desert," attached to a family in a way she has never been before (*TP*, 187). It is striking that the most idealized vision of family in all of these works appears in the form of Gordimer's imagined Muslim country, and it is a vision of family based in the sense of kinship among a single sex. At the center of this at-homeness for Julie is, as well, the dream of green in the desert, a project of irrigation inspired by the vision of an oasis: lushness, growth, birdlife, the "coexistence of wonder and possibilities" (*TP*, 211). But Abdu will leave. Not for him the disputes about religion, politics, and revolution in which his friends engage; not for him the dry, unforgiving desert; not for him the vision of his mother, who fought for education, boiling water to keep the family clean. His dream of "possibilities" lies elsewhere. Separated by their dreams, their idea of true Home, they are nonetheless alike. They each seek emancipation in the other's world. "Like me, like me," Abdu understands, though in a rage at Julie's resistance, "she won't go back to where she belongs" (*TP*, 262).

Emigration in *The Pickup* is a two-way movement in which each of these lovers must travel to get Home, to a different home. Abdu keeps thinking that for Julie, the spoiled child, these various relocations are just another "adventure," a kind of play, but here there is no distinction between adventure and homecoming. Julie is as free to travel as any heroine we have encountered so far, but for her this form of freedom is virtually meaningless. What she seeks is a place where she is made to feel "consciousness of self," a place where her difference from those around her creates, paradoxically, the kind of self-awareness and alertness that leads her to a sense of peace (*TP*, 117). Gordimer leaves us with the question of how to locate the self in a world of economic, religious, and ideological contrasts, where individual tastes and needs often get lost. Is Julie's insistence that she has found a home among women whose scope of movement is severely limited more or less self-deluding than her husband's belief that his happiness lies in the opportunities afforded by a thriving capitalist land? Are the liberal notions that women should be free and no man subject to another's will adequate premises for a life of contentment? Or are these notions that typically underpin received ideas about relocation too rooted in place and culture, too cognizant of global differences, not alert enough to the idiosyncratic demands and desires of the individual traveler?

Raised in the United States but born in London some thirty years after Anita Desai's birth and more than forty years after Nadine Gordimer's, Jhumpa Lahiri claims a "sense of exile" inherited from her Indian parents, immigrants to the West. She grew up between two worlds—the Calcutta of her parents and grandparents, whom she visited regularly, and suburban New England—and cast such a first-generation American as the central and eponymous protagonist of her novel *The Namesake*. But her most poignant and original characters are the displaced Indian women who make their lives tentatively and sometimes agonizingly in the United States. She writes as the child of immigrants about the condition of being an immigrant, as someone still not fully at home in the country of her own birth, a country alien to her parents and the members of their generation. That generation felt a burdensome "longing for a lost world," but the problem for their offspring—for her—is that "they feel neither one thing nor the other." "I have never known," she has said, "how to answer the question 'Where are you from?'"[16] Through figures of immigrant women who struggle to establish a satisfying bicultural existence, and children who listen intently to the stories of displacement told by their elders, Lahiri manages to represent in her fiction the quandary of being neither Indian nor American, neither one thing nor another. Assimilation into the new culture can be problematic or even cataclysmic—devastating for the parents and disorienting for the children, who find themselves wanderers still, even into the first generation.

Lahiri's first collection of stories, *The Interpreter of Maladies* (1999), is filled with maps. In "When Mr. Pirzada Came to Dine," Lilia, the Boston-born child narrator, recalls the regular visits to her home of Pirzada, a Bengali, during the year of the Civil War in Pakistan. The world, its politics and geography, take on new meaning for Lilia as a result of these visits: "Every now and then I studied the map above my father's desk and pictured Mr. Pirzada on that small patch of yellow [Pakistan], perspiring heavily, I imagined, in one of his suits, searching for his family. Of course the map was outdated by then."[17] In "Sexy," Dev shows his lover Miranda where Bengal is on a map in the *Economist* and later takes her to the Mapparium in Boston's Christian Science Center, his favorite place in the city. They stand on a transparent bridge in the middle of a room of "glowing glass panels . . . shaped like the inside of a globe," and Dev points out the countries, like Siam, that no longer exist, as well as the deepest point of the ocean (*IM*, 90). Later in the story a child, Rohin, whose father has left his mother for someone he has met on a plane, attaches himself to Miranda and insists that she look at an almanac with him and quiz him on capitals of the world.

These characters, mainly but not exclusively children, strain to figure out where they belong on the map, trying to get straight where they and those around them have come from, as if working out their identities through a geography lesson. Where, indeed, is the location of the self? Without the map in her father's study, it is hard for Lilia to imagine how much Mr. Pirzada misses his wife and children or, indeed, to understand how far her own parents have journeyed. The recitation of capitals gives Rohin a sense that he can control his uncontrollable and disintegrating world. As Miranda comes to realize, these replicas of the world, of space and geography, like her security in Dev's love for her, are illusions, unreliable and shifting. Siam is now Thailand; parts of Pakistan have become Bangladesh; the map above Lilia's father's desk is out-of-date; Dev has gone back to his wife; Rohin's father has found a new romantic life by means of the very vehicle that brings the immigrant back and forth from home; and Rohin inappropriately uses a word—"sexy"—that his father had used for a woman on a plane to describe Miranda. Understanding the world of one's parents is here inseparable from grasping their itineraries, as if the condition of the child, whether first-generation or not, is always one of disorientation and psychic wandering.

In the story "Mrs. Sen's," in another intimate relationship between an adult woman and a child confidant, Lahiri focuses on the agonizing dislocation of the immigrant adult. The boy, Eliot, placed in the after-school care of Mrs. Sen, is himself at sea and alone, living with a taciturn, emotionally distant single mother. Mrs. Sen's alienation, however, is of operatic proportions by comparison, though the child likely sees his loneliness reflected in hers. Like Desai and Gordimer, Lahiri gets at the wider phenomenon of dislocation through wifely domestic chores and rituals. Eliot watches, mesmerized, as Mrs. Sen chops vegetables while seated on a newspaper on the floor of the living room:

> Instead of a knife she used a blade that curved like the prow of a Viking ship, sailing to battle in distant seas. . . . She took whole vegetables between her hands and hacked them apart: cauliflower, cabbage, butternut squash. She split things in half, then quarters, speedily producing florets, cubes, slices, and shreds. She could peel a potato in seconds. . . . Her profile hovered protectively over her work, a confetti of cucumber, eggplant, and onion skins heaped around her. (*IM*, 115)

Later, Mrs. Sen works the same magic on the fish she brings home from the market. Spreading out the newspaper wrapper and clutching her blade, she "inspected her treasures" and "stroked the tails, prodded the bellies, pried apart the gutted flesh" (*IM*, 127). On the most intimate terms with her adored mackerels, Mrs. Sen delights in preparing and eating all the parts of the fish—tail, eggs, head, everything (*IM*, 124).

In Eliot's eyes, Mrs. Sen seems a type of warrior, "sailing to battle in distant seas" with her formidable weapon, the curve of which mimics the sinuous profile of a marauder's vessel. Her mastery and authority, her fierceness—even bellicosity—and adventurousness, her panache and sensual pleasure in executing these tasks, delight him, as do her stories of communal food preparation at home ("Eliot understood that when Mrs. Sen said home, she meant India") (*IM*, 116). These memories afford Eliot and the reader the opportunity to see Mrs. Sen's past and current lives simultaneously and to see both the continuities and the disquieting gaps between them. On the eve of large family celebrations, she tells the spellbound child, Mrs. Sen's mother would send out a call to the neighborhood women to bring their blades and gather to sit in a large circle on the roof of the building, "laughing and gossiping and slicing fifty kilos of vegetables throughout the night" (*IM*, 115). There, in India, as in Gordimer's mythical Muslim country, women's lives and work are full of chatter and company; here, in Massachusetts, the silence and loneliness are punishing. The partitioning and isolation of domestic life for Lahiri's Mrs. Sen (as for Desai's Patton family and Gordimer's Summers family) rob women's work of pleasure and imprison them in their separate, maddening cubicles.

The mobility of migration does not redeem Mrs. Sen; indeed, it isolates her from female community, now inadequately replaced by a child. She requires a different sort of mobility altogether—a way of getting to the fish market, now that her husband refuses to take her. He insists that, like other women in America, she learn to drive herself. At first hopeful that the car will take her out and even back home ("Could I drive all the way to Calcutta?" she asks Eliot, her constant companion during driving practice), Mrs. Sen has an accident and retreats from the world, from trips to the fish market, even from babysitting for the boy (*IM*, 119). Utterly defeated, she withdraws into permanent seclusion and aloneness.

Like the maps and airplanes of these stories, Mrs. Sen's automobile signifies a life in transit: exhilarating and alienating, liberating but terrifying. In the last story in the collection, "The Third and Final Continent," the protagonist-narrator has emigrated from India, sailed to England across the Arabian Sea, the Red Sea, and the Mediterranean Sea, and, five years later, in 1969, settled in Boston. His pixilated but kindly landlady speaks to him incessantly of that year's moon landing, an event forever after associated in his mind with his arrival on the "third continent." To his son in later years, he avers that anything is possible. He knows this to be true because the astronauts spent three hours on the moon and, in an achievement possibly more unexpected than that, *he* has lived in "this new world" for nearly thirty years (*IM*, 198).

The feats and failures of transportation in these stories make their way into Lahiri's first novel, *The Namesake*, where trains become her principle emblem for the leitmotif of dislocation and a life in between. (The director Mira Nair uses bridges in the film version of the novel to convey the same in-betweenness. This works well visually though without the same confounding sense of movement through time and space that trains and planes suggest.) Although the entire Ganguli family feels itself "in transit," especially after returning to the United States in a disorienting twenty-four-hour journey from India, and though Gogol, the son, lives uncomfortably suspended between immigrant parents attached to a culture that is not his and a contemporary American life that is his but not wholly, the most compelling character in relation to the phenomenon of displacement in the narrative is Ashima, Gogol's mother. The world of *The Namesake* occupies a temporal middle ground between the immigrant generation of Mrs. Sen and the largely first-generation characters in Lahiri's second story collection, *Unaccustomed Earth*. Though Gogol, born in Massachusetts, is the novel's eponymous hero, his parents, Ashoke and Ashima, account for much of the story's affective power. Ashima begins in the condition of estrangement common to many of the immigrant women of the *Interpreter* collection, and her story, like theirs, is evoked through the bodily and domestic life of wife and mother.

As the novel opens in Cambridge, Massachusetts, she contemplates "motherhood in a foreign land" and prepares a mélange—or, more appropriately, a masala—of Rice Krispies, Planters peanuts, red onion, and green chilies in an effort to reproduce a cheap Indian snack to satisfy her pregnant cravings.[18] Through the birth and rearing of two children, the premature death of her husband, relocation to the Friedanian suburbs ("more distressing than the move from Calcutta to Cambridge had been"), employment as a librarian, and the trials of being a perpetual foreigner, Ashima also becomes something of an American (49). She learns to roast a turkey in November, hang a wreath in December, and color eggs in the spring. These mundane acts of domestic celebration, stripped of their religious or even historical meaning, carry a weight beyond their apparent ordinariness and superficiality. They represent concessions to the new life and a creative, emotional investment in its domestic culture but also signify that Ashima has taken charge of her circumstances and surroundings.

Ashima reproduces and then transcends the estrangement of characters like Mrs. Sen, not merely because she partly assimilates to American life but because she ultimately chooses in-betweenness, the condition into which she had initially, unwittingly fallen. Late in the novel she muses that she has had an "unexpected life" and inhabits a world and home that still bear a touch of the unfamiliar. But as she has taken charge of the domestic customs of Christian America, so too does she now claim responsibility for this improvised, hybrid life (280). The condition of deracination, widowhood, and aloneness has made her into a different kind of woman, a woman able and now even anxious to live "without borders," without a permanent address, without her own private domestic space (276). A woman with two adult American children, she decides to spend half the year in Calcutta and half in the United States.

Prepared to be "a resident everywhere and nowhere" (ibid.), Ashima has grown into and embraced an unexpected, accidental state of being—in Lahiri's extranovelistic words, "neither one thing nor the other." Lahiri uses this phrase to describe her own generation, however, not the generation of her immigrant parents and Ashima. Through the figure of Gogol's mother, the writer finds the meaning and identity of rootlessness and claims them as her own. Unlike Mary Antin, author of an earlier kind of immigrant story, who insisted on a clear distinction between her pre- and post-immigrant selves and even uses different pronouns—"she" and "I"—to refer to them in *The Promised Land*, Lahiri and characters like Ashima hold on defiantly to their continuing ambiguous and multiple identities. "My parents' refusal to let go or belong fully to either place [the United States or India]," Lahiri has written, "is at the heart of what I, in a less literal way, try to accomplish in writing. Born of my inability to belong, it is my refusal to let go."[19] She continues to search out forms and stories that allow her to investigate this condition of not letting go, of being, in effect, an inhabitant of multiple places and cultures. For her second collection of short stories, Lahiri chose a title—*Unaccustomed Earth*—and an epigraph from "The Custom-House," Hawthorne's prologue to *The Scarlet Letter* (1850). The passage she cites marks a different, earlier migration but hails transplantation as a necessary state. "Human nature will not flourish, any more than a potato," Hawthorne writes, "if it be planted and replanted, for too long a series of generations, in the same worn-out soil. My children have had other birthplaces, and, so far as their fortunes may be within my control, shall strike their roots into *unaccustomed earth*."[20]

Perhaps the most extreme example in Lahiri's oeuvre thus far of this inability—or refusal—to belong is Kaushik, the journalist born in India, schooled in the United States, and lately living in Italy, whose death ends *Unaccustomed Earth* in the story "Going Ashore." "I don't live anywhere at the moment," he tells a Swedish man he meets on a beach in Thailand just before he drowns in what appears to be a tsunami. Citizen of nowhere, he may be Lahiri's ultimate and, in this imagining, most calamitous version of living in-between.[21] But she continued her experiments with representing existences in limbo. Following in the footsteps of Anita Desai, Lahiri produced a second novel, *The Lowland* (2013), which is split between India and the United States. Like *Fasting, Feasting*, it tells the story of siblings—in this case two brothers—whose lives take radically different paths. Set in the 1960s and beyond, it follows the course of Subhash, who emigrates to the United States, and Udayan, who stays in India to foment political revolt. Though the American brother returns to India in the wake of his sibling's death, the narrative toggles back and forth between the two countries until the very end. Lahiri's latest venture, a collection of autobiographical essays, reflects yet another adopted home—Rome—and was written in Italian. *In altre parole* (*In Other Words*), which was published in the United States in February 2016, was translated into English, one of Lahiri's native languages, by someone else (Ann Goldstein).[22] Her in-betweenness, now linguistic as well as geographical, continues, and her points of identification multiply.

By choosing to shrink the space of women's lives to a narrow, domestic (and often suburban) realm, and by juxtaposing two alternative domestic cultures, Desai, Gordimer, and Lahiri are able to make broad and complex statements about the politics of gender in a wide, multinational context. Desai exposes the sexual politics of both East and West, beginning with what an American reader would consider the more obvious oppressions of Indian life and then moving on to a subtler but ultimately more shocking delineation of the pathologies of American femininity. She complicates ideas of want and plenty, troubles easy assumptions about the superiority of what passes for advanced cultures, and imagines possibilities for joy among the deprived and dismissed daughters of rigidly patriarchal societies. Gordimer follows suit, though her provocations are more radical than Desai's. She questions liberal shibboleths about why we emigrate and where emigration should take us, and, beyond that, she demonstrates that liberal structures of thought and behavior are flimsy and fragile. For Gordimer, sexual politics are another symptom of modern culture, and their gravity pales in comparison to that of other kinds of discrimination or to the psychic deformities of capitalist culture. Sexuality and relations between the sexes are the ground on which a variety of political dynamics can be dramatized and explored and not simply a focus for understanding the oppression of women.

Jhumpa Lahiri, the youngest and most contemporary of these writers—and the only one who has grown up in the United States—is also the least overtly political or ideological in her portraits of migrating women. Though she, like the others, represents the deficiencies of life in the privileged West, she is more interested in psychic displacement, adaptation, and the state of in-betweenness her female protagonists occupy. More than Desai and Gordimer, she begins to define a new kind of multinational identity, even as she registers the deficiencies and even calamities of a life transplanted. Prompted by the disbanding of family life—through loss or the passage of time—some of her characters, principally Ashima, seem to emerge into a new state of independence and affiliation. They are able to sustain more than a single cultural allegiance, or perhaps it's more accurate to say that they surmount and even reject the need for an identity tied to one nation and one place. To some extent, Desai's and Gordimer's characters also transcend the bounds of national identity: Uma takes the American poet Ella Wheeler Wilcox as her lodestar and Julie chooses her home in a culture that is remote on many levels from the place where she was born. And, in the end, all three—Ashima, Uma, and Julie—discover a coveted state of existence beyond and outside of conjugal life.

These writers widen the sphere of fiction in pursuit of a notion of self not easily defined or located, a self not reliably fixed on maps that are themselves unreliable. Through split narratives, palimpsest, and renderings through memory, they go beyond questions of immigration and geography to existential questions of belonging and to an exploration of individual, rather than national, identity. In this they echo Cather, who declared that the history of every country begins in the heart of an individual; Gertrude Stein, who averred that every writer lived inside herself; and Tess Slesinger's Elizabeth in *The Unpossessed*, who claims that she belongs "anywhere and nowhere." Our multinationals insist, however, that individual identity, idiosyncratic and self-created though it may be, is not ultimately separable from national culture, even national origins. Traveling inward, to the kitchens, bedrooms, and living rooms of isolated family dwellings, they move outward to consider radical displacements and the spanning of enormous distances and, beyond that, to imagine how, within and without boundaries, it might be possible to locate the self.

PART II: WORLD POLITICS

We turn from the politics of home—the domestic narratives that nonetheless reflect wider struggles of dislocation and oppression—to the world political stage where the legacies of colonialism can end in revolution, conflagration, or slaughter. Leaving the suburban homes of the Pattons, the Smales, the Summers, and Mrs. Sen, we now take up narratives in which survival itself cannot be taken for granted. Some of these narratives are also split, spanning continents and following immigrants to a new world, but others, like Gordimer's *The Conservationist* and Edwidge Danticat's *The Farming of Bones*, zero in on a society in transition or collapse.

In such cases, locating the self becomes not only a more complicated but a more dangerous enterprise. The very act of imagining that it might be possible to find the "exact location of a person" and having found it, to fully inhabit it, attests to women's ability and, in fact, their determination to "create dangerously."[23] This is how Danticat, appropriating the title and injunction of one of Albert Camus's polemical lectures, describes the power, indeed, the obligation of the immigrant artist to give those suspended between separate, often rival cultures what is often denied them—a voice, a distinct identity, and a place of their own.

This is a heartening prospect, but one that does not go unchallenged, even, as we shall see, by those writers most invested in its ultimate realization. The challenge may be posed in the form of a leading, but not quite rhetorical, question: Does the possibility of locating, indeed, *settling* the self in a "home country" of one's own discovery or creation represent a genuine augury of the multinationalist's social future, or is it a mirage conjured by wishful, if commendably utopian, thinking? The answer in any given instance largely depends on whether one is isolated from the greater world or struggling, often haplessly, to make one's way through and within it. Outside the confines of the family dwelling (or compound), space not only expands, it segments into diverse, often competing spheres of influence and aspiration. The affections and devotions nurtured in the intimate spaces of the kitchen, living room, or bedroom are often set aside, disregarded, or in extreme, but not infrequent, cases nullified in the transactions of the marketplace, the calculations of the boardroom, the policies and plans of those in power. It is in this wider, variegated sphere that the stability of Tradition, whose first and last safeguard is the home, confronts modern forces of transformation and unrest. Their clash profoundly unsettles long-established relations obtaining between inside and outside, private and public, home and world. The home increasingly loses its authority as a bastion of Tradition, while the greater world just beyond the threshold of home appears more vital and appealing, but also more overwhelming, even threatening, in its multifariousness.

How overwhelming? Diligently reading the *New York Times* gives some sense of how fragmented the world appears to those trying to locate their place within it. This, at least, is the way knowledge of the teeming world comes to Biju, the economic migrant from the backwaters of West Bengal. His struggles to make a new life in the cosmopolitan melting pot of lower Manhattan are depicted with a kind of jesting despair in Kiran Desai's *The Inheritance of Loss*, another geographically divided and culturally splintered novel that reflects the immigrant experience. It is in reading the *Times* that Biju encounters the names and hears of the grievances of countries and oppressed populations he never knew existed:

> Former slaves and natives. Eskimos and Hiroshima people, Amazonian Indians and Chiapas Indians and Chilean Indians and American Indians and Indian Indians, Australian aborigines, Guatemalans and Colombians and Brazilians and Argentineans, Nigerians, Burmese, Angolans, Peruvians, Ecuadorians, Bolivians, Afghans, Cambodians, Rwandans, Filipinos . . . [the list goes on for half a page, making it most likely that the reader will remember the daunting number rather than the specific names of the world's various peoples] . . . Zambians, Guinea-Bissauans, Cameroonians, Laotians, Zairians coming at you screaming colonialism, screaming slavery, screaming mining companies screaming banana companies oil companies screaming CIA spy among the missionaries screaming it was Kissinger who killed their father and why don't you forgive third-world debt; Lumumba, they shouted, and Allende; on the other side, Pinochet, they said, Mobutu; contaminated milk form Nestlé, they said; Agent Orange; dirty dealings by Xerox. World Bank, UN, IMF, everything run by white people. Every day in the paper another thing![24]

The diverse nations, tribes, and ethnicities of the world register as little more than dismal entries in a catalog of wrongs, to which new outrages are added daily. What Biju hears resounding through this avalanche of bad news are the primal screams of cultures in distress, of countries ravaged by modernization, military adventurism, and economic imperialism. The din of the world is such that it is hard for Biju to formulate the questions that sound so distinctly and urgently in the quiet interiors of *The Pickup*, *Fasting, Feasting*, and *The Namesake*, questions that Gordimer reports haunted her as a "colonial" writer unsure of her own location on the political and moral map of world literature: "What [is] my place? Could it know me?"

The adventuring heroines and stalwart pioneers of the nineteenth and early twentieth centuries who traveled to distant lands in search of freer, more consequential lives may have asked themselves the first question, but not the second. Once they found or made their place, it knew them, as Ántonia's place knows her; or as Sweetwater knows Captain Forrester; or as America knows Mary Antin, a young Jewish immigrant born again on its shores. These peripatetics were the makers, not the casualties, of modernity, who confidently took up their role as imaginative and dedicated agents of futurity.

But a more uncertain future awaits the immigrants whose travails and losses are chronicled by Kiran Desai and Edwidge Danticat. The displaced and dispossessed who populate their more overtly political fictions are exposed and vulnerable to every conceivable evil, from the prejudices and injustices visited upon those of low social or economic status (like Biju) to the wrenching indignities endured by refugees from political tyranny (as recounted in Danticat's *The Dew Breaker*) to the outright massacre of targeted populations (the subject of Danticat's *The Farming of Bones*, a fictional retelling of the massacre of Haitians ordered by Trujillo, the dictator of Haiti's neighbor, the Dominican Republic, where many Haitians sought work as harvesters of sugarcane). Casualties rather than makers of change, they experience modernity not as the creation of a new life but as the destruction of the old. Political refugees, they flee the autocratic "Papas" who, in a cruel parody of fatherhood, imprison and slaughter their children.

This mounting loss of agency and choice represents a dispiriting development in the history and literature of migration. It becomes harder, sometimes impossible, to sustain the hope that the private self, in pursuit of personal happiness and prosperity, and the public self, whether voluntarily or forcibly caught up in geopolitical movements and events, can be joined in common purpose. This was the hope that sustained the nation-building emigrants who sought their fortune and happiness in the New World. That hope wanes for those aspiring to build a life or create a modern nation in the postcolonial world, even among those who stay at home. Gyan, the other lower-caste male protagonist of *Inheritance of Loss* who is determined to "rise" to a higher economic and social rank, initially believes that his love for Sai, an upper-class, socially cloistered young woman he is tutoring, will not conflict with his gradual involvement with local insurgents agitating for a land and country of their own. (Their slogan, "Gorkhaland for the Gorkhas" is another primal scream of the world's dispossessed.) A serious, perhaps fatal miscalculation, as Gyan comes to realize: "The trouble was that he'd tried to be part of the larger questions, tried to become part of politics and history. Happiness had a smaller location."[25]

Happiness has traditionally been located in the home, but this private sanctuary is increasingly defenseless against the encroachment of modernity, with its new freedoms and new forms of servitude, its promise of economic prosperity but also threats of exploitation and spiritual impoverishment. Modernization irreversibly changes the look and undermines the values, indeed, the stable character of the reassuringly familiar world of tradition, that smaller location that Jewett called the parish and Cather identified as the patria. The imminent disappearance of the patria as both a social reality and as an imaginative locale is the most catastrophic loss recorded in the multinational novel. The patria or neighborhood that conferred identity and inspired allegiance from Virgil's Mincio to Cather's Red Bluff recedes before the advancing tide of modernization; familial and social ties are stretched to the point of snapping by the relations forged by the cash nexus, international markets, transnational political movements, and the "social" media that usurp the place and role of the local gossip or newspaper as a source of news. The parish is replaced by the global village, in which everyone is connected but no one feels at ease, much less at home, with one another.

The multinational novels that turn outward, toward history and politics, are thus not as sanguine about the future as those in which the self contemplates and pursues its happiness in the smaller and more sheltered locations of home and patria. Yet in these novels, too, fiction serves as a mode of prophecy, as well as cultural and ideological critique. Their clear-eyed, often bleak depiction of the hardships of diasporic existence is brightened by the promise of another order of life in a country that is yet to be born. Imagining this promised land is the self-appointed mission of those women writers who "create dangerously." Much depends on this creative effort, nothing less than the reclamation of the patria, what Salman Rushdie, in a phrase shadowed by the sorrow of the exile, calls the "imaginary homeland."

Femaleness, the embodied lens of gender, is both a help and a hindrance in these imaginative excursions into the wider world. Gordimer, who has written about both the journey inward and the voyage out, is an exemplary instance of how a woman writer may call upon her femaleness to create dangerously. This was no idle metaphor in the South Africa in which Gordimer came of age as a writer. "It was not only the ninety-plus categories of offence described by the censorship laws that silenced people," she recalls. Writers opposed to apartheid were also "silenced by the necessity for secrecy; for by the thread of an ill-considered word might hang a life—the speaker's, the writer's, or that of another."[26]

Reflecting on her own historical situation, Gordimer credits the "thread" of her femaleness for showing her a way out of her social and imaginative isolation as a white South African "colonial" debarred "not by land and sea, but by law, custom, and prejudice" from "the great continuous to-and-fro of life" just beyond the gate of her suburban enclave. "The only genuine connection with social form," she writes, "was through my femaleness. . . . Rapunzel's hair is the right metaphor for this femininity; by means of it I was able to let myself out and live in the body, with others, as well as—alone—in the mind."[27] Gordimer does not regard femininity as a sexual masquerade, a complex performance of cultural codes, nor does she consider it to be the artful sublimation of innate sex traits into bodily gestures that please and allure. Femininity for her incorporates and transcends these meanings. It is active and manifest in her work not as a sex characteristic but as an existential disposition and imaginative readiness to be and to commune with other people. Rapunzel's hair is both a part of the self and a means to reach beyond it, the means and the metaphor for experiencing the life of the body and the life of others.

Femaleness so exalted comes perilously close to the primal stuff of fairy tales. Gordimer acknowledges as much in figuring her youthful, protonovelistic self as a Rapunzel held captive by apartheid's rigidly enforced divisions in race and class, but also by her own treasured solipsism (which ensures that she can be alone in the mind). Thus, however right Rapunzel's hair may be as a metaphor for the creative femininity that links and affiliates the young Gordimer to the outer world and its social forms, it is insufficient as an image for the tangle of feelings, motives, perceptions, and strategies that prompt the mature novelist's more subtle and deeper penetration into the life of bodies, selves, communities, and nations. Rapunzel's hair may be strong enough to let her out of her confined existence, but it can hardly be relied upon to support and steady her once she has descended into "the great continuous to-and-fro of life."

Gordimer elsewhere fashions a different, more radical metaphor to convey her historical plight as a writer seeking her place and her obligations in the bustling multiracial, multicultural world. Her source this time is not a fairy tale, but Camus's unfinished, posthumous novel, *Le Premier Homme*, whose protagonist, Jacques, is a white colonial born and raised in Algiers, a Frenchman, even though he has never been to France. Gordimer sees her childhood self mirrored in the fictional Jacques, for whom "the premise is: Colonial." A stark, arguably reductive premise on which to posit an identity, yet nonetheless, in and behind that geopolitical label, Gordimer discovers "the story of who I am": "The one who belongs nowhere. / The one who has no national mould" (*WB*, 120). Gordimer not only finds the premise of her story in *Le Premier Homme* but also finds the precept for creating—dangerously—a postcolonial identity: "The precept is: if he is not to be the dangling participle of imperialism, if he is not to be the outsider defined by Arabs—a being non-Arab—what is he? A negative. In this sense, he starts from zero. He is the constructor of his own consciousness. He is The First Man" (*WB*, 121). So defined, the "one who belongs nowhere" is not only without a place and a national patrimony, but he is also without a recognized value—zero here designating the moral emptiness of a being without any place or tradition to claim and to mold him. "Let us not worry about gender" in applying this precept and in adopting this model, Gordimer advises, or we would lose the sense of zero as a starting point rather than as an endpoint. Zero is the place where the old life and the old grammar are expunged; zero is where the "dangling participle of imperialism" suddenly becomes a subject constructing his own consciousness. It is here, at zero, where loss becomes gain, where the artistic consciousness is born, a second birth that allows Gordimer to escape the confinements and definitions imposed by law, custom, and prejudice. For Gordimer, then, Jacques's story charts a positive trajectory for her own unfolding story: "I was to come to the same necessity; to *make myself*, in the metaphor of the First Man, without coherent references, up on his own two legs, no model on how to proceed" (*WB*, 121).

That new consciousness is feverishly at work in *The Conservationist*, Gordimer's own favorite work and certainly her most radical experiment in novelistic self-location. In her effort to create dangerously, Gordimer not only did not worry about meeting conventional gender and narrative expectations but actually welcomed the chance to jettison all references to her own femininity and antiapartheid, liberal politics. The risk she took involved not so much the story she wanted to tell as the way she wanted to tell it. Her story, after all, was rather an old one, at least for Gordimer: the story of South Africa during the last days of apartheid. But the perspective and manner of its telling were disturbingly new in the best modernist manner. The novel is told primarily from the point of view of a white South African male named Mehring, an international businessman and weekend farmer who is gradually losing his mental hold on reality despite enjoying a privileged and secure location in his country's racist regime. The success of this narrative strategy depended on Gordimer's ability to imagine the thoughts, fantasies, presumptions, and eventual disintegration of a consciousness thoroughly repugnant to her, but in some ways also like her. Mehring, the narrative tells us, is of German origin— "[f]rom South West. A long way back—,"[28] thus calling attention to how remote, both in space and time, Mehring is from his ancestral roots. In other words, the quintessential colonial.

Mehring, however, is the colonial figured not as the First but as the Last Man. He is the economic Insider and cultural Outsider struggling to defend his power and preserve his identity during the fraught days of the interregnum, when apartheid South Africa was in its death throes and a new postcolonial nation was struggling to be born. The novel chronicles his efforts to conserve his farm, his refuge from the pressures of city life and the stresses of his job, as it comes under a series of natural assaults: first a drought, then a fire, finally a flood. But the most serious threat to his hegemony is the unaccountable appearance of a dead native on the edge of his property. The dead man, without any mark or possession that can identify him, is in some ways the most powerful figure in the novel. As a portent and uncanny agent of Mehring's ultimate undoing, his unexplained appearance on the farm confirms Gramsci's observation that "in the interregnum there arises a great diversity of morbid symptoms."[29]

It is, in fact, his morbidity that marks Mehring as the quintessential figure of the interregnum. That morbidity is expressed by a diversity of symptoms, all of which can be traced, although never completely reduced, to his compulsion for mastery—over his land, his workers, his mistress, and his son. His dubious moral claim to the land is somewhat bolstered by the role and obligations he willingly assumes as a conservationist, an identity the novel's title confers on him, with how heavy an irony is not as easy to determine as one might think. Yet despite his efforts to preserve the farm as a viable ecosystem, the earth itself seems to rebuke his efforts to work and fructify it: "broken into, the earth gives up the strong musty dampness of a deserted house or violated tomb" (*TC*, 226). Working the land is here adjudged to be inseparable from defiling it. The conjoined images of home and tomb insinuate something not only unnatural but unholy about Mehring's presumption to own and rule over the "the home that is the earth itself," the mythic ground from which life arose and to which it is destined to return. Such acts of "breaking in" structure the novel and advance its theme of intrusion and violation, a theme that is elaborated in different, but overlapping, registers: as a secular crime against property, but then more compellingly, as a desecration of the sacrosanct earth.

The novel begins with an apparently minor break-in—the theft by local native children of "[p]ale freckled eggs" (*TC*, 9), an image redolent of germinating life, but also of the fragile impermeability of Mehring's intact consciousness. This act of trespass is followed immediately by another, more unnerving one: a dead man, known to no one on or off the farm, is discovered in a bed of reeds at the farthest verge of Mehring's property. "How is happen?" (*TC*, 15), his native caretakers quizzically ask. The novel will never answer that question. The body lying among the reeds remains an uncanny presence that at times seems to have arrived as an emissary from another world.

The form and the events of the novel suggest that he very well may be. "Dead, dead finish" (ibid.), Mehring is assured by his caretaker. On the contrary, the story is not finished but just beginning, and the dead man will be resurrected many times in Mehring's mind. The dead man also opens up the novel to another dimension of reality, one represented by nine quotations from the Reverend Henry Calloway's 1879 *Religious System of the Amazulu*, which are interspersed between the narrative sequences of the novel.[30] These quotations maintain their own place and integrity in the sequence of events. They never enter the primary narrative, nor do they form part of the consciousness of any of the characters. Even the narrator (as opposed, of course, to Gordimer, the author) seems unaware of their existence until the last paragraph of the novel, which invokes the spirit if not the letter of the Amazulu belief system in the ritual burial of the dead man: "They had put him away to rest, at last he had come back. He took possession of this earth, theirs. One of them" (*TC*, 267). These lines, which reinstate the unknown man to his ordained place in the tribal and cosmic order, have the cadence and efficacy of a benediction, resanctifying an otherwise accursed earth.

This extension of the novel into transcendental realms complicates and enriches the ecological theme of conservation explicitly evoked by the title. The religious sense that the earth has its own order and sanctities complements the novel's lyrical paeans to the indigenous fecundities of the South African veld, as symbolized by those pale freckled eggs. Home in this ecological context is reconceived and reconfigured as a habitat. The narrator assumes the guise and authority of a naturalist interpreting human behaviors that otherwise seem aberrant or outright mad. "Everything," she assures us, "has its range[,] and the most random seeming creatures are shown by studies to have a topography of activity from which they never depart, although they may appear to casual observation to weave and backtrack aimlessly, almost crazily, free" (*TC*, 75). "Almost crazily" becomes a certainty as the naturalist-narrator tracks Mehring's routine movements within his habitat. His movements become increasingly erratic and unpredictable as the novel progresses, and Mehring, as if in internal flight from that dead man down in the reeds, wanders further afield from the "normal" topography of his mental activity.

The resulting changes in Mehring's topography of activity lead him to new perceptions, not so much about himself as about the world he thought he had mastered. He becomes aware of the land as a living reality that has its own language and syntax: "things come to life before his eyes as the syntax of a foreign language suddenly begins to yield meaning" (*TC*, 133). In concert with, at times in counterpoint to, this newly acquired fluency in the language of the earth, Mehring begins to roam more freely in his mind, revisiting the past, recalling the circumstances of his failed marriage, his tense relation to his son (whom he suspects has homosexual leanings), and his emotionally fraught exchanges with his "Gypsy" mistress, who echoes Gordimer's liberal politics and whose desire to get into Mehring's bed seems intended as an ironic commentary on Gordimer's desire to get inside his head.

The narrator's own topography of activity also begins to widen and expand. She no longer focuses so obsessively on Mehring's consciousness and ranges out to encounter those whose habitat overlaps his—the Amazulu natives, the first inhabitants of the land and its true conservators, and the Gujarati-speaking Indians, immigrants who bring their mercantile traditions to Africa and are also excluded from apartheid's white hierarchy of power and influence. At the novel's end, she abandons Mehring completely as a locus of identification and of story, but not before following him as he descends into madness. The penultimate chapter culminates in Mehring's psychotic break when, waiting at a stoplight, he sees himself being lured by a young hitchhiker to a dump site on the outskirts of the city where he is/will be robbed and murdered. The incident is narrated as if it is already happening and Mehring is commenting on his own life at the very moment of its extinction.

But Mehring doesn't lose his life, only his home, such as it was, in the narrative. The coffin being made in the first sentence of the final chapter is meant, we learn after an initial confusion, not for him but for the unknown dead man who is finally being laid to rest. Mehring himself is never mentioned again by name; he is referred to only as "the farmer," who, we are told, is on his way to "one of these countries white people go to" (*TC*, 266). With his departure, the narrative serenely turns its attention to the burial of the unknown man. In his ritual interment, the novel finds its ending, but also its vision for the future. In *The Conservationist*, Gordimer remarked in an interview:

> [T]here's a resurrection theme, and that is also a political theme. At the end of the book there's a disguised message. The slogan of the biggest banned liberation movement, a kind of battle cry widely adopted, is the African word *mayibuye*. This means, "Africa, come back." You can see the whole idea of resurrection is there. And if you look at the end of *The Conservationist* you'll see that this thought is reworded, but it is actually what is said when the unknown man is reburied: that although he is nameless and childless, he has all the children of other people around him; in other words, the future. He has people around him who are not his blood brothers and sisters but who stand for them. And that he has now been put with proper ceremony into his own earth. He has taken possession of it. There's a suggestion of something that has been planted that is going to grow again.[31]

As Gordimer says, the African slogan "Africa, come back" is echoed, translated, and invested with new meaning in the novel's final narrative declarations: "They had put him away to rest, at last he had come back." The "at last" intimates that the return of the unknown man to the earth is a fulfillment of a prophetic hope that Africa will "come back" and be restored to those who have always called it home.

As political prophecy, this is not only moving but prescient. The dismantling of apartheid, which began with ongoing negotiations from 1990 to 1993 between President de Klerk's government and the African National Congress and culminated in the 1994 democratic election that brought Nelson Mandela to power, came two decades after the novel was published (1974). But Gordimer does not limit the theme of resurrection to its immediate historical and political situation. Resurrection retains its transcendental import in the novel's ceremonial closing lines that keep the ancient traditions alive.

This religious meaning may be itself resurrected from a passage from Calloway not quoted by Gordimer but active in her evocation of the Amazulu belief system—the passage that expounds the Amazulu creation myth. It concerns Unkulunkulu, "the most Ancient Man" to whom the Amazulu trace their origin:

> The old man say, Unkulunkulu came into being, and gave being to man. He came out of a bed of reeds. He broke off from bed of reeds. The children ask, "where is the bed of reeds out of which Unkulunkulu came." For men now have gone into every country; in which of them is the bed of which from which Unkulunkulu broke off? They say in answer, "Neither do we know."[32]

Like the waiting place that lies at the limits of Jewett's country of the pointed firs, the bed of reeds is that mythic locus, ordinarily invisible and by many discredited, where spirits go to and fro between the lower and the upper world. The location of that bed of reeds remains unknown, lost to us, as the Amazulu myth tells us, because the Ancient One, who gave being to man, broke off from the seedbed of Creation even as he broke into human history. It falls to the First Man, constructing out of his own consciousness, to take us back to that mythic place of creation and spiritual transit—the First Man, that is, as reconceived and embodied by a female writer determined to venture out into the world and to make, one day, her own place within it.

"All artists," writes Edwidge Danticat, "writers among them, have several stories—one might call them creation myths—that haunt and obsess them."[33] Danticat's personal myths are drawn from the blood-soaked history of Haiti, the former French colony that, through an appallingly violent revolution, transformed a population of slaves into the world's oldest black republic, a historic achievement that was subsequently diminished by military coups, occupation by American forces, and the dictatorial rule of Papa Doc and Baby Doc Duvalier. Born in Haiti, Danticat had not one but two native tongues, French and its colonial offspring, Kreyòl (Haitian Creole), a patois born out of the exchanges between African slaves and their French-speaking masters. Although English, the language in which she was educated and first learned to write, remains her literary language, the oral rhythms and traditions of her native Kreyòl infuse her prose. This bilingualism determines her own special, rather precarious location as a Haitian American writer. Danticat's parents immigrated to America when she was eight; she joined them four years later, a separation that may have intensified her feeling of not being fully at home in either world. In representing the Haitian experience at home and abroad, Danticat writes both from the standpoint of a native informant with an insider's knowledge of customs and beliefs, and from the more detached but never disinterested perspective of "outside" observer. This blurs and finally splinters the perspectives, as well as the continuity of her narratives, making it difficult, if not impossible, to locate her at the core of her own work.

Creativity is in fact linked in her mind and in her work to a spiritual readiness for movement and travel. This is the organizing precept that defines the story of who she is: "The nomad or immigrant who learns something rightly must always ponder travel and movement, just as the grief-stricken must inevitably ponder death."[34] There is that cadence again; learning rightly is the premise of, and preparation for, creating dangerously, the adverb having in both instances the force of a directive. (In her epigraph to *The Dew Breaker*, Danticat, quoting Osip Mandelstam, will enjoin her readers to "Read it . . . quietly, quietly"). It is not enough, then, merely to learn; the immigrant artist must take pains to learn rightly. Given how much depends on this imperative, Danticat is clear about what is involved in fulfilling it. Learning rightly demands that one must "ponder" the exigencies of movement, a word that suggests the burden in acquiring and in living with such knowledge, just as the equipoise of the sentence balances the thought of movement outward and elsewhere with the grief of leave-taking, whether of a country or a person, both being ways that death enters and asserts its power over our lives.

This association of new beginnings with death suggests that a mythical, not historical, logic governs Danticat's creative ponderings. Yet the two are fused in her own mind, as she reveals in discussing how the execution of Marcel Numa and Louis Drouin, dissenters who worked to bring down the regime of dictator François "Papa Doc" Duvalier, became an originary event for her in "its heartrending clash of life and death, homeland and exile."[35] These public deaths assumed the grandeur of a creation myth in her mind, since they spoke to her of the full depth and extent of loss—the loss of life, home, and homeland.

Danticat perceived the rudiments of another vital creation myth in the 1937 slaughter of thousands of Haitian workers ordered by the Dominican dictator Rafael Trujillo. This massacre is the historical subject of her 2008 novel, *The Farming of Bones*, a title that suggests the grim husbandry of Trujillo's genocidal campaign against people with darker skin, but literally translates the Kreyòl term for the life of cane cutters, "tray trè pu zo, the farming of bones."[36] The title is the first sign of Danticat's resolve to write a historical narrative that echoes the idiom and reflects the experience of those who suffer rather than inflict violence. She risks, even courts, unreliability in handing her novel over to a first-person narrator, a woman who accepts that, for her, as for the other wayfarers of the Haitian diaspora, "It's either to be in a nightmare or to be nowhere at all" (*FB*, 2). An objective, third-person narrator would be better qualified to analyze the historic causes and dreadful, recurrent motifs of this nightmare, but not what it feels like to be trapped within it. A third-person narrator would lack, that is, the emotional authority of Amabelle Désir, whose very name seems chosen as an amulet against the misfortunes that threaten human love and desire. (The book is partly dedicated "in confidence" to her, as if the novel was born of a secret communication between Danticat and her own creation.) That she is the servant and not just the namesake of love is confirmed in the novel's opening when Amabelle, a Haitian domestic who serves an aristocratic Dominican household, delivers her mistresses' twins, a boy and a girl who is smaller and darker, and a few minutes younger than her brother. These children enter the novel less as full-fledged characters than as allegorical personifications of those stark oppositions—light and dark, Spanish and French—that fuel the historic enmity between the two nations that share the island of Hispaniola. In what may be intended simply as a historical irony or, more passionately, as Danticat's imaginative retaliation against the racial ideology that motivated Trujillo's genocidal campaign, the boy who inherits the pallid aristocratic looks of the Spanish masters dies in infancy, while the dark-skinned daughter thrives—even grows in stature!—despite the eugenic taint that makes her mother fearful, as she confesses to Amabelle, that she might be "mistaken for one of your people" (*FB*, 12).

Their birth certificates underscore the extent to which their birth is celebrated for its symbolic rather than human significance. The task of recording their birth falls not to Amabelle but to Papi, the children's grandfather, an avid supporter of General Franco in the Civil War raging in Spain. It is he who inscribes "ceremoniously in his best script the time and place of the births, noting that it was on the thirtieth of August, the year 1937, the ninety-third year of independence, in the seventh year of the Era of Generalissimo Rafael Lemonades Trujillo Molina, Supreme Commander-in Chief, President of the Republic" (*FB*, 17). With hardly a qualm, the children Amabelle helped bring into the world are delivered over to history, which is dominated by generalissimos with the will and force to impose their own narratives upon it.

To counter the nightmare of history that she is compelled to witness and recount, Amabelle sets aside entire chapters of her narrative to describe the healing effect of her love for a cane cutter, whose profession is honored by the title. She intermittently withdraws from her historical narrative into the achingly small and haunted location where she can recall and still imagine what happiness was and still might be. It is in this sanctuary that she ponders the name and story that would never be remembered but for her devotions.

These devotions take the form of a quasi-ritualistic chant of the novel's opening sentence—"His name is Sebastian Onius"—that with each repetition brings the dead lover and his story back to life:

> His name is Sebastian Onius and his story is like a fish with no tail, a dress with no hem, a drop with no fall, a body in the sunlight with no shadow.
>
> His absence is my shadow, his breath my dreams. New dreams seem a waste, needless annoyances, too much to crowd into the tiny space that remains.
>
> Still I want to find new manners of filling up my head, new visions for an old life, waterless rivers to cross and waterfall caves to slip into over a hundred times each day. (*FB*, 281)

For Amabelle, the smaller location in which happiness abides has contracted into a space so tiny that it can only contain the shadow, not the substance, of her old loves and new dreams. Yet this is where Danticat chooses to forge her creation myth, knowing that her story may have no end, no tail, no hem, no final fillip to consecrate the human losses her fiction memorializes.

The image that anchors this creation myth is the memory Amabelle carries with her into exile. It is an image of "the giant citadel that loomed over my parents' house in Haiti, the fortress rising out of the miter-shaped mountain chain, like two joined fists battling the sky" (*FB*, 46). The tiny space in which Amabelle stores memories of her old life suddenly expands to accommodate a structure that aligns the sanctity of the parent's house with the strongholds of power. The instinct to fight or answer back one's oppressors, dormant for most of the novel, finally bursts through Amabelle's rather hushed narration, which normally "speaks quietly, quietly," in the voice of someone who fears detection and reprisal. A new vocabulary, more grand and more confident, floods Amabelle's otherwise unruffled and unpretentious prose—giant, citadel, miter.

Her suddenly emboldened rhetoric culminates in an image of two joined fists, clenched in a proud gesture of defiance.

This conjoined image of home and citadel, of home *as* citadel, locates *The Farming of Bones* within the vicinity, if not the precincts, of myth. But it is through language, in fact, through a single word, that Danticat hopes to secure her novel a permanent place there. The word is not grandiose, but utterly commonplace—parsley, *perejil* in Spanish, *pèsi* in Kreyòl. All the more horrific, then, that this word determines who lives and who dies. In a historical note appended to the novel, Danticat reports that the Dominican soldiers devised a linguistic test to identify Haitians who might have "passed" as Dominicans. They asked those they suspected of being Haitians to pronounce the word "perejil." "The trilled rolling 'r' does not exist in Haitian Creole," Danticat writes, "so Haitians would pronounce the word 'peweril' rather than 'perejil.'" Their faulty pronunciation condemned them to death. This linguistic test is a modern variant of the ancient Gileadites' use of the word "shibboleth" to identify the Ephraimites, whom they defeated in battle and then hunted down for slaughter. (The Ephraimites could only manage "sibboleth.") Danticat makes this connection explicit in the epigraph of the novel, taken from Judges 12:4–6, which recounts the death of forty-thousand Ephraimites who could not sound the "sh" any more than the Haitians could manage the rolling "r." This biblical precedent locates the Dominican atrocities of 1937 within a world history of massacres.

This linguistic and phonetic trial is the final ordeal the Haitians must endure before they reach the safety of their homeland. Amabelle provokes this crisis but is not herself at the center of it. That place is taken by Odette, a woman who has accompanied Amabelle in her flight and who Amabelle inadvertently drowns by covering her mouth so that they might swim undetected across the Massacre River to the opposite home shore. The pathos of this episode is intensified, but also transformed into a heroic register, when Odette manages, with her parting breath, to mouth "pesi,"

> not calmly and slowly as if she were asking for it at a roadside
> garden or open market, not questioning as if demanding of

the face of Heaven the greater meaning of senseless acts, no effort to say "perejil" as if pleading for her life. (*FB*, 203)

Amabelle, who is beginning to learn rightly the force as well as the meaning of words, ponders the impact of this dying declaration:

> The generalissimo's mind was surely as dark as death, but if he had heard Odette's "pesi," it might have startled him, not the tears and supplications he would have expected, no shriek from unbound fear, but a provocation, a challenge, a dare. To the devil with your world, your grass, your wind, your water, your air, your words. You ask for perejil, I give you more. (ibid.)

Odette's "pesi" is the "Let there be light" of Danticat's creation myth. Used "to wash a new infant's hair for the first time and— along with boiled orange leaves—a corpse's remains one final time (*FB*, 62), "pesi" is an ordinary word that invokes "the larger miracles in small things, the deeper mysteries" of the commonplace, the domain of daily life. These deeper mysteries are also invoked in the fairy tale of Rapunzel, a figure Gordimer had invoked to represent her nascent artistic consciousness of the world of other people. As Marina Warner has pointed out, parsley is the herb from which Rapunzel derives her name (e.g., Persinette) in the Italian and French variations of the fairy story that predate the versions of the Brothers Grimm.[37]

Although Odette shows Amabelle how to defy power, she does not point the way to those "waterless rivers" on whose shores Amabelle might glimpse "new visions for an old life." The figure who seems to lead the way into that new world is someone hardly at home in this one, a "tall, bowlegged old man with a tangled gray beard, wearing three layers of clothing padded with straw" (*FB*, 285)—a comic scarecrow, a grizzled magus out of a fairy tale. The locals call him "Pwofesè," the Professor, but what he professes is not knowledge but vision: "I am walking to the dawn," he serenely tells anyone who asks him where he is going. In the closing pages of the novel, he stops for a moment to gaze upon Amabelle who, returning to the Massacre River, the scene of so much horror, floats in its waters, "cradled by the current, paddling like a newborn in a washbasin" (*FB*, 310). The symbolic equation of the river with uterine waters is obvious, as if Danticat could find no path to rebirth and renewal except through the time-tested routes of mythic commonplaces.

Yet there is another possible way of reading this moment, so saturated with the imagery of rebirth. Perhaps the risk of cliché is one of the perils the artist confronts in creating dangerously. The novel's final moments gesture toward this possibility. Amabelle reports that the Professor, a sorrowful scarecrow of a man, perhaps a figure for Haiti itself, turns away from the scene he has just witnessed and resumes his solitary way: "He, like me, was looking for the dawn" (ibid.). Is one or both of them deluded in thinking that the dawn will deliver them from the nightmare of history?

For the dawn holds its own terrors, as Danticat's next novel, *The Dew Breaker*, reveals. There is grim poetry in this title, which, like *The Farming of Bones*, is taken from Kreyòl, a language overburdened with the names and tales that inspire horror. The "dew breakers" is the Kreyòl word for the torturers of Papa Doc Duvalier's paramilitary force, the Tonton Macoutes, themselves named after the bogeyman in Haitian folklore "who abducted unruly children at night and put them in his knapsack."[38] In the novel, the Tonton Macoutes are abetted by a high-ranking woman in Duvalier's military regime who yearns to establish her own female cadre of torturers, to whom she would give the name Fillette Lalo, after a fabled Haitian bogeywoman who eats children (*DB*, 216). These bogeymen and women stride out of Haitian folklore into the living history that Danticat's novel records, frightful allegories of Duvalier's cannibalization of his own people.

The Dew Breaker domesticates these allegories as familiars of every Haitian household, thus making them more, not less, frightful. *The Conservationist* and *The Inheritance of Loss* were also novels that began with the fact and the looming specter of home invasion, but though such intrusions of malevolent forces, whether in the form of uncanny bodies or political marauders, are morally unsettling, they do not undermine the foundations of the home, which remain intact at novel's end. Not so in *The Dew Breaker*, a novel that recounts the story of a man, a house, and a country divided against itself. The title character is portrayed as split in two, at once predator and prey, both the agent and the victim of state terror. He is a man who appears to be an ordinary Haitian immigrant living in the United States with his wife and daughter but is actually living incognito, trying to escape his past as a Tonton Macoute. Among his victims, we eventually learn, is his wife's brother; in fact, this murder is what initiates, in a kind of gruesome turn on the courtship plot, his noticing, then marrying her. The home they establish as immigrants in New York is less a refuge from history than a traumatic site whose foundations are soaked in blood.

In her later works, like *The Pickup*, Gordimer seemed more optimistic than in her earlier fiction that the utopian hope voiced in William Plomer's poem to "go to another country . . . And start again" might one day be realized. Lahiri's fiction and, more recently, her literary renaturalization as a speaker, writer, and translator of Italian, open up yet another space to locate the multinational self. But any such efforts to start again in another country or to forge and sustain multiple cultural affiliations prove unavailing for Danticat's characters, haunted as they are by the unmitigated calamity of Haitian history and the diaspora of its peoples. The dew breaker is a demonic symbol and incarnation of this cultural fracturing that slaughters any private or public hope for starting over on more open, if not always more innocent, ground.

In breaking the peace and promise of dawn, the dew breaker also disrupts the prospect of a unified narrative. The trauma he has inflicted and the trauma he suffers shatter both the core and the continuity of his story. At first the novel does not seem a novel at all but a series of stories set both in Haiti and America, arranged in no particular order and having no apparent relation to one another except as they illustrate the catastrophic disintegration of Haiti's civil society under Duvalier. Danticat has suggested that one way to read her splintered narrative might be to see it as a "fragmented collage with as many additions as erasures." The novel contains just such an image in the wanted poster that calls for the apprehension of Emmanuel Constant "FOR CRIMES AGAINST THE HAITIAN PEOPLE." Constant, who created a death squad after a military coup sent the Haitian president Jean-Baptiste Aristide into exile, is real, as were his crimes, which included "circling entire neighborhoods with gasoline, setting houses on fire, and shooting fleeing residents" (DB, 79), some of whom had their faces scalped. Constant, a torturer in exile and in hiding, is a demonic double of the dew breaker, around whom the separate characters and their stories eventually come—or rather are pieced—together.

Constant's crimes are historical "additions" to the collage Danticat quietly, dangerously constructs. But they also represent the inevitable "erasures" made by a traumatized or guilty memory. Even boldface caps cannot keep the public record of Constant's crimes intact. Deletions, sometimes outright expurgations, are inevitable, subject to the vandalism of time: "After a while, the letters and numbers started disappearing so that the word rape became ape and the 5 vanished from 5,000, leaving a trio of zeros as the number of Constant's casualties" (DB, 79). This is one way that a culture inherits loss—its history is slowly and irrecoverably expunged by time, neglect, and the sheer fatigue of adding one more story to the annals of horror. Greater than the fear that history will repeat itself is the fear that it will be lost forever. This historical dread closes the novel, whose final pages are given over to Anna, the wife of the dew breaker who murdered her brother. Caught between her daughter's newfound knowledge of her father's monstrous past and her own hopes to redeem that past, Anna laments that "the most important relationships of her life were always on the verge of being severed or lost, that the people closest to her were always disappearing." The last image that occupies her mind and closes the book is the memory of her brother's burning "in the prison yard at dawn, leaving behind no corpse to bury, no trace of himself at all" (DB, 242).

In closing her novel with such an image, Danticat confronts the likelihood that her own textual collage, a plaintive representation of the past in all its pain, disorder, and incomprehensible cruelty, is itself fated for extinction. This possibility does not discourage her, but acts, as she says, as a "powerful muse" that forces her to "sit down and express something from very deep within."[39] Yet Danticat is also aware of the temptation of the artist to make the tragedies of history "your own private catharsis."[40] Danticat faces this temptation in her treatment of the dew breaker's daughter, Ka, the only character allowed to tell her story in the first person and the only "modern" artist in the novel. Ka, Kreyòl for "good angel," is a sculptor who attempts to render what she perceives to be her father's noble character in an iconic wooden figure. Her father steals the sculpture and consigns it to the depths of a lake, unable to tolerate the falsity, the inadvertent blasphemy of her adulatory conception of him.

That Ka does not continue as a narrator for the stories that succeed hers signals Danticat's refusal to write as the dutiful daughter of Haiti, creating idealized images of its brutal and brutalizing history. She insists on more radical and at the same time more traditional, even ancient models for her preternatural art, which does not so much record history as redream it. She populates the novel with revenants, night talkers, and funeral singers, figures indigenous to Haitian folk culture who are believed to have access to the world of dreams and the realm of the dead. These figures form a kind of confraternity of immigrant artists, exiled from the daytime reality that hides as many wrongs as it exposes. Their major burden is to keep the past from disappearing, to keep it alive and give it words, which often means keeping open the paths and links to the spirit world.

For Danticat, the rite of art is invariably and inevitably a rite of remembrance. Such rites are not the particular provenance of any one culture or set of traditions or beliefs. For her own rites, Danticat draws on two ceremonial models outside Haitian traditions, both from the Egyptian Book of the Dead. The first is the Negative Confession, a ceremony that precedes the weighing of hearts, when final judgment is rendered. The Negative Confession gives "the dead a chance to affirm that they'd done only good things in their lifetime" (DB, 22). The other is the rite for Driving Back Slaughters, a ritual that repels and subdues real as well as imaginary monsters. The first ritual is performed in the private, domestic precincts of the novel, portraying, and in portraying, absolving the dew breaker as a monster. Read as a Negative Confession, the story of the dew breaker tells a conversion narrative in which the murderous torturer who took so many lives is born again in a new world as a husband and father capable of doing good things. Driving Back Slaughters is the rite that advances Danticat's political aim in the novel—to drive those monsters slaughtering their own people out into the open, where they will be indicted and condemned for their crimes against the Haitian people.

These rituals provide Danticat a way not just to record and judge the past but to envision an "afterlife" for her characters and for a traumatized Haiti. Through them she is able to convert the horrendous history recounted in *The Dew Breaker* into what one chapter title announces as "The Book of Miracles." In this book the dew breaker is condemned for his deeds but also saved by the love of and for his wife and daughter, both hailed as good angels who can "make him take root" (*DB*, 25). That is one miracle. The other miracle encompasses the possibility that he may be restored to his patria and be henceforth rooted in the daily, nontraumatic life of his people

Still, stories, unlike the history out of which they are made, have to stop. The question, as Gyan says, is where.[41] There are two points where we might consider stopping our account of multinationals struggling to make a new life for themselves in the great and unfamiliar world opening before them. Both are thresholds where they encounter the forces that are changing the life, and ultimately the character, of their patria. The first is from *The Inheritance of Loss*. It comes in the only chapter prefaced by a date—27 July 1986—a day of riot and insurrection. Gyan, who we discover at novel's end has collaborated with the Gorkhan insurgents, is walking through the local marketplace when he suddenly finds himself caught up in the swift movements of history:

> As he floated through the market, Gyan had a feeling of history being wrought, its wheels churning under him, for the men were behaving as if they were being featured in a documentary of war, and Gyan could not help but look on the scene already from the angle of nostalgia, the position of a revolutionary. But then he was pulled out of the feeling, by the ancient and usual scene, the worried shopkeepers watching

from their monsoon-stained grottos. Then he shouted along with the crowd, and the very mingling of his voice with largeness and lustiness seemed to create a relevancy, an affirmation he'd never felt before, and he was pulled back into the making of history.

Then, looking at the hills, he fell out of the experience again. How can the ordinary be changed?[42]

Gyan is pulled, then pulled apart, by the forces sweeping him into the force field of history, where shouts of peoples and cultures in distress reverberate with a largeness and lustiness that create their own relevancy. These are the shouts of revolution, clamoring to change, ideally transfigure, the ordinary. But even as he joins his voice to these revolutionary shouts, Gyan is momentarily arrested by "the ancient and usual scene" of shopkeepers. The scene, though ancient (we would say "traditional") is hardly a usual one, however. It is disturbed and disordered by the shopkeepers' fear that the trades and trading indigenous to their patria will be eradicated by revolution, modernization, and incursions of the global marketplace. How does one change the ordinary? Perhaps the question should be: How does one change the ordinary without destroying the patria?

The second stopping point would leave us not looking backward on worlds that are disappearing over the course of a single lifetime but looking forward to the transfiguration of the ordinary into a new patria. Danticat has repeatedly expressed her willingness to belong nowhere and to go anywhere, perhaps no more poignantly than in an interview during which she paused to reflect on a line from a poem by Gustavo Pérez Firmat that has special meaning for her: "I belong nowhere else." Danticat then goes on to confess that she herself might say, "I belong nowhere else at this particular time. Because who knows? I might migrate somewhere else in the future and adopt the language of that place. Once you leave the place where you were born, it's easier to leave the place where you live at any time."[43]

Migration is no longer a destiny imposed or endured but a vocation that is chosen. Such dislocations are necessary, Danticat contends, if one is to create, dangerously, creation myths for the future. Their imaginative readiness to move to another place, to accept and even affirm the fact that they may belong nowhere, is what distinguishes the writers we have called the multinationals as the First Men and Women of a new world order.

CONCLUSION

Promised Lands

ᕮᖇᕮᕪ

"To discover the exact location of a 'thing' is a simple matter of factual research. To discover the exact location of a
person: where to locate the self?"
— Nadine Gordimer, *The Pickup*[1]

GORDIMER'S QUESTION IS A GOOD ONE, perhaps the overriding
question for women writers contemplating the world before them,
but it is not an easy one to answer. Women writers take different
routes and devise their own rites of passage to discover the promised land where the self is free and the imagination empowered to
enter what George Eliot called "the great movements of the world."
This great tradition of women writers and their public lives begins,
as we have seen, with the will to adventure, a determined rejection
of domestic life, and a departure to places unknown: to sea, to
Labassecour, to the Levant. Our early heroines set sail, sometimes
recklessly or impulsively, but always taking pleasure in desert-
ing an incommodious, constraining home and watching a natal
land retreat behind them. As she embarks on the Channel crossing
that separates her from England, Charlotte Brontë's Lucy Snowe
is neither "depressed [nor] apprehensive." On the contrary, she
feels "animated and alert" at the prospect of what Gordimer calls
"pulling up anchor." These heroines and their progeny repeatedly
abandon home in order to find a better one or, to be more precise,
to find some fuller version of themselves, a mission, or a vocation.
To locate the self is as urgent for them as for the masculine adventurers of epic, except that the wide world of feverish movement,
heroic action, and public engagement throws roadblocks before

the woman wanderer that her male counterpart seldom encounters. Among these barriers is the very idea, enshrined in myth and fantasy, that a man's home cannot possibly prosper without the presiding spirit and presence of woman. Translated into a vision of woman's writing that does not reflect the historical record, this myth also generates the idea of a literary tradition that is domestic, housebound, even trapped.

Our chapters are filled, however, with departures: Harriet Martineau to the United States to write of abolition; the slaves in her story "Demerara" to Liberia; Linda Brent to the North; Willa Cather and Sarah Orne Jewett's characters to new territories, new patriae; Mary Antin to America; Vera Brittain to the Mediterranean to nurse soldiers; Martha Gellhorn first to Czechoslovakia, then Italy and Germany to cover the horrors of war; Jhumpa Lahiri's Indian women to the estranging West; Edwidge Danticat's Haitian émigrés to flee torture and seek elusive respite from the past. Some of these women are adventurers, others exiles or refugees. We called them peripatetics in our introduction to evoke both the omnipresent pattern of departure and the entrenched habit of itinerancy or perpetual movement. As Danticat suggests in *Create Dangerously*, the process of emigrating invites more wandering— the "nomad or immigrant who learns something rightly must *always* ponder travel and movement," she insists.[2] Not only is discovery of self or true Home problematic and even tenuous, but this discovery, or search, often takes the form of creating, writing, recording, and reporting back—activities that never really find a terminus. Engagement with the wider world—in debates on slavery; in the embrace, but also the critique, of reformist, sometimes outright revolutionary politics; in thinking peace during times of war; in chronicling the separation, as well as the joyous heroic adventure, of migration and resettlement—leads to writing and more writing, to an open-ended project of "creating dangerously" for women. It also simultaneously determines their lasting sense of themselves as political beings. The political consciousness, created in time of catastrophe, of a Harriet Beecher Stowe, Vera Brittain, or Martha Gellhorn, does not fade into complacency or find easy resolution.

This restlessness and sense of perpetual itinerancy coexists in our writers, however, with dreams of a promised land: not exactly a return to the paradise that Mother Eve was forced to abandon but a place of freedom imagined and not yet achieved. This place might be the modest dream of egalitarian marriage, as in Harriet Beecher Stowe's formulation of "spiritual partnership" between husband and wife. "There can be no home," she protested, "without liberty." For the slave characters Stowe created in her fiction, the stakes were infinitely higher and their freedom of a more fundamental kind. Eliza and George Harris flee first to Canada and then to Liberia to escape the bonds of slavery and achieve the status of full personhood. In *Dred*, fugitive slaves gather at the Dismal Swamp, likened by Stowe to the wilderness the Israelites were forced to inhabit before they could reach the promised land. In the case of these exiles, the land of Canaan—or the Garden of Eden—may exist north of the US border. It does not yet exist in New York State, as Harriet Jacobs's Linda Brent makes clear, or in any place where she remains vulnerable to recapture or cannot "sit with [her] children in a home of [her] own." Toni Morrison offers a fleeting glimpse of one Edenic location for the fugitive slaves of *Beloved*—the clearing where Baby Suggs preaches, more a promise than a realization of paradise. There, Sethe "claim[s] herself," at least for a short while. Even a "freed self" is in need of claiming.

The vision of emigrating to a promised land echoes in Elizabeth Gaskell and Mary Antin as well. Gaskell ends *Mary Barton* with exile to Canada for Mary and Jem Wilson, disgraced and shut out of employment in Manchester. As if to signal the flight into fantasy she takes in this conclusion, Gaskell renders the backwoods of Canada a pastoral retreat, a return to Eden. The narrator evokes this place as a vision of her own, a picture she sees in her mind's eye:

> I see a long low wooden house [the narrator tells us], with room enough, and to spare. The old primeval trees are felled and gone for many a mile around; one alone remains to overshadow the gable-end of the cottage. There is a garden around the dwelling, and far beyond that stretches an orchard. The

glory of the Indian summer is over all, making the heart leap
at the sight of its gorgeous beauty.[3]

Mary and Jem, as first woman and man, occupy a space as far
from the industrial north of England as Gaskell can imagine: not
just pastoral but "primeval," with the perfect amount of shade, a
garden ringing their hand-hewn cottage, and an orchard of trees
from which they can eat without fear of sin and fall. Mary has recovered from the physical crisis caused by her public shaming and,
as if to prove it, has given birth to a healthy, crowing child. This is
a new Eden, postlapsarian but without sin.

Antin, like the American pioneers who went West and claimed
another country, a patria of their own, fuses the fantasy of rebirth
into freedom with the reality of leaving a land of oppression for
one that she can call her own—"my country." She calls her immigrant's memoir *The Promised Land* to signal the extent of her
hopes and their grand fulfillment and, like those born into American slavery, to call on the biblical trope of wandering in the wilderness and arriving at the destination of true Home. Antin, born into
exile, *goluth*, could not locate a homeland until she emigrated. So
radically separate are the two phases of her life that she calls her
older self, the subject of her memoir, Mashka, and declares that
woman's life at an end. She discovers the location of self and a new
identity in a wholly strange culture, in what for other migrants and
immigrants might seem an alienating world.

In the era of multinationalism, the hope of a promised land
may still exist, but it is viewed more often than not with skepticism, if not suspicion. Julie and Abdu, Gordimer's lovers in *The
Pickup*, seek a promised land in their union, in each other, in love-
making, and in "another country / Not yours or mine." They find
it nowhere, especially not in each other, for their points of origin
foster in them wholly disparate notions of what a promised land
might be. As if by negation, each lover's experience of homeland
generates an opposite dream of paradise. Writers like Gordimer,
Desai, Lahiri, and Danticat refuse the simple idea of a promised
land, a one-way flight from oppression or deprivation, and aim to

undermine, even debunk, the belief in "pulling up anchor" as an easy answer to existential angst or even social chaos. Past traumas migrate alongside—and within—the immigrant; hunger in one country turns out to be a reflection of gluttony and excess in another; deracination can be reproduced at home or abroad, as can complacency.

Setting sail and relocation may not be the final answers for the late twentieth- and twenty-first-century women writers we consider here, but being in transit, eschewing a stationary home, and turning the condition of exile and in-betweenness into art may be. Lahiri's Ashima chooses to live "without borders," a citizen of no one place, and Lahiri herself continues to live and write in a variety of places and languages. Danticat's Ka, agonized daughter of a former Haitian torturer, and many of the other characters in *The Dew Breaker* create art—sculptures, totems, songs, shrines—to tell their personal stories and the stories of their people. Gordimer's Julie will try to live as a stranger in an alien culture in order to be more herself. Out of the reality of a newly configured globe, these writers have remapped the world, created a new kind of literary geography, and forged selves that defy familiar notions of belonging.

Thinking back through the writers and their protagonists profiled in this book, however, we note that this strain of imagining a promised land as a place not yet conceived starts long before our own time. The peripatetics, pioneers, wanderers, and Exaltadas we have offered here are all, to one degree or another, dreamers and visionaries. This may be most apparent in the Americans, with their utopian and transcendental leanings. Margaret Fuller's Exaltadas occupy not a land unknown but a state of being unrealized: a state of heroic activism within a cadre of other political revolutionaries, all women. But even in the British tradition, with its more inveterate realism and materialist inclinations, it is not only Pemberley or the little cottage at Ferndean or the schoolroom in Labassecour that constitute a new (and indeed, utopian) idea of home but also a kind of indeterminate and unanchored space— Anne Elliot's imagined shipboard existence, Deronda's anticipated voyage to a nation that does not exist, Mrs. Ramsay's reveries of travel in nonhuman form, and Vera Brittain's dreams of a pacifist, socialist state. Departing from familiar ground—slamming the door on domestic life, seeing the shores of home fade in the distance, and hailing the world, whether real or imagined, before them—seems the crucial moment for all.

Notes

INTRODUCTION: THE PERIPATETICS

1. Vera Brittain, *Testament of Youth* (New York: Penguin, 2005), 98.
2. Both classic and postmodern accounts of the novel assign women a similar role. Ian Watt, in his seminal account of the rise of the novel, blames conservative tendencies in women writers and readers for the "characteristic weakness and unreality to which the form [of the novel] is liable" (Watt, *The Rise of the Novel* [Berkeley: University of California Press, 1971]), 299. Nancy Armstrong, in her Foucauldian treatment of so-called domestic fiction, cautions that women are loath to acknowledge the power they have as "shapers and enforcers of bourgeois domestic life" (*Desire and Domestic Fiction* [New York: Oxford University Press, 1987]), 251.
3. See Ellen Moers, *Literary Women: The Great Writers* (New York: Doubleday, 1976), 36–41.
4. Elizabeth Barrett Browning, *The Letters of Elizabeth Barrett Browning*, ed. Frederick G. Kenyon (London: Smith, Elder, 1897), 2:110–11.
5. Lionel Trilling, "Emma and the Legend of Jane Austen," in *Beyond Culture* (New York: Viking, 1968), 54. Trilling is actually quoting this phrase—which he wholeheartedly endorses—from an anonymous critic in the *North British Review*.
6. Gillian Beer wrote famously of Eliot's need for her heroines to "endure their own typicality." See Beer, "Beyond Determinism: George Eliot and Virginia Woolf," in *Women Writing and Writing about Women*, ed. Mary Jacobus (London: Croom Helm, 1979), 88.
7. Willa Cather, *One of Ours* (New York: Knopf, 1922), 299.
8. Ibid., 299.

CHAPTER 1: ADVENTURE

1. Virginia Woolf, *To the Lighthouse* (San Diego: Harcourt, Brace, 1981), 62.
2. Mary Seacole, *Wonderful Adventures of Mrs. Seacole in Many Lands* (Oxford: Oxford University Press, 1988), 2, 4.
3. John Ruskin, *Sesame and Lilies* (New Haven: Yale University Press, 2002), 77.
4. Karen R. Lawrence, *Penelope Voyages: Women and Travel in the British Literary Tradition* (Ithaca: Cornell University Press, 1994).
5. Paul Zweig, *The Adventurer: The Fate of Adventure in the Western World* (New York: Akadine Press, 1974), 68–69.
6. Ibid., 12.

7. Virginia Woolf, *A Room of One's Own* (Orlando, FL: Harcourt, Brace, 2005), 66–69.

8. Ibid., 70.

9. Woolf, *To the Lighthouse*, 6–7.

10. Virginia Woolf, "Professions for Women," in *Women and Writing*, ed. Michèle Barrett (San Diego: Harcourt Brace Jovanovich, 1979), 59–60.

11. Elaine Showalter, *A Literature of Their Own: British Women Novelists from Brontë to Lessing* (Princeton: Princeton University Press, 1977), 73.

12. Charlotte Brontë, "Biographical Notice of Ellis and Acton Bell," in *Wuthering Heights*, ed. Pauline Nestor (London: Penguin, 2003), xlix.

13. Mary Wollstonecraft, *Vindication of the Rights of Woman* (London: Penguin, 1982), 131, 121–22.

14. Ibid., 105–7.

15. Ibid., 79.

16. Mary Wollstonecraft, *Letters Written during a Short Residence in Sweden, Norway, and Denmark* (Lincoln: University of Nebraska Press, 1976), 162. Further citations are given parenthetically by page number in the text.

17. Mary Wollstonecraft, *Maria, or The Wrongs of Woman* (New York: W. W. Norton, 1975), 103.

18. Ibid., 28, 135.

19. Ibid., 153.

20. Ellen Moers, *Literary Women: The Great Writers* (New York: Doubleday, 1976), 126.

21. Jane Austen, *Pride and Prejudice* (New York: Penguin, 2003), 228. Further citations are given parenthetically in the text as *P&P* followed by the page number.

22. Susan Fraiman, "Jane Austen and Edward Said: Gender, Culture, and Imperialism," *Critical Inquiry* 21 (Summer 1995): 811.

23. Jane Austen, *Persuasion* (New York: Penguin, 1998), 10. Further citations are given parenthetically in the text as *P* followed by the page number.

24. Brian Southam, *Jane Austen and the Navy* (London: Hambledon and London, 2000), 282.

25. Virginia Woolf, *The Common Reader* (New York: Harcourt, Brace and World, 1953), 147.

26. Mary Ellis Gibson, "Henry Martyn and England's Christian Empire: Rereading *Jane Eyre* through Missionary Biography," *Victorian Literature and Culture* (1999): 435.

27. Charlotte Brontë, *Jane Eyre* (New York: Penguin, 2006), 126.

28. Lawrence, *Penelope Voyages*, 26–27.

29. Charlotte Brontë, *Villette* (London: Dent, 1983), 2. Further citations are given parenthetically in the text as *V* followed by the page number.

30. Alfred Lord Tennyson, "Ulysses," in *The Poems and Plays of Tennyson*, ed. Christopher Ricks (London: Longmans, Green, 1969), 565, lines 59–61; Zweig, *Adventurer*, 61.

31. George Eliot, *Middlemarch* (New York: Penguin, 1994), 838.

32. George Eliot, *The Mill on the Floss* (New York: Penguin, 2003), 516.

33. George Eliot, *Daniel Deronda* (New York: Penguin, 1995), 185. Further citations are given parenthetically in the text as *DD* followed by the page number.

34. Anna Jameson, *The Diary of an Ennuyée* (Boston: Houghton Mifflin, 1885), 18.

35. Seacole, *Wonderful Adventures*, 4.

CHAPTER 2: EMANCIPATION

1. Elizabeth Barrett Browning, *The Letters of Elizabeth Barrett Browning*, ed. Frederick G. Kenyon (London: Smith, Elder, 1897), 2:110–11.

2. Ibid., 259; emphasis added.

3. George Eliot, *The George Eliot Letters*, ed. Gordon S. Haight (New Haven: Yale University Press, 1955), 6:301.

4. In her indispensable book, *Joyous Greetings: The First International Women's Movement, 1830–1860* (Oxford: Oxford University Press, 2000), Bonnie Anderson writes: "Of all these internationalist ideas [humanity, rights, equality, freedom] that they applied to women's situation, 'emancipation . . . the catchword of the day,' . . . proved the most significant and widely used" (114).

5. See Raymond Williams, *Culture and Society* (Harmondsworth: Penguin, 1968), 99–119.

6. Elizabeth Gaskell, *Mary Barton* (Harmondsworth: Penguin, 1970), 38. Further citations are given parenthetically in the text as *MB* followed by the page number.

7. Bonnie S. Anderson, *Joyous Greetings: The First International Women's Movement*, 16–18.

8. Harriet Beecher Stowe, *Uncle Tom's Cabin* (New York: W. W. Norton, 1994), 388. Further citations are given parenthetically in the text as *UTC* followed by the page number.

9. Harriet Beecher Stowe, *Dred: A Tale of the Great Dismal Swamp* (Chapel Hill: University of North Carolina Press, 2000), 316.

10. Ibid., 446.

11. Margaret Fuller, *"These Sad But Glorious Days": Dispatches from Europe, 1846–1850*, ed. Larry J. Reynolds and Susan Belasco Smith (New Haven: Yale University Press, 1991), 164–65.

12. George Eliot, "Three Novels" and "Silly Novels by Lady Novelists," in *The Essays of George Eliot*, ed. Thomas Pinney (New York: Columbia University Press, 1963), 325, 319.

13. Elizabeth Gaskell, *The Life of Charlotte Brontë* (Harmondsworth: Penguin, 1985), 483.

14. Eliot, "Woman in France: Madame de Sablé," in *Essays*, 55.

15. George Sand, "Review of *Uncle Tom's Cabin*," in *Uncle Tom's Cabin*, 462.

16. Quoted in Winifred Gérin, *Elizabeth Gaskell: A Biography* (Oxford: Oxford University Press, 1980), 230.

17. Harriet Martineau, *Writings on Slavery and the American Civil War*, ed. Deborah Anne Logan (DeKalb: Northern Illinois University Press, 2002), 42. Further citations are given parenthetically in the text as *WS* followed by the page number.

18. See Deborah Anne Logan's introduction to Martineau's *Illustrations of Political Economy: Selected Tales* (Toronto: Broadview, 2004).

19. Ibid., 42.

20. Harriet Martineau, *Illustrations of Political Economy: Selected Tales* (London: Charles Fox, 1834), 20, 30. Further citations are given parenthetically by page number in the text.

21. Clare Midgley, *Woman Against Slavery: The British Campaigns, 1780–1870* (London: Routledge, 1995), 97.

22. Harriet Jacobs, *Incidents in the Life of a Slave Girl* (Cambridge, MA: Harvard University Press, 1987), 1. Further citations are given parenthetically in the text as *ILS* followed by the page number.

23. Regarding Lydia Maria Childs as editor of Jacobs's narrative, see Jean Fagan Yellin's introduction to *Incidents*, xiii–xxxiv.

24. Jacobs, *Incidents*, 113; Stowe, *Uncle Tom's Cabin*, 94.

25. Lisa Surridge, "Working-Class Masculinities in *Mary Barton*," *Victorian Literature and Culture* 28, no. 2 (2000): 339.

26. Stowe, *Dred*, 236.

27. Elaine Showalter, *A Jury of Her Peers: American Women Writers from Anne Bradstreet to Annie Proulx* (New York: Knopf, 2009), 109.

28. Jennifer Fleischner, *Mastering Slavery: Memory, Family, and Identity in Women's Slave Narratives* (New York: New York University Press, 1996), 5.

29. Deborah M. Garfield, "Earwitness," in *Harriet Jacobs and "Incidents in the Life of a Slave Girl": New Critical Essays*, ed. Deborah M. Garfield and Rafia Zafar (Cambridge: Cambridge University Press, 1996), 107.

30. Stowe, *Dred*, 439.

31. In Joan D. Hendrick, ed., *The Oxford Harriet Beecher Stowe Reader* (Oxford: Oxford University Press, 1999), 488.

32. Ibid., 490.

33. Stowe, *Dred*, 446, 405.

34. For the tense relationship between Jacobs and Stowe, and Stowe's knowledge of Jacobs's garret hiding place, see Deborah Garfield, "Conclusion: Vexed Alliances; Race and Female Collaborations in the Life of Harriet Jacobs," in *Harriet Jacobs and "Incidents in the Life of a Slave Girl,"* 283–85.

35. William L. Andrews, ed., *Six Women's Slave Narratives* (Oxford: Oxford University Press, 1988), 3.

36. Anita Goldman, "The Tender of Memory: Restructuring Value in Harriet Jacobs's *Incidents in the Life of a Slave Girl*," in *Harriet Jacobs and "Incidents in the Life of a Slave Girl,"* 242.

37. Toni Morrison, *Beloved* (New York: Signet, 1991), 29. Further citations are given parenthetically by page number in the text.

CHAPTER 3: PIONEERS

1. Moers's term is also the title of chapter 7 in *Literary Women* (New York: Doubleday, 1976), 122–41.

2. Ibid., 197.

3. Willa Cather, *My Ántonia* (Boston: Houghton Mifflin, 1954), 197. Further citations are given parenthetically in the text as *MÁ* followed by the page number.

4. Willa Cather, *O Pioneers!* (Boston: Houghton Mifflin, 1988), 9. Further citations are given parenthetically in the text as *OP* followed by the page number.

5. "For we think back through our mothers if we are women." Virginia Woolf, *A Room of One's Own* (Orlando, FL: Harcourt, Brace, 2005), 82.

6. Willa Cather, *A Lost Lady* (New York: Vintage, 1990), 45.

7. George Eliot, *Middlemarch* (New York: Penguin, 1994), 3.

8. Sarah Orne Jewett, *Country of the Pointed Firs*, in *Novels and Stories* (New York: Library of America, 1994), 413. Further citations are given parenthetically in the text as *CPF* followed by the page number.

9. Charles Olson, *Call Me Ishmael* (Baltimore: Johns Hopkins University Press, 1997), 15. Hermione Lee first called attention to this passage as key to understanding Cather's nativist art in *Willa Cather: Double Lives* (New York: Vintage, 1989), 6.

10. Willa Cather, *The Song of the Lark* (Boston: Houghton Mifflin, 1988), 199. Further citations are given parenthetically in the text as *SL* followed by the page number.

11. Mary Antin, *The Promised Land* (New York: Penguin, 1997), 1; emphasis in original. Further citations are given parenthetically in the text as *PL* followed by the page number.

12. Gertrude Stein, *Paris France* (New York: Liveright, 1970), 2.

13. Zora Neale Hurston, *Their Eyes Were Watching God* (Urbana-Champaign: University of Illinois Press, 1978), 50. Further citations are given parenthetically in the text as *TE* followed by the page number.

14. Willa Cather, preface to *Alexander's Bridge* (New York: Meridian, 1987), xxv.

15. Henry James, *The Ambassadors* (New York: Penguin, 1986), 218.

16. Willa Cather, preface to *The Best Stories of Sarah Orne Jewett* (Boston: Houghton Mifflin, 1925), xviii.

17. Elaine Showalter, *A Jury of Her Peers: American Women Writers from Anne Bradstreet to Annie Proulx* (New York: Knopf, 2009), 183.

18. See ibid., 194–95, for a thorough and sensible account of the controversies attending this passage, which accuse Jewett of harboring racist and ethnocentric sentiments and being complicit with the militaristic rhetoric and ambitions of American imperialism.

19. Gertrude Stein, *The Making of Americans* (New York: Dalkey Archive, 2006), 3.

20. Ibid., 27.

21. Frederick Turner, "Pioneer Ideals and the State University," http://xroads.virginia.edu/~Hyper/TURNER/chapter10.html.

22. Marilynne Robinson, *Housekeeping* (New York: Farrar, Straus and Giroux, 1990), 192. Further citations are given parenthetically by page number in the text.

23. Marilynne Robinson, *Gilead* (New York: Farrar, Straus and Giroux, 2004), 246.

24. Marilynne Robinson, "My Western Roots," in *Old West–New West: Centennial Essays*, ed. Barbara Howard Meldrum (Moscow: University of Idaho Press, 1993). Available at https://www.washington.edu.

25. Marilynne Robinson, "Wilderness," in *The Death of Adam: Essays on Modern Thought* (New York: Picador, 2005), 247.

26. Robinson, "My Western Roots."

CHAPTER 4: WAR

1. Vera Brittain, *Testament of Youth* (New York: Penguin, 2005), 292. Further citations are given parenthetically in the text as *TY* followed by the page number.

2. Rose Macaulay, *Non-Combatants and Others* (London: Hodder and Stoughton, 1916), 222. Further citations are given parenthetically in the text as *NC* followed by the page number.

3. Rose Macaulay, "Many Sisters to Many Brothers," in *Cambridge Poets of the Great War*, ed. Michael Copp (Cranbury, NJ: Rosemont, 2001), 72.

4. Virginia Woolf, *Three Guineas* (Harmondsworth: Penguin, 1982), 46; emphasis added.

5. See, for example, David Mitchell's discussion of the Pankhursts' involvement in the war effort in *Women on the Warpath* (London: Jonathan Cape, 1966), 45–83 and 271–301.

6. Radclyffe Hall, "Miss Ogilvy Finds Herself," in *The Penguin Book of First World War Stories*, ed. Barbara Korte and Ann-Marie Einhaus (London: Penguin, 2007), 242; Mrs. Humphry (Mary) Ward, "Wordsworth's Valley in War-Time," in *The Book of the Homeless*, ed. Edith Wharton (New York: Charles Scribner's Sons, 1916), 153.

7. Edith Wharton, "Writing a War Story," in *The Collected Short Stories of Edith Wharton*, ed. R.W.B. Lewis (New York: Charles Scribner's Sons, 1968), 364.

8. Mitchell, *Women on the Warpath*, 197.

9. Sandra Gilbert, "Soldier's Heart: Literary Men, Literary Women, and the Great War," in *Behind the Lines: Gender and the Two World Wars*, ed. Margaret Rudolph Higonnet and Jane Jenson (New Haven: Yale University Press, 1987), 216.

10. Ibid., 214.

11. Virginia Woolf, *A Room of One's Own* (Orlando, FL: Harcourt, Brace, 2005), 74.

12. Ibid., 77.

13. Ibid., 93.

14. Virginia Woolf, *To the Lighthouse* (San Diego: Harcourt, Brace, 1981), 132.

15. Rebecca West, *The Return of the Soldier* (New York: Penguin, 1998), 6.

16. Ibid., 7.

17. Hermione Lee, *Edith Wharton* (New York: Knopf, 2007), 486. See chapters 14 and 15 of Lee's biography for a fascinating account of the full extent of Wharton's war activities.

18. Edith Wharton, *Fighting France: From Dunkerque to Belfort* (Gloucester: Dodo Press, 2007), 54, 59.

19. Ibid., 62.

20. Ibid., 76.

21. Lee, *Edith Wharton*, 496.

22. Samuel Hynes, *A War Imagined* (New York: Atheneum, 1991), 126–29.

23. Clair Tylee, *The Great War and Women's Consciousness* (London: Macmillan, 1990), 114.

24. Suzanne Raitt, "'Contagious Ecstasy': May Sinclair's War Journals," in *Women's Fiction and the Great War*, ed. Suzanne Raitt and Trudi Tate (Oxford: Oxford University Press, 1997), 67. See also Raitt's biography of Sinclair, *May Sinclair: A Modern Victorian* (Oxford: Oxford University Press, 2000).

25. Raitt, "Contagious Ecstasy," 67, 69; Tylee, *The Great War*, 132–33.

26. Rebecca West, "Miss Sinclair's Genius," in *The Young Rebecca: Writings of Rebecca West, 1911–17*, ed. Jane Marcus (Bloomington: Indiana University Press, 1982), 305.

27. Hynes, *A War Imagined*, 95.

28. May Sinclair, *A Journal of Impressions in Belgium* (New York: Macmillan, 1915), 53, 177. Further citations are given parenthetically by page number in the text.

29. May Sinclair, *The Tree of Heaven* (New York: Macmillan, 1917), 80. Further citations are given parenthetically in the text as *TH* followed by the page number.

30. Suzanne Raitt, "May Sinclair and the First World War," *Ideas from the National Humanities Center* 6, no. 2 (1999): 42.

31. Virginia Woolf, *The Diary of Virginia Woolf*, ed. Anne Olivier Bell (New York: Harcourt Brace Jovanovich, 1982), 4:177; emphasis added. See also Marion Shaw, "'Alien Experiences': Virginia Woolf, Winifred Holtby and Vera Brittain in the Thirties," in *Rewriting the Thirties*, ed. Keith Williams and Steven Matthews (Harlow, UK: Addison Wesley Longman, 1997), 37–52.

32. Woolf, *Three Guineas*, 118.

33. Ibid.

34. Marina MacKay makes the most convincing and nuanced argument that the "belatedness of Woolf's war awakening makes it impossible to superimpose the pacifist polemic of *Three Guineas* on her last novel." See "Virginia Woolf and the Pastoral Patria," in *Modernism and World War II* (Cambridge: Cambridge University Press, 2007), 30.

35. "The Few: Churchill's Speech to the House of Commons," Churchill Society, London, http://www.churchill-society-london.org.uk/thefew.html. "In the last war," Churchill reminded the nation, "millions of men fought by hurling enormous masses of steel at one another. 'Men and shells' was the cry, and prodigious slaughter was the consequence. In this war nothing of this kind has yet appeared. It is a conflict of strategy, of organisation, of technical apparatus, of science, mechanics, and morale."

36. Elizabeth Bowen, postscript to the first US edition of "The Demon Lover," in *The Mulberry Tree: Writings of Elizabeth Bowen*, ed. Hermione Lee (New York: Harcourt, Brace, 1988), 96.

37. Ibid., 97.

38. Woolf, *Diary*, 5:263.

39. Woolf, *Three Guineas*, 125.

40. Woolf, *Diary*, 5:297.

41. Virginia Woolf, "Thoughts on Peace in an Air Raid," in *Collected Essays, Vol. 6: 1933–1941*, ed. Stuart N. Clarke (London: Hogarth Press, 2011), 242.

42. Woolf borrows this phrase from Lady Astor, the first woman member of Parliament. Lady Astor's warning against unconscious Hitlerism was offset by her own more or less conscious Hitlerism as expressed in her appeasement politics, reinforced by her association with the so-called Clivedon set, a coterie of British aristocrats who saw Hitler as a "solution" for the problem of Jews and communists. Woolf ignores the provenance of the phrase and the fascist politics subtending it. She is more interested in excoriating the male "fighting instinct," which she condemns as an alibi for "the rage for acquisition" that drives men "to desire other people's fields and goods perpetually; to make frontiers and flags; battleships and poison gas, to offer up their own lives and their children's lives" (*Room*, 38).

43. Woolf, *Diary*, 5:285.

44. Elizabeth Bowen, "Summer Night," in *Collected Stories of Elizabeth Bowen* (New York: Vintage, 1982), 590. Further citations to Bowen's stories from this edition are given parenthetically in the text as *CS* followed by the page number.

45. Martha Gellhorn, "Introduction, 1959," in *The Face of War* (New York: Atlantic Monthly Press, 1988), 2.

46. Bowen, postscript to "The Demon Lover," in *The Mulberry Tree*, 95.

47. Virginia Woolf, *The Years* (New York: Harcourt, Brace, 1965), 422.

48. Gertrude Stein, *Wars I Have Seen* (London: Brilliance Books, 1984), 75.

49. Woolf, *Room*, 82.

50. Virginia Woolf, *Between the Acts* (San Diego: Harcourt Brace Jovanovich, 1969), 188. Further citations are given parenthetically in the text as *BA* followed by the page number.

51. Bowen, postscript to "The Demon Lover," in *The Mulberry Tree*, 96.

52. In her postscript to "The Demon Lover," Bowen identifies this as one of her wartime stories in which the ghost might be "subjective purely." Nonetheless, she insists that these ghosts are "certainties" that "fill the vacuum for the uncertain 'I'" (*The Mulberry Tree*, 98).

53. Bowen, postscript to "The Demon Lover," in *The Mulberry Tree*, 96; emphasis in original.

54. Woolf, *Diary*, 5:242.

55. Iris Origo, *War in Val D'Orcia* (Boston: David R. Godine, 1984), 120.

56. Ibid., 58.

57. Gellhorn, *The Face of War*, 6.

58. Bowen, postscript to "The Demon Lover," in *The Mulberry Tree*, 99.

59. Martha Gellhorn, *A Stricken Field* (Chicago: University of Chicago Press, 2011), 93. Further citations are given parenthetically in the text as *SF* followed by the page number.

60. A letter from Prague to her New York editor, dated July 4, 1938, and reproduced in her afterword to *A Stricken Field*, 305–6.

61. Spain, Gellhorn writes in her affecting, bitter afterword to the novel, "was my Cause: Spain was what I believed in and I could not bear to watch the suffering any longer. My work was useless, none of my articles had saved anyone. When I saw the starved withered babies in the Barcelona Children's Hospital and the eyes of the silent wounded children, I decided to get out. Leave Europe, leave history. I could not help anyone; I could remember for them." *A Stricken Field*, 310.

62. E. M. Delafield, *The Provincial Lady in Wartime* (Chicago: Chicago Academy, 1986), 1, 7.

63. Olivia Manning, *Levant Trilogy: "The Danger Tree," "The Battle Lost," and "The Sum of Things"* (London: Penguin, 1982).

64. Ibid., 333.

65. Gellhorn, *Point of No Return* (Lincoln: University of Nebraska Press, 1995), 330. Further citations are given parenthetically in the text as *PNR* followed by the page number.

66. Gellhorn, *The Face of War*, 2.

67. Ibid., 337.

CHAPTER 5: POLITICS

1. Aristotle, *Politics*, 1276b 28–29.

2. Ibid., 1317a: 40-1317b13.

3. Margaret Fuller, *Woman in the Nineteenth Century* (New York: W. W. Norton, 1971), 33. Further citations are given parenthetically by page number in the text.

4. Joan Didion, foreword to *Political Fictions* (New York: Knopf, 2001), 7.

5. Lionel Trilling, "A Novel of the Thirties," in *The Last Decade: Essays and Reviews*, ed. Diana Trilling (Oxford: Oxford University Press, 1979), 16.

6. Tess Slesinger, *The Unpossessed* (New York: Feminist Press, 1984), 93. Further citations are given parenthetically in the text as *U* followed by the page number.

7. See Janet Sharistanian's fine afterword to *The Unpossessed* (366–70) for a fuller consideration of Slesinger's biography, one that situates Slesinger in the social and professional milieu that informed her beliefs.

8. Trilling, "A Novel of the Thirties," in *The Last Decade*, 16.

9. Elizabeth Hardwick, introduction to *The Unpossessed* (New York: New York Review of Books, 2002), ix.

10. Mary McCarthy, *The Company She Keeps* (New York: Avon Books, 1981), 114. Further citations are given parenthetically in the text as *CSK* followed by the page number.

11. Mary McCarthy, *A Charmed Life* (New York: Harcourt, Brace, 1992), 117 and 53.

12. Randall Jarrell, *Pictures from an Institution: A Comedy* (Chicago: University of Chicago Press, 2010), 188.

13. Frances Kiernan, *Seeing Mary Plain* (New York: W. W. Norton, 2000), 181, 189.

14. Grace Paley, "Faith in the Afternoon," in *Grace Paley: Collected Stories* (New York: Farrar, Straus and Giroux, 1994), 147. Further citations from this edition are given parenthetically in the text as *GP* followed by the page number.

15. Joan Didion, *Democracy* (New York: Simon and Schuster, 1984), 18. Further citations are given parenthetically in the text as *D* followed by the page number.

16. Mary McCarthy, "Love and Death in the Pacific," *New York Times*, April 22, 1984.

17. Joan Didion, "Doris Lessing," in *The White Album* (New York: Farrar, Straus and Giroux, 1979), 123.

18. Ibid., 134.

19. Ibid., 123.

20. Mary McCarthy, "The Art of Fiction," *Paris Review* 27 (Winter–Spring 1962); interview by Elizabeth Sifton.

CHAPTER 6: MULTINATIONALS

1. Nadine Gordimer, *The Pickup* (New York: Penguin, 2002), 47–48. Further citations are given parenthetically in the text as *TP* followed by the page number.

2. Maggie Gee, "Anita Desai in Conversation with Maggie Gee," *Wasafiri* 42 (2004): 8.

3. George Eliot, *Impressions of Theophrastus Such* (Edinburgh: William Blackwood and Sons, 1879), 338.

4. Anita Desai, "Various Lives," in *Lives in Translation: Bilingual Writers on Identity and Creativity*, ed. Isabelle de Courtivron (Basingstoke: Palgrave Macmillan, 2003), 11–12.

5. Ibid., 16.

6. Florence Libert, "An Interview with Anita Desai, 1 August 1989, Cambridge, England," *Journal of Postcolonial Writing* 30 (1990): 54.

7. Corinne Demas Bliss, "Against the Current: A Conversation with Anita Desai," *Massachusetts Review* 29, no. 3 (Fall 1988): 537.

8. Desai, "Various Lives," in *Lives in Translation*, 13.

9. Gee, "Anita Desai in Conversation," 8.

10. Anita Desai, *Fasting, Feasting* (Boston: Houghton Mifflin, 1999), 17. Further citations are given parenthetically in the text as *FF* followed by the page number.

11. Alex Tetteh-Lartey, "Arts and Africa: An Interview with Nadine Gordimer," in *Conversations with Nadine Gordimer*, ed. Nancy Topping Bazin and Marilyn Dallman Seymour (Jackson: University Press of Mississippi, 1990), 282.

12. Robert Boyers, Clark Blaise, Terence Diggory, and Jordan Elgrably, "A Conversation with Nadine Gordimer," in Bazin and Seymour, *Conversations*, 192–93.

13. Ibid., 193.

14. Ibid., 203.

15. Nadine Gordimer, *July's People* (New York: Penguin, 1982), 117. Further citations are given parenthetically in the text as *JP* followed by the page number.

16. "Jhumpa Lahiri on her Debut Novel," About.com: Hinduism, http://hinduism.about.com/library/weekly/extra/bl-jhumpainterview.htm.

17. Jhumpa Lahiri, *Interpreter of Maladies* (Boston: Houghton Mifflin, 1999), 41. Further citations are given parenthetically in the text as *IM* followed by the page number.

18. Jhumpa Lahiri, *The Namesake* (Boston: Houghton Mifflin, 1999), 6. Further citations are given parenthetically by page number in the text.

19. Jhumpa Lahiri, "Trading Stories," *New Yorker*, June 13 and 20, 2011, 83.

20. Jhumpa Lahiri, epigraph, in *Unaccustomed Earth* (New York: Knopf, 2008), emphasis added.

21. Ibid., 328.

22. Rachel Donadio, "Académie Française Honor Highlights Fluid National Allegiances among Writers," *New York Times*, June 6, 2015.

23. Edwidge Danticat, *Create Dangerously: The Immigrant Artist at Work* (Princeton: Princeton University Press, 2010).

24. Kiran Desai, *The Inheritance of Loss* (New York: Grove, 2006), 134.

25. Ibid., 272.

26. Nadine Gordimer, *Writing and Being* (Cambridge, MA: Harvard, 1995), 21. Further citations are given parenthetically in the text as *WB* followed by the page number.

27. Nadine Gordimer, preface to *Selected Stories* (London: Jonathan Cape, 1975), 11.

28. Nadine Gordimer, *The Conservationist* (New York: Penguin, 1978), 49. Further citations are given parenthetically in the text as *TC* followed by the page number.

29. Gordimer cites this line from Gramsci's prison notebooks in "Living in the Interregnum," in *The Essential Gesture: Writing, Politics and Places* (Harmondsworth: Penguin, 1989), 262. She also uses it as the epigraph to *July's People*.

30. We are grateful to Samuel Hynes, who first drew our attention to the importance and significance of these quotations.

31. Nadine Gordimer, interview, *Salmagundi* 62 (Winter 1984).

32. Henry Callaway, *The Religious System of the Amazulu* (Springvale, South Africa: Natal, 1870). Available at http://sacred-texts.com/afr/rsa/rsa01.htm (30).

33. Danticat, *Create Dangerously* (New York: Vintage, 2011), 5.

34. Ibid., 16.

35. Ibid., 5.

36. Edwidge Danticat, *The Farming of Bones* (New York: Penguin, 1999), 55. Further citations are given parenthetically in the text as *FB* followed by the page number.

37. Warner's observation comes in a response to Alison Lurie's review essay on Rapunzel stories, *New York Review of Books*, July 17, 2008.

38. Edwidge Danticat, *The Dew Breaker* (New York: Vintage, 2005), 214. Further citations are given parenthetically in the text as *DB* followed by the page number.

39. Edwidge Danticat, "My Turn in the Fire," *Transition* 93 (2002): 117.

40. Ibid.

41. Kiran Desai, *The Inheritance of Loss*, 143.

42. Ibid., 157.

43. Danticat, "My Turn in the Fire," 123.

CONCLUSION: PROMISED LANDS

1. Nadine Gordimer, *The Pickup* (New York: Penguin, 2002), 47.

2. Edwidge Danticat, *Create Dangerously*, 16; emphasis added.

3. Elizabeth Gaskell, *Mary Barton* (Harmondsworth: Penguin, 1970), 465.

Suggestions for Further Reading

Austen, Jane
Emma
Mansfield Park
Persuasion
Pride and Prejudice
Sense and Sensibility

Bird, Isabella
Journeys in Persia and Kurdistan

Bowen, Elizabeth
The Demon Lover and Other Stories
Eva Trout or Changing Scenes
The Heat of the Day
The House in Paris

Brittain, Vera
Testament of Youth

Brontë, Charlotte
Jane Eyre
Shirley
Villette

Browning, Elizabeth Barrett
"A Curse for the Nation"
"The Runaway Slave at Pilgrim's Point"

Cather, Willa
A Lost Lady
Death Comes for the Archbishop
My Ántonia
O Pioneers!
One of Ours
Song of the Lark

Danticat, Edwidge
Breath, Eyes, Memory
Create Dangerously: The Immigrant Artist at Work
The Dew Breaker
The Farming of Bones
Krik? Krak!

Desai, Anita
  Baumgartner's Bombay
  Clear Light of Day
  Fasting, Feasting
  In Custody

Desai, Kiran
  Hullabaloo in the Guava Orchard
  The Inheritance of Loss

Didion, Joan
  A Book of Common Prayer
  Democracy
  The Last Thing He Wanted
  Slouching Toward Bethlehem (essays)
  Where I Was From
  The White Album

Eliot, George
  Adam Bede
  Daniel Deronda
  The Essays of George Eliot (ed. Thomas Pinney)
  Felix Holt, The Radical
  Middlemarch
  The Mill on the Floss

Ellmann, Mary
  Thinking about Women

Fuller, Margaret
  "These Sad But Glorious Days": Dispatches from Europe, 1846–1850
  Woman in the Nineteenth Century

Gaskell, Elizabeth
  The Life of Charlotte Brontë
  Mary Barton
  North and South

Gellhorn, Martha
  The Face of War (reportage)
  Point of No Return
  A Stricken Field
  The View from the Ground (war reporting of five decades)

Gordimer, Nadine
  Burger's Daughter
  The Conservationist
  The Essential Gesture (essays)
  July's People
  The Pickup

Writing and Being (essays)
Living in Hope and History (essays)

Gilbert, Sandra
"Soldier's Heart: Literary Men, Literary Women, and the Great War"

Gilbert, Sandra, and Susan Gubar
The Madwoman in the Attic

Gilman, Charlotte Perkins
Herland

Hall, Radclyffe
"Miss Ogilvy Finds Herself"

Herbst, Josephine
Pity Is Not Enough
The Executioner Waits
Rope of Gold

Hurston, Zora Neale
Dust Tracks on a Road
Their Eyes Were Watching God

Jackson, Mattie
The Story of Mattie J. Jackson

Jacobs, Harriet
Incidents in the Life of a Slave Girl

Jameson, Anna
The Diary of an Ennuyée

Jewett, Sarah Orne
The Country of the Pointed Firs

Kingsley, Mary
Travels in Africa

Lahiri, Jhumpa
In altre parole (*In Other Words*)
Interpreter of Maladies
Lowland
The Namesake
Unaccustomed Earth

Lawrence, Karen
Penelope Voyages: Women and Travel in the British Literary Tradition

Lee, Hermione
Edith Wharton
Virginia Woolf

Leonowens, Anna
The English Governess at the Siamese Court

Lessing, Doris
The Golden Notebook

Macaulay, Rose
"Many Sisters to Many Brothers"
Non-Combatants and Others
The Towers of Trebizond
The World My Wilderness

Manning, Olivia
The Balkan Trilogy
The Levant Trilogy

Martineau, Harriet
Illustrations of Political Economy
Writings on Slavery and the American Civil War (ed. Deborah Anne Logan)

McCarthy, Mary
Birds of America
Cannibals and Missionaries
A Charmed Life
The Company She Keeps
The Groves of Academe
The Group
Memoirs of a Catholic Girlhood
The Oasis

Moers, Ellen
Literary Women

Morrison, Toni
Beloved
Paradise
Song of Solomon

O'Connor, Flannery
The Complete Stories
Wise Blood

Origo, Iris
A Need to Testify
War in Val D'Orcia

Paley, Grace
Collected Stories

Porter, Katherine Anne
Flowering Judas and Other Stories
The Old Order: Stories of the South

Pale Horse, Pale Rider
Ship of Fools

Robinson, Marilynne
Gilead
Housekeeping
Home
Lila

Seacole, Mary
Wonderful Adventures of Mrs. Seacole in Many Lands

Showalter, Elaine
A Jury of Their Peers
A Literature of Their Own

Sinclair, May
A Journal of Impressions in Belgium
The Tree of Heaven

Slesinger, Tess
The Unpossessed

Smith, Stevie
Over the Frontier

Spacks, Patricia
The Female Imagination

Stein, Gertrude
The Making of Americans
Wars I Have Seen

Stowe, Harriet Beecher
Dred: A Tale of the Great Dismal Swamp
Uncle Tom's Cabin

West, Rebecca
"Miss Sinclair's Genius"
The Return of the Soldier

Wharton, Edith
The Book of the Homeless
Fighting France: From Dunkerque to Belfort
The Marne: A Tale of the War
A Motor-Flight Through France
A Son at the Front
"Writing a War Story"

Wollstonecraft, Mary
Letters Written during a Short Residence in Sweden, Norway, and Denmark
Maria, or The Wrongs of Woman
A Vindication of the Rights of Woman

Woolf, Virginia
  Between the Acts
  The Common Reader
  "Professions for Women"
  A Room of One's Own
  Three Guineas
  To the Lighthouse

Index